PUERTO RICO'S
FIGHTING 65th
U.S. INFANTRY

Fort Brooke, Puerto Rico, 1950. Troops of the 65th practicing for Armed Forces Day Parade. U.S. ARMY PHOTO

PUERTO RICO'S FIGHTING 65th U. S. INFANTRY

FROM SAN JUAN TO CHORWAN

W. W. HARRIS,
Brigadier General, U.S. Army (Ret.)

PRESIDIO PRESS

This edition printed 2001

Copyright © 1980 by Presidio Press

Published by Presidio Press, Inc.
505 B San Marin Dr., Suite 160
Novato, CA 94945-1340

Library of Congress Cataloging-in-Publication Data

Harris, William Warner, 1907–
    Puerto Rico's fighting 65th U.S. Infantry.

    Includes index.
    1. Korean War, 1950–1953—Regiment histories—United States—
65th Infantry. 2. United States. Army.
65th Infantry. I. Title.
    DS919.H37   951.9'042   79-26889
ISBN 0-89141-056-2 (hardcover)
ISBN 0-89141-753-2 (paperback)

Printed in the United States of America

To the people of Puerto Rico,
who produced the brave men of the glorious
65th United States Infantry Regiment.
Viva Borinqueneers!

CONTENTS

1

SAN JUAN

This is a story of pride and prejudice.

This is an account of the all-Puerto Rican 65th United States Infantry Regiment.

This is the history of that regiment's first year of combat in the Korean War, and I was the regimental commander.

No ethnic group has greater pride in itself and its heritage than the Puerto Rican people.

Nor have I encountered any that can be more dedicated and zealous in support of the democratic principles for which the United States stands. Many Puerto Ricans have fought to the death to uphold them.

In 1949, when I was first assigned to Puerto Rico as the commander of the 65th United States Infantry Regiment, I would not have believed these statements.

As a matter of fact I was outraged at what I considered being sent to pasture for two years to command what the Pentagon brass referred to as a "rum and Coca Cola" outfit. I would be less than honest if I did not admit that, at the time, I agreed with that opinion.

Like any other eagle colonel in the regular army, aged forty-two, I was ambitious. Going to the West Indies to command the Puerto Rican Regiment was not my idea of either where or how to prove my command ability.

There was no question about it in my mind; the Pentagon was relegating me to obscurity.

But humans being what they are, there are few among us who can lay claim to reading the future, and I was not one of them. It's just as well, for my story would be difficult to tell and even more difficult to believe if I had not had a part in that great adventure.

I had seen and heard of battalion-size units (approximately 850 officers and men) of the 65th Infantry Regiment when I was assigned to General Eisenhower's Allied Force Headquarters (AFHQ) in North Africa (later moved to Italy). I was responsible for conducting the operational planning for the invasion of Southern France. That operation, code name Anvil, was a ten-division (three American and seven French) assault up the Rhone Valley designed to link up with the cross-channel landing in Normandy. Both forces were then to come under command of General Eisenhower's new Supreme Headquarters Allied Powers Europe (SHAPE), which he later set up in London.

In the selection of available and battle-tested U.S. units that could be withdrawn from the campaign in Italy and used in Anvil, the 65th was not even considered. It had not been employed as a complete unit in combat and therefore had not been blooded.

At the time, one battalion was deployed along the French-Italian border in the Alps. Its mission was to provide warning should the German Army in Italy attempt to cross over from there into Southern France.

But the probability of such a maneuver by the Germans was considered very remote. Lt. Gen. Mark W. Clark's Fifth United States Army and the British Eighth Army had them too heavily engaged. The Axis Powers were not going anyplace, unless it might be to withdraw back into Germany.

Another of the battalions of the regiment was positioned on the northern tip of the island of Corsica near the village of Bastia. Its mission was to give the alert should the Germans attempt to recapture that island.

Again, there was only the slightest possibility of such a maneuver by the Germans. But we did not care to risk even a remote possibility that they might attempt it. We had planned that the initial assault divisions for Anvil would be staged, or based, on that island just prior to the attack.

The last of the three battalions of the regiment had already been allocated to Lt. Gen. A. W. ("Sandy") Patch, who was to command the United States Seventh Army (three U.S. divisions) in Operation Anvil. (The other seven divisions included in the operation were to be under command of General de Lattre de Tassigny, later a marshal of the French Army.) General Patch's staff assigned the battalion the mission of guarding Seventh Army headquarters. Such duty is commonly referred to as the "Palace Guard."

As the millions of Americans who are and have been in the service could tell you, the missions given to the Puerto Rican 65th Infantry were not those assigned to gung ho outfits. Only troops with a reputation as fighters were trusted with combat missions.

But, as I now know, the tasks allocated to the Puerto Ricans were the result of our own poor knowledge of history. We had forgotten, if in fact we ever knew, that the people of Puerto Rico were fierce warriors who had successfully held off invaders of their island long before this country gained its independence. As early as the sixteenth century, various nations attempted to colonize Puerto Rico as a link with the New World. France, Denmark, Holland, and England all tried and failed. The Dutch did manage to burn San Juan in 1625, but they were never able to take the entire island.

The British, who had defeated the great Spanish Armada in 1588, were probably the most persistent in their attempts to establish a base there. In 1595 Sir Francis Drake tried and failed. In 1598 the Earl of Cumberland tried again. He did manage to occupy the country for five months but was eventually driven off by an epidemic. Lt. Gen. Sir Ralph Abernathy was the last of the British to undertake the job. He had overpowered Trinidad in 1797, but he was soundly thrashed by the Borinqueneers when he invaded the harbor of San Juan.

At the time I received my orders to go to Puerto Rico, I was chief of staff of the 17th Airborne Division. Although we were not the same group of men who had fought with the 17th during World War II, the tradition and spirit of those great warriors had been rekindled in the officers and men of our division.

The 17th was being inactivated in order to cut down on Department of Defense expenditures. The personnel were being scattered to the four winds, and I was going to command the all-Puerto Rican 65th United States Infantry Regiment.

I was familiar with the World War II record of the 65th, and I knew that the Puerto Ricans had not established a reputation then as combat soldiers. I had also been on the Department of Army staff at the Pentagon, and I knew the feeling about them there.

But by the time the ship arrived in New Orleans, I had pretty well reconciled myself to my fate. The trip to Puerto Rico was pleasant and even though I had been reluctant to take the post I was at the ship's railing when the island bobbed up above the surface of the water.

There really wasn't much to see. A few buildings penetrated the skyline, but barely. There was nothing spectacular about either the city or the countryside. The city was obviously Spanish in architecture, and the countryside seemed scrawny and barren except for what looked like small cinder-block houses dotting the hillsides. There were lots of coconut trees, mostly along the water's edge, but I saw little other vegetation anywhere.

Later I was to learn the reason for the country looking so scraggly. Puerto Rico sits astride the path of the violent tropical hurricanes that sweep through the Caribbean every year, and 1949 had been the year a big one hit.

As we headed into the deep-water port of San Juan, the most prominent buildings in view were La Fortaleza and El Moro Castle. Both buildings are perched on high ground that extends out into the ocean like a finger giving warning to intruders. Built by the Spanish in the late sixteenth century as the governor's residence, they also provided the ramparts from which the people defended their island against marauding pirates and other aggressive colonizers. I did not know it at the time, but El Moro was later to be both my residence and my headquarters.

As we stepped down from the gangplank onto the dock, I was astounded but delighted to find some old friends there to meet us. I had certainly not expected to see anyone whom I knew, but to find Lt. Col. and Mrs. George ("Chick") W. Childs and his family there was a real surprise. Childs and I had served together on the Department of Army staff, and I thought very highly of him.

The two enlisted men standing beside Childs wore the insignia of the 65th. They were Sgt. Augustin Ramos, whom Childs introduced as my personal enlisted assistant, and Cpl. Victor Vargas, who had been assigned as the driver of my official car. A long and lasting friendship among the three of us began with this dockside meeting.

Childs had arranged for two official cars to transport the families, and he and I rode in his own personal car so that we could talk in private during the almost three-hour trip to Losey Field, where my headquarters were to be. Childs told me that he was the senior lieutenant colonel and regimental executive.

I realized that he was not being rank conscious, only stating a fact that would be helpful for me to know. It meant that by actual seniority he was the second in command, in addition to being the executive officer. And knowing Chick, I was delighted to have him in that position. Brig. Gen. Edwin L. Sibert was the commanding general, Antilles Command, and my immediate superior. His headquarters were in San Juan.

I told Childs what I had seen and heard of the 65th during the Second World War and learned in return that the Puerto Ricans were not given worldwide assignments. As a result they were not sent to either their basic school or to Leavenworth.

The Leavenworth to which Childs referred was the army's Command

and General Staff College which trained company and field-grade officers in the fundamentals and principles of command and staff work. It is a must, if an officer aspires to senior rank. Only those who have demonstrated their potential for high command are sent there.

If it was Pentagon policy not to train Puerto Ricans then it was also no wonder the Puerto Ricans did not have a better reputation. It seemed to me about as stupid a policy as I had ever heard. Though I was to try many times to get that policy changed over the next two years, it was not until I returned to the personnel division of the Pentagon after the war in Korea that I was able to get anything done about it. Then, I finally managed to get Puerto Ricans sent to Leavenworth and to their basic school, like Fort Benning for the infantry officers and Fort Sill in Oklahoma for artillery students. I was also able to get them worldwide assignments.

I learned a lot more about the Puerto Ricans and the 65th Infantry as we drove toward Losey Field, and the more that I learned, the more I sympathized with them. It was becoming quite clear to me that as far as the military authorities were concerned, we were treating the Puerto Ricans as second-class citizens.

I discovered, for the first time, that the 65th was really not a regiment after all, for we had only two battalions while full-strength organization called for three. This understrength would pose quite a problem, of course, if we were ever committed to combat — heaven forbid. Then to make matters even worse, these two battalions were widely separated geographically. The 2nd Battalion was stationed at Henry Barracks in the mountains, sixty miles from the 1st Battalion, which was at Losey Field. I was chagrined over this last piece of news, for it was further indication of my being shanghaied to the boondocks to command a regiment that existed in name only, and with not too good a name at that. Having the two battalions separated by such distance was going to further complicate an already complicated training problem.

I was more upset to learn that we had no mortar company. In those days, the TO/E *(Tables of Organization and Equipment)* of an infantry regiment contained one company of three platoons, each equipped with four 4.2-inch mortars, which provided the regimental commander with his own built-in artillery support. Organized and equipped so that the company as a whole could be employed as a single-fire unit in direct support of the regiment or the individual platoons parceled out to the battalions, a mortar company was a very effective weapon in the hands of the regimental commander. These units were particularly useful in searching out defiladed areas which could not be hit by the low-angle, direct-fire artillery pieces.

Then, just to compound our difficulties, we were short some essential organizational equipment, particularly vehicles. This would materially reduce our battlefield mobility.

These were all major deficiencies. I estimated they would reduce our combat capability by at least 40 or 50 percent. Not that the 65th was going off to war or anywhere, but a commander must evaluate his command somehow, and combat capability is the best gauge to use because it has the lowest common denominator — estimated combat effectiveness.

Childs and I discussed all this in those first few hours and then turned to the question of the personnel in the 65th. Chick said that in his opinion we had as good commanders and staff as most units in the States.

"Let's start with St. Clair," he began, "who commands the 1st Battalion at Losey Field. He is probably younger than Dammer, who commands the 2nd Battalion at Henry Barracks, and is probably the more extroverted of the two. I believe that 'Saint' was in the class of '39 at West Point and that Dammer came into the army as a Thompson Act officer."

"Dammer," he continued, "commanded a battalion at Anzio [the Italian beachhead where we made an amphibious landing to get in behind the Germans, and they came very near to throwing us back into the sea] and has a fine war record."

"Headquarters Company is commanded by a Puerto Rican named Mendes, and he knows his job too. Then the Service Company is commanded by Maj. Carno Ramirez — he's also your S-4. [staff officer, supply] Carno is a hard worker. You'll never have to worry about the 65th needing anything, provided it's available of course, for we are on the bottom of the totem pole when it comes to getting anything from the States — the whole Antilles Command is in the same fix. Carno has been trying to get additional trucks for a long time, but they just aren't available. I'll say this, though; I don't believe you'll find any vehicles that get more loving care than ours do. Sometimes I wonder how he keeps them running."

He also told me that General Sibert had to make a trip to one of the other islands. He was responsible for all of the islands in the Antilles chain, even through we didn't have any troops on any of the other islands.

I learned some more dismal facts in addition to our lack of a mortar company. We didn't have a medical company either — that is, one that could be called a medical company. The personnel were scattered all over the island running the dispensaries for all of the units.

I hadn't expected this regiment to be the best in the army, but hoped that at least it would be a full command. Well, there wasn't anything I could do about it. Chick went on about the staff.

"Our S-1 [personnel officer] is 'Mac' MacCaughey, a Continental who knows the personnel business inside and out. Then there's 'Johnny' Czares who is the S-2 [intelligence officer]. We don't have too much intelligence activity, but what he does have to do, he does well. I guess his main job is keeping up with our mobilization assignment."

I asked what that was.

"Well, we have plans to go charging off to ——— [classified information] to protect American oil interests. We keep plans updated to either fly the regiment to that country or to go by surface transportation. I think three Liberty Ships are set up for that purpose."

"Where would the Pentagon expect to get the air lift from?" I asked. Chick didn't know.

"That's the damndest mobilization assignment I ever heard of. Have you ever seen the size of the lake where all of those oil wells are located?"

"No, sir, I haven't."

"Well, by God, I have. When I was in GHQ [General Headquarters in Washington, D.C., which was responsible for running the war for the first few years] I participated in making a study for that requirement, and if I remember correctly, there were some five infantry divisions assigned to that mission. I can also tell you that the 65th was not a part of that task force either."

"We have it now. I just finished reading the plan."

All I could hope was that we wouldn't have to implement it. We could no more protect those oil wells than fly to the moon (which was only a Jules Verne fantasy then).

Chick continued telling me about the staff.

"Our S-3 [plans and training officer] is (Major E.G.) Jerry Allen, a real pro. Allen's assistant, a senior staff officer, is Major Max Figueroa. He and his wife, Margo, are the salt of the earth and a great stabilizing factor in the relations between the Puerto Ricans and the Continentals. Max also does a creditable job as assistant S-3 even though he has never gone to Leavenworth."

At this point we arrived at Losey Field. It looked small. There certainly wasn't enough room to train a regiment, not even one two-thirds the size of the 65th. There didn't seem to be more than fifty acres at the most, and almost all of that was occupied by buildings of one sort or another. We were going to need more real estate than this, even to practice close-order

drill. I made a note to inquire about training grounds. I noticed, too, that
there were only a few soldiers moving about on the post. This was unusual, for on a normal stateside installation at this hour of the day, the
men would be marching back to barracks from afternoon drill. Then I
suddenly realized why — Puerto Rico is in the semitropics, and the services normally dispense with afternoon training in such climates. The
rum and Coca Cola must certainly get an early start in the 65th.

Thinking about rum and Coca Cola reminded me about the old World
War I infantry colonel who said he would not tolerate any "nipping" in
his regiment. He told the new officers who joined the unit that he could
appreciate the fact that a man needed a shot of good liquor when he
awakened in the morning, for that was what started him off properly. He
further agreed that it might be necessary for a man to have a short pick-
me-up in the midmorning, and then of course it was accepted practice for
a man to have an appetizer or two just before lunch. Further it was the
social thing to do for a man to gather with his friends for several drinks
before dinner. And, he continued, he had no objections if a man took a
couple of drinks right before retiring for the night. But, he wanted to
make it quite clear, he would not tolerate anyone nipping on the whiskey
bottle all day long. I thought about that colonel as we walked over to the
reception; I wondered how many nippers we would have in the 65th.

As it turned out, the reception was a complete success. I not only met
all of the officers of the regiment and their wives, but I was also able to
talk at some length with the Puerto Ricans, and I was surprised at what I
learned about them. I had imagined them being somewhat provincial in
their views, limited in their knowledge of world affairs, and resentful of
the *Americanos*. Instead, I found that they were a sophisticated group of
conversationalists who spoke better English than I did Spanish. Rather
than being resentful of the Continentals, they were delighted that we were
a part of their beloved regiment.

I made some other startling discoveries that evening too. I found the
Puerto Ricans were as proud of the fact that the 65th was a part of the
U.S. Army establishment as they were of their own history and heritage.
This new knowledge gave me a better understanding and made me feel
sympathetic, though it did not change my opinion as to what kind of
soldiers they would make. That evaluation would have to await the test
of time and the training fields.

I thought of some of these things as I lay in bed that night. With the
arrival of daybreak, I was up, had my breakfast, and was on the way to
my office at what I thought would be an early hour. I had hoped to get
there before other members of the headquarters staff arrived so that I

could look around and evaluate the orderliness and state of police of the Command Headquarters Building. This would be a good indication of what the rest of the organization was like.

Instead of arriving early, it appeared as though I had walked in during the midmorning, for the headquarters was a beehive of activity. I learned that headquarters opened at seven every morning except Sunday, when there was only a duty officer to take any calls or handle any emergency.

My first directive, signed by General Porter (Maj. Gen. Ray E. Porter, the commanding general, U.S. Army Headquarters, Panama Canal Zone, which included all troops in the Antilles as well), involved a test which would take place in three weeks. It was to last three days and cover these subjects: The "School of the Soldier," "Close-Order Drill," "Stripping and Assembling of Weapons," "Preliminary Rifle Marksmanship Training," "Scouting and Patrolling," and "The Tactics and Techniques of Employing the Squad and Platoon." In other words, the basic military subjects.

I decided to use The Infantry School method in getting ready for these tests. Instead of having the company commanders responsible for training their units in all of these subjects, I would select the instructors from the regiment and make them responsible for all training in their assigned subjects. I told Chick and he agreed. I then met with the noncommissioned officers and told them about the training tests first, for they were uppermost in my mind at the moment. Then because this was probably one of the few times that I would have all of the headquarters noncommissioned officers together at one time, I told them of the importance that I attached to their positions of authority in the regiment. In summing up I said that any regiment was only as good as the senior noncommissioned officers wanted it to be, and that I hoped they wanted to make the 65th one of the best; that they would have their first opportunity to demonstrate this desire in helping the regiment get ready for the inspection.

Finally I told them that the order about being tried by court martial if anyone spoke Spanish, which I learned had been issued by my predecessor, was rescinded. I did, however, remind everyone that English is, after all, the official language of the United States Army, and that any communications directed to the headquarters would be in English. Furthermore, should the regiment ever participate in maneuvers with other U.S. Army troops, we most certainly would have to speak English to be understood. Lastly I urged that everyone continue to attend the spoken English course that General Sibert had set up to help them. Following this discussion I learned for the first time that English was taught in the Puerto Rican schools; I was surprised to hear this.

I felt greatly encouraged after that meeting, and I guess that one of the biggest surprises was my first glimpse of those twenty or so men waiting there for me. For some reason, I had expected that long hair and sideburns would be standard equipment. Instead, everyone there was clean-shaven and dressed in well-tailored, neatly pressed uniforms. They looked like what they were supposed to be, senior noncommissioned officers in the United States Army.

I studied the training directive in detail. The emphasis was on basic training. There are those who think that battles are won by the side that produces the most troops and the biggest cannon at the proper place and proper time. While this doctrine is generally true, it is really the infantry soldier who closes with the enemy in the final struggle, and is the deciding factor between defeat and victory on the battlefield.

In the first of the subjects on the test, Item 3, "The School of the Soldier," the objectives were twofold: first, to teach the soldier the correct posture and carriage; secondly, and more important, being required to conform to these rigid standards, the soldier is subjected to the first of many disciplines that he must learn in his physical and mental conditioning for combat.

"Close-Order Drill," Item 4, was designed to perfect a man's timing and precision and his immediate response to commands, which is another of the disciplines used to train the combat soldier to survive.

The "Stripping and Assembling of Weapons," Item 5, follows in the natural order of training events. Here the man learns to care for and to husband the tools of his profession. If a soldier's weapons will not function because they are dirty, rusty, or have a broken part, that soldier is in trouble. It's that simple.

The "Preliminary Rifle Marksmanship," Item 6, is intended to teach the individual soldier the fundamental principles of how to shoot his weapon without firing a shot: how to hold the weapon, how to align the sights, how to hold his breath while he squeezes the trigger, how to follow through after the shot is squeezed off (keeping the eyes and the sights aligned on the target after the shot is fired).

Item 7, "Scouting and Patrolling," is probably the one most important lesson in the combat infantryman's military training. It brings together all of the elements of his other training that are designed to teach him how to survive on the battlefield. It is here that the soldier learns how to be cautious and alert to his surroundings; how to search for and locate his enemy without being discovered himself. He learns how to read and to take full advantage of the terrain, particularly all available cover and concealment, for the battlefield is a very lonely and naked place. It is here, too, that the combat infantryman learns how to move about over a desolate area without stumbling into an enemy minefield or other booby trap set to snare him or blow him to bits. He learns how to look at the ground in front of him before he takes each step, to make sure he is not stepping on a mine or about to strike a trip wire that will set off a demolition charge. He learns how to creep and crawl equally as carefully and how to avoid making a noise that will reveal his presence to an enemy soldier who might be waiting for him nearby. Finally, this training sharpens the man's animal instincts to look for and be wary of other human signs, just as our ancestors did when they moved westward and had to be prepared for any hostile encounter with man or animal.

Lastly, Item 8, is called "The Tactics and Techniques of Employing the Squad and the Platoon." Here the man learns how a leader employs and controls his unit in combat. For example, using the principles and techniques learned in scouting and patrolling, a platoon locates a small enemy force deployed in a defensive position on the top of the hill to its front. One solution the platoon leader may employ to destroy that force is to divide his unit into two parts, using one part as a base of fire to keep the enemy down and pinned to the ground, while he maneuvers the other part to the rear of the enemy and takes him by surprise.

While the directive did not contain all of the subjects a combat soldier needed to know, it did encompass the most basic ones he had to master in order to live and to fight — the combat soldier's two principal problems. Such instruction, in this age of rocketry and nuclear weapons, may seem to some like training the American soldier to fight in the Stone Age, yet all of the sophisticated weaponry that was available during the Korean War was of little use to us, and the same was true in Vietnam. Battles and wars are won by squads and platoons, not the strategy of the high command.

I discussed these subjects and the training test in general with the commanders during my inspection trips. I found all of them in complete agreement with the idea of setting up the new instructional system to prepare for it. When I later found that the staff also agreed, the directive which Childs had prepared was issued, and training got under way.

After watching the system in operation for several days, it appeared that we were accomplishing what we had set out to do: improving the quality and depth of the instruction, establishing a higher level of competence, and making that level more uniform throughout the regiment. By concentrating on only one subject, each instructor was able to improve upon his own pedagogy by thinking up new and more interesting ways of presenting it, as well as increasing his own knowledge of that particular subject.

This improved expertise also stimulated the men's interest in what might otherwise have been dull and dreary instruction. Soldiers who have been in the service for any length of time, like anyone else, soon tire of hearing the same subjects repeated year after year, lose interest, become bored and indifferent. Instructors must therefore use their imagination in such instances and vary their methods and techniques. The officers whom we had selected to conduct the training were certainly doing just that, for the interest level among the troops was very high. As a result, they worked harder to prepare themselves for the tests, and by the time the team from Panama arrived, they felt that they were ready.

The tests themselves were conducted in what appeared to be a series of county fairs, like the jousting tournaments of medieval England when that original welfare worker, Robin Hood, and his co-workers, Friar Tuck and Little John, might have been in their prime. Each setup, under the supervision of one of the officers from Panama, had a tent fly to provide some relief from the sun for the "king's men and their helpers." Each area was roped off and had a big sign indicating what test would be conducted at that station. Then, to add some color to the scene, the inspection team had placed numerous company guidons and standards and flags throughout the area. It was, however, the sudden appearance of many of the men's families, particularly those with children, who came to watch the show that made the entire affair look more like a holiday celebration than an official inspection.

Each examination was conducted in a different way. Some were given in the form of written tests. At other stations the contestants were required to observe a demonstration, for example a man stripping and assembling an automatic rifle. Then they were directed to mark on their papers the answers to certain True or False questions that pertained to the demonstration. Some of the tests required the contestants to demonstrate their knowledge of the subject by actual performance.

On the whole, we thought that the exercise had been conducted very well. It had also been very comprehensive in its coverage, and when it ended, none of us had any real idea how well we had done. But a critique had been scheduled for the afternoon of the last day, and we were told then what our overall score was: satisfactory, good, excellent, or superior.

We all assembled at the appointed hour in the conference room and listened with bated breath, or at least I did, while each team member critiqued his part of the test. As time passed, it was evident that we had not done too badly, for there were not many derogatory remarks made about our performance. When the last man completed his comments, the chief inspector rose to give the summation. I must admit that my heart gave several extra flip-flops, for what he was about to say would be the verbal, but nevertheless official, report he would make to Generals Sibert and Porter. I guess that our pride was at stake, mine included.

"Gentlemen, I'll make my remarks brief and to the point. The aggregate grade made by the 65th was superior. You made the highest numerical score of any troops in the entire Panama area. Congratulations."

2

OPERATION PORTREX:
THE VIEQUES MANEUVERS

I had become aware of the Puerto Ricans' strong feeling of self-respect and dignity the night of our first reception. I became even more conscious of it during the meeting with the noncommissioned officers. This type of test inspection had never happened to them before, even though it was standard procedure in other units. They had taken it as an expression of confidence, which it was, though no specific point had been made in that regard. They had also readily accepted this apparently new responsibility and exercised it wisely and carefully.

In turn, the other men of the regiment soon began to show what they could do — not in a showy pretentious manner, but in a quiet, modest, and self-effacing way. And the results were outstanding. As a matter of fact, I do not believe that our infantry-school methods had done any more than polish off the rough edges of an already well-trained outfit.

The cancellation of the order about speaking Spanish also had an immediate and effective impact on the men. Though it was no more than the fair and logical thing to do, the response to this revocation amazed me. It now seemed to be a matter of pride for everyone to demonstrate in even greater degree that my confidence was not misplaced.

This newly found spirit made for a happier command, and it occurred to me that my tour of duty might at least turn out to be a pleasant and enjoyable one, even though I might not have the opportunity to demonstrate my command ability. There were many places to visit and sights to see, and my family and I could at least enjoy a two-year sojourn in travel throughout the Caribbean area.

But that concept didn't hold up very long. As a matter of fact, it lasted about two weeks, and then we received another directive. This time it was from the Department of Defense.

This long and detailed document announced that we were to participate in the largest, joint amphibious-airborne maneuver ever staged by the department during peacetime. It was to start the latter part of February 1950 and last for seven days, with emphasis on the play of ground troops. It was to be a free maneuver, which meant that umpire control of the troops would be kept to a minimum. In such exercises the ground troops of each side are permitted to advance in an attack formation or to assume a defensive posture without interference from the umpires. The maneuvering of troops or establishment of defensive positions is made under protection of planned artillery fires and/or aerial bombardment, just as in actual combat, except that firing of weapons is simulated. When first contact is made between opposing forces, the umpires assess the "casualties" sustained by personnel, vehicles, tanks, and other hardware. They evaluate the tactical maneuvers and then direct the advance, and withdrawal, of the side which has accumulated the most, or least, vantage points.

There would be some eighteen hundred Marine Corps officers assigned as umpires. Most of them had seen combat in the Pacific during the war, so this looked like it was going to be a carefully evaluated maneuver.

The area selected for the exercise was to be the small three-mile long and narrow island of Vieques, which is located just four miles or so off the northeast shore of Puerto Rico. Actually the island is a part of Puerto Rico, but the U.S. Navy and Marine Corps had established something of a squatters right over it. They used it as a target area for the long guns of the Caribbean Fleet and as a place where the marines could practice their amphibious landings.

The scenario called for "Aggressor" (who had captured the island and enslaved the inhabitants) to be the defenders, while the "Liberating Force" from the United States was to drive Aggressor into the sea and reestablish order in this Western-oriented republic.

Aggressor ground forces were to be composed of troops from the Antilles Command; the 98th Anti-Aircraft Artillery Battalion; the 504th Field Artillery Battalion; the 65th Infantry Regiment, augmented by one battalion from the 33rd Infantry Regiment in Panama; and other ancillary service and supply troops from the Panama area (ordnance, signal, engineer, military police). The 65th was to be the largest single unit of the Aggressor ground forces and was to be commanded by Brig. Gen. Edwin L. Sibert, commanding general, Antilles Command.

The Liberating Force was to consist of the United States 3rd Infantry Division (reinforced), which was probably the most decorated fighting unit in either World War I or World War II. If recollection serves me correctly, Sgt. Alvin York, the Medal of Honor winner, was its most famous member during the First World War; and Audie Murphy was the most highly decorated member during World War II. This unit was to be augmented with sufficient naval, air, and other troops so that its superiority in numbers and military capability would be in the order of about four to one over Aggressor. In addition, one battalion of the famous 82nd Airborne Division was to be attached to the 3rd Division. All ground troops of the attacking force were to be commanded by the 3rd Infantry Division commander, Maj. Gen. Percy W. Clarkson.

It was clearly evident from this allocation of superior numbers and power to the attacking force that Aggressor was expected and scheduled to lose the battle. Confirmation of our predetermined fate came in the form of personal letters to me from friends in the Pentagon. They informed me that the regimental commanders of the 3rd Infantry Division were even then making bets as to which of them would capture me and end the battle. This was going to be a "fun maneuver," or so they thought.

On the other hand, we were determined that if we were defeated and driven off the island, the 3rd was going to have to fight like hell to do it. When the officers and men of the regiment learned about the letters and the bets on capturing me, they became even more determined that it would not happen. Since the 65th was to be the major force or Aggressor, this determined attitude was even more important because our success or failure would pretty well determine the overall outcome of the maneuver.

In reading the script I noted that Aggressor was to be entrenched in defensive positions in the center portion of the island. The eastern portion was to be used as an impact area for a real, live preinvasion naval and aerial bombardment, which was expected to soften up Aggressor. Further description of this bombardment stated that the Department of Defense had devised an "ingenious" method of evaluating its effectiveness in assisting the ground troops to land on a hostile shore. I never learned what this method was, except the Department of Defense might have been referring to the use of the eighteen hundred umpires. Possibly I should have never mentioned it, but I am only relating what the directive stated.

Plans called for us to install fortifications in this impact area which were replicas of the barricades, demolitions, and other obstacles constructed on the beaches and around our defensive positions. Then, upon completion of this "death blow" from the sea and the air, an administrative halt to the maneuver would be declared while the umpires evaluated the damage to the fortifications and assessed the effectiveness of the bombardment.

Following closely upon the heels of this action — the script continued — the assault forces would be put ashore in the huge U.S. Navy landing craft (LSTs) and the air force troop carriers, called flying boxcars. Then by a combination of skillful tactical maneuvers and the overwhelming power of the supporting naval and air bombardment, the Aggressor would be annihilated, and the suffering natives would be liberated. As Shakespeare said in *As You Like It*, "All the world's a stage and all the men and women merely players." So it was in this case, except that the actors in this scenario did not completely follow the script.

After I had read the directive and discussed it with Childs, we both agreed that the staff should study it in detail. Following that, we would have a meeting to discuss and formulate our outline plans. In the meantime I made a number of notes that I wished to use as the basis for these discussions:

A. As Sibert's senior commander, I expected that we would be called upon to assist him in both the selection of the general area where we would make our stand and the organization of the ground for its defense. This would require that we set an early date for a reconnaissance of the island of Vieques.

B. Detailed planning for organization of the defensive positions would require selection of specific locations for the automatic weapons. Around these, we would place the battalion, company, and platoon strong points, or defensive positions for the riflemen. Close-in protection for these men would be provided by barbed-wire entanglements, demolitions, and artillery and mortar barrages. Air bombardment would be called in, if we had air superiority, which I doubted.

C. We would make a careful study of the ground and locate dominant points of the terrain on which we could place the automatic weapons and the strong points. We must locate them where the crews of the automatic weapons and the individual riflemen would have an unobstructed view of all approaches to their positions. Any shrubs, trees, or other vegetation that might obstruct this view would have to be removed.

D. Defiladed approaches, which could not be seen by the men in the strong points, would be covered by mortar and artillery fires; these weapons had to be concealed from air observation and be within range of their targets.

E. Reserve forces should be located in positions from which they could be quickly and effectively moved to any portion of the defensive area. Routes from these positions to the strong points had to be reconnoitered.

F. Command Posts (CPs), the nerve centers of the commander's communications (command and control), must be dug in on reverse slopes, in defilade, to protect them from the long-range naval guns and the ground-based artillery, and they must be camouflaged for protection from air observation.

G. Observation Posts (OPs) would be located on high ground and similarly protected.

H. Beach obstacles, such as wire entanglements, demolitions, and tank and vehicle traps, must be prepared to impede or at least slow up the progress of the amphibious landing forces. Automatic weapons and artillery fires should be planned for quick concentration on those areas, while the obstacles held them in massed formations.

I. Possible drop zones (DZs), where parachute troops could land, must be reconnoitered and given special attention. We would plant petards or pikes in those areas to impale the descending paratroopers and barbed wire in loose coils, with booby traps and other demolitions, to impede their escape while we concentrated our heavy weapons and artillery fires on them. We would then send in our reserves to engage them in hand-to-hand combat. This was grisly business, but as General Robert E. Lee once said, "It is well that war is so terrible—we would grow too fond of it."

J. Having completed all of this, we would then spend several days, at least, rehearsing commanders and troops in the tactics and techniques of the attack and the defense, particularly the latter, for that would be our primary role in this maneuver.

K. And one final note regarding the operation of the staff and the commander during the exercise: I had seen the staff of some headquarters in both maneuvers and combat operate like a side show at a circus — barking out instructions to subordinate headquarters, talking among themselves in voices loud enough to be heard two miles away. I would insist that the noise level in all headquarters be kept to a very low pitch. A quiet, orderly headquarters can usually operate more efficiently.

Although I did not make a note to the effect, I decided that I would be on the lookout for any of my battalion commanders wandering around the battlefield when the fighting was critical. I had seen many commanders in combat doing just that in their attempts to influence the action, giving orders to squad and platoon leaders when they should have been concerned with the employment of their companies. In more cases than not, these same commanders would be out of communication with their own headquarters. This can be disastrous when they are needed to make a decision that only they should make.

By some strange reasoning that escapes me completely, I have even seen some very senior commanders who feel that their presence on the immediate battlefield, in the thick of the fight, demonstrates their command ability and, even worse, their bravery. Such cavalier performance is sometimes necessary, but as a general practice it accomplishes nothing. In my opinion, such actions are not included in the role of a senior commander. When a critical battle is in progress, he should be in constant communication with all of his immediate subordinate commanders. In most situations this can best be accomplished from his own headquarters.

I estimated that it would probably take us the better part of four months to accomplish all of the work that I had listed, and the staff would probably have many more items that would require acting on. This meant that we should make plans to move to Vieques at an early date, probably before Christmas, since the maneuvers were scheduled to begin in late February.

Later in the week we had a conference on the new directive. I started it with a few remarks about being glad to have another project, for it would provide us with something to do other than routine training. I covered all of the items in my notes and then emphasized the importance of good communications. Reliable communications is the secret of success in any military operation. History is replete with incidents where communications was the difference between victory and defeat; the naval battle at Leyte Gulf in the Pacific comes to mind. Then I made a remark really intended as a jest, "Wouldn't it be something if we could whip the 3rd Division?" Of course the humor of my statement was not lost on the assembled officers, for they all smiled; and someone said that we had about as much chance of beating the 3rd Division as a snowball had in hell, which was a pretty accurate statement.

The next few months were busy ones. We did detailed planning, reviewed the tactics and techniques of employing the company and battalion in both the attack and the defense, repaired our equipment, and made preparations for our move to Vieques in mid-November. We found the island to be sandy and rugged, with little vegetation except some scrubby, nondescript brush and literally thousands of coconut trees. We also found a hundred or more *jiberos* (truck farmers) living there with their families, which surprised me. Apparently the navy's big guns didn't bother them in the least, for later, during the progress of the maneuver, we saw them hoeing away as if nothing unusual were happening.

Fortunately the Antilles headquarters had constructed a tent camp for us, which relieved us of that housekeeping chore, and we were able to get an early start on preparing our defensive positions. Our first problem was to select the specific area where we wished to establish these positions, and this choice would depend in large measure on our evaluation of the beaches. Soft, sandy areas where the seaward slopes were gradual and the water shallow and smooth were considered the most favorable to land amphibious forces. These were rated highest when we made our reconnaissance.

Having charted these likely landing spots, we then carefully traced the defiladed approaches leading from them to the high ground. Those routes which could not be covered by rifle fire were marked for the special attention of the artillery and mortars.

These tactical walks also served several other purposes, for we were able to select the most logical locations on the high ground for our automatic weapons and strong points. Once these positions were determined, we allocated zones of responsibilities to the battalion commanders. They in turn assigned specific missions to the company commanders, who allocated selected areas to the platoon leaders. Then the platoon leaders assigned certain responsibilities to the sergeants; finally the work of digging the foxholes and positions for the automatic weapons was done by the privates. As President Truman had once said about his office, "The buck stops here."

We had also noted on these reconnaissances that the growth of coconut trees extended almost from the water's edge to a line about a hundred yards inland. We decided to use them in our defense of the beaches. We would cut them down, leaving about a seven-foot stump, and not completely sever the trunk so that the entire thicket could be interlaced with barbed wire and demolitions. We hoped to make this the initial obstacle which would stop the landing forces at least long enough for us to place heavy concentrations of artillery and mortar fire on them. If we could destroy the landing forces or at least slow them down or disorganize them here, we would have a better chance to deal with them later. The task of preparing these defenses was assigned to the reserve battalion, and work was begun immediately. Additionally, the reserve battalion was assigned the mission of digging and camouflaging a large number of tank traps to further reduce the invaders' mobility and firepower.

Next we directed our attention to selecting areas where airborne troops could be dropped. This requires open ground with no trees or other underbrush that might injure the descending paratroopers and someplace where the prevailing winds are no stronger than fifteen or twenty miles per hour. This is a dangerous operation, and the paratroop commander must select his DZ (drop zone) with great care. He must, of course, pick an area in close proximity to the defending forces as well, so that he may close with them within a reasonably short time after hitting the ground. With these criteria in mind, we selected several possible DZs, and initiated the preparation of the ground at once. I noted later that the men who were working on this project went about it with a great deal of enthusiasm.

The next major problem was to select our successive defensive positions to the rear, should we be pushed back from our initial beach defenses, which we fully expected would happen. We had to insure that each successive position was within small-arms and mortar range of the position just in front of it so we could protect our withdrawing troops. Our final position would be in the form of a circle for a perimeter defense, or last stand, like General Custer at the Little Big Horn.

Having tentatively selected these battle lines, we then located positions for our reserve forces where they could be deployed quickly and effectively to any point in our defenses. Both principal and alternate positions were selected.

Artillery and mortar fires were then planned, and locations for the weapons were made by the commanders of those units. Priorities were established for the concentration of fires so that initial coverage could be given to the beaches, the approaches from them to our defensive positions, the DZs, the close-in protection of our strong points, and, finally, the massive barrages which would be called down on top of these strong points should they be overrun and occupied by the enemy.

With the basic decisions made regarding our defenses, we located and started construction of the underground command posts from which the commanders would control and influence the action. Preparation of these became a work of art.

I had informed the headquarters commandant that I planned to have about ten to twelve staff officers and men in my command post at one time; that we would need three and possibly four different locations, one for each of the successive defensive positions. In addition to personnel, we would have folding desks and chairs, file cabinets, telephones, radios, and other paraphernalia in these control centers. All of this would require at least a sixteen- or eighteen-foot square hole in the ground. These should be on the reverse slopes of the hills to protect us from the direct fire of the navy's heavy guns.

When I later inspected the four CPs, I found that the underground rooms were large enough to permit fifteen or twenty people to live in them indefinitely, even under the most hazardous conditions. The ten-foot holes had been covered with eight-inch poles and these in turn covered with metal sheets. Finally, eight to ten inches of dirt had been placed on top so that they were camouflaged from the air. On the inside, electric lights had been installed, electric fans were in operation, and tables and chairs had been neatly arranged to look like any other comfortable living room.

Equal care and work had gone into construction of the positions for the crew-served weapons and the individual foxholes so that maximum protection from fire and observation was afforded the occupants. As one news reporter later described the maneuver, "The Puerto Ricans of the defensive forces, who began by building installations that were really impregnable, went about behaving as though they were in the business of blood, sweat, and tears. Their camouflage was excellent, their fields of fire were properly arranged, and they did not mind staying up all night."

When we completed construction of our fortifications, we started a series of rehearsals to sharpen our timing in the employment of the reserve forces, the shifting of the supporting mortar and artillery fires, the withdrawing of forces to successive defensive positions to the rear, and other defensive measures. We also spent considerable time exercising our communications, which consisted of telephone, radio, runner, signal flags, sun mirrors, and smoke signals. I am told that the signal officer actually obtained some carrier pigeons but that one of the cooks had mistakenly used them for dinner because he thought they had been delivered as part of the daily rations. At any rate, we had multiple means of communicating, and we learned to use all of them.

We conducted refresher training for the medical company personnel and the line company aid men, none of whom had worked together as a unit since World War II. As mentioned, they had been operating dispensaries all over the island and needed to be retrained in the methods and techniques of caring for the sick and wounded on the battlefield. They had to be brought up to date on the use of field expedients, such as the construction of a litter by strapping rifles together and stretching the canvas top of a jeep between them to hold a casualty. They needed to learn how to lash several of these improvised stretchers to a jeep, so that they could get the wounded off the battlefield and back to the field hospitals quickly. It is highly important for a soldier to know that he will receive expert and immediate medical care should he be wounded.

Since we had no mortar company, it was decided that we would only organize a small group and designate it the fire-control center of the company. They would plot the fire missions for the mortars and the employment of the weapons, and their firing would be simulated.

But it was not all work and no play prior to the maneuvers, for we arranged for the men to return to Puerto Rico to visit their families, and they made side trips to the islands of St. Thomas and St. Croix. We started a hot-stove league of baseball, which is even more of a national sport in Puerto Rico than it is in the United States.

The officers were able to enjoy some free time as well. For my part, I went fishing. I had mentioned to my assistants Ramos and Vargas, that I liked to fish, so they arranged to take me one day. It had been decided that we would go on a Saturday. I suggested that we get an early start, like about four in the morning, when the fish usually bite the best.

"We don't have to go so early, sir," Ramos said. "We can catch them any time, sir," he continued.

Since they both seemed convinced that we could do pretty well at any hour of the day, I figured that they knew what they were doing and there was no use debating the subject. So it was decided that we would leave immediately after breakfast.

At the agreed hour both of them drove up in front of my tent in a jeep and away we went. I noted that there were no fishing poles or other gear, and I commented about it. But they both assured me they had everything that was needed, and I dropped the subject.

I guess we had been driving for about forty-five minutes when we stopped at an old wooden dock well hidden in a cove on the south side of the island. The ships spars that had been used to construct this ancient anchorage were waterlogged and decayed, and it was obvious that it had been there for many years. I thought at the time that it looked like something Captain Kidd might have built to harbor his long boats when he and his pirates came ashore for the water and other provisions they had stashed in nearby caves.

As we walked out onto the pier, I again asked about the fishing equipment.

"We have it, sir," Vargas said with a big grin on his face.

When I looked at Ramos for confirmation, he, too, was grinning like a Cheshire cat.

"OK, fellas, what's the gag?" I asked, knowing that they were up to something. I had hardly gotten the words out of my mouth when Ramos showed me four or five blocks of TNT, the half-pound type used by the army engineers in their demolition work.

"This is it, sir."

I am sure that I must have had a startled look on my face when I asked, "Isn't that a bit illegal?"

"No, sir," they both answered.

"This is the way we always fish, sir," Ramos replied. "We don't have any laws about fishing here, sir," he continued.

And when I thought about it, I guessed that he was right. Certainly the navy would not have gone to the trouble to establish any laws on the island when all they wanted was something to shoot at. Nor would the Puerto Rican government have been expected to exercise any control of this little piece of land while the U.S. Navy was using it for this purpose.

At any rate, Ramos inserted a detonator and let fly. After the explosion, a large number of big white fish appeared on top of the water and bellied over, dead. Vargas then dived in and retrieved our "catch," and that's the way we fished. With two or three more blasts, we had all that we could use, and my only fishing expedition on the island of Vieques was over. However, I was to plan another deep-sea fishing trip with General Sibert later, and that one turned out to be quite a surprise too.

Time passed quickly. Christmas had come and gone, and the start of the maneuver was close at hand. Last-minute preparations were just being completed when a large influx of observers suddenly descended upon us. They were mostly military personnel from the Pentagon, but there were also a number of news reporters present among them, and everyone wanted to see our battlefield positions. I had not seen so many kibitzers since the invasion of Southern France.

By nightfall of the last day before the maneuver, the visitors had departed from the combat zone, and the sea gulls had gone to roost. Peace and quiet reigned over the front lines, and this gave us a last-minute chance to check our communications nets, post our sentinels and observers, and hopefully to get some rest before the battle began.

However, there was little sleep for me that night. I rolled and tossed on my field cot and thought about the possible outcome of the maneuver. I only hoped that we would not be ingloriously chased to the water's edge, there to be dunked and given the *coup de grâce* at the hands of the hilarious victors. It was almost a welcome relief when I heard the first navy shells come screeching over our heads at dawn and heard them land with an ear-splitting blast in the impact area. Not to be outdone by the navy, the air force bombers unleashed a continuous string of explosives that literally shook our CP.

We should be safe enough, I thought, unless the navy gunners or air force bombardiers made a mistake, which was always a possibility. The impact area was about a thousand yards off to our left, but even so, a slight error in the gun settings or flight pattern could make this maneuver more realistic than we had bargained for.

My field telephone rang at almost the same instant the bombs began to hit. "Fantastic Six here," I said, using the code name assigned to me as the Aggressor commander of the 65th Royal Fusiliers.

"Bolero Six, sir," came the voice of St. Clair, the commander of my 1st Battalion. I had to laugh when he gave his code name, for I thought that we sounded like a Spanish dance team. The commander of the 2nd Battalion was named "Conga," the third commander was called "Fandango," and the separate company commanders named "Mambo," "Rumba," "Samba," and "Tango."

"The assault boats are about one hundred yards offshore, sir," St. Clair reported as he described how he could barely see them in the early morning mist. "Looks like about a battalion, sir, and headed right for the beaches in front of us."

So we had made at least one good selection of where the enemy might land. But there was no certainty that the other eight infantry battalions would land there, or the supporting troops either. As a matter of fact, I was sure that the other rifle troops would land on a broad front to permit the engineers, tanks, artillery, and other supporting units to come ashore quickly, which is the usual procedure. They would probably do their best to land the bulk of the division by no later than noon of the second day.

When St. Clair completed his report, I alerted the artillery and makeshift mortar company commanders to be prepared, on call, to fire their preplanned barrages onto the beaches. At the same time, Allen notified the other commanders of the situation. For the moment, at least, we could do nothing but wait and see what developed.

Several hours passed before I heard any other really important news. We had of course received a running account from the forward observers and the battalion commanders, but it was not until about noon that Bolero Six again notified me of what was happening.

"Colonel, we have just been informed by the umpires that the landing force has been held up by our beach defenses, and that they have been assessed 40 percent casualties. The umpires told me that instead of knocking holes in our defenses, the bombings had made them completely impassable. They said that our beach defenses are the best that they have ever seen — even better than what the Japanese threw at them in the Pacific."

When I repeated St. Clair's statements to the staff, there was a rebel yell that could have been heard by the crews of the enemy ships at sea. We had stopped the mighty 3rd Division, at least temporarily, that is.

"That's great," I said to St. Clair. "What happens now? Did the umpires say where we go from here? I wondered what took them so long to make their evaluations. Yours is the first news that we have had since early morning."

"Sir, one of the umpires is right here, would you like to talk to him?"

"Yes, please," I replied.

"This is the senior Aggressor umpire," came the voice on the other end. "As Bolero Six has said, we made the survey in the impact area and have come to the conclusion that the assaulting forces would not have been able to breach your beach defenses before they would have been completely wiped out by your artillery and mortar fires. The naval gun fire and aerial bombardment only make your beach obstacles harder to penetrate. We have decided to call an administrative halt to the maneuver so that your troops can clear several paths through the obstacles and the assaulting troops can come ashore."

"How soon do you wish us to start?" I asked.

"Just as soon as you can get your troops down here to the beaches," was the answer.

"Thank you. We'll get started right away. By the way, I understand that the landing forces were assessed 40 percent casualties."

"That is correct. As you probably know, before the maneuver started we checked your preplanned artillery and mortar fires as well as the fields of fire of the automatic weapons and the riflemen, so we were able to determine the effects of those fires quickly. The evaluation of the bombing in the impact area required more time."

"We thank you for the information. We'll have our troops go to work on those beach obstacles right away. How many lanes do you want us to cut?"

"Eight or ten will be sufficient. When you have completed that job, another administrative move will permit the attacking troops to come ashore."

I then called Conga Six and directed Dammer to start the beach-clearing work in his sector. In the meantime, Childs had given the same instructions to St. Clair, on the right half of our positions.

This was going to pose a problem: if the 3rd Division had not been able to cut their way through, how were we going to accomplish the job? After some discussion it was finally decided to hitch some tanks to the mass of tangled rubble and literally pull it apart. With that plan and the help of wire cutters and some heavy-duty saws, we were finally able to clear the required number of lanes by late afternoon.

Stopping the assault forces at the water's edge had proved at least two important facts. First, that such beach defenses can be made almost impregnable, strong enough to withstand even the heavy shelling from the navy's big guns and the pounding of the air force bombers. The Japanese had done the same thing at Tarawa, and when the marines tried to go ashore, they were literally cut to ribbons. Secondly, it proved once again, at least up to this point in the maneuvers, that the Puerto Ricans could hold their own with the best-trained soldiers that the United States Army could put into the field. They had been put to the test in this initial phase of the maneuver and had shown what they could do.

After we had cleared the required number of lanes, the landing forces were permitted to continue their landings ashore, not because of their own military prowess or skill but by courtesy of the umpires.

The enemy build-up ashore continued, and by the time word finally reached us that the maneuver was again "live," some six or seven battalions were storming our positions. We immediately resumed our artillery and mortar barrage on the beaches. We really poured it on them. When they finally came within range of our automatic weapons and rifles, those men opened up with devastating effect.

Progress of the attacker was slow that first twenty-four hours, and no really critical situations developed as far as we were concerned. I suspect that the enemy spent most of that first night reorganizing and consolidating positions, while continuing the build-up in preparation for an early morning assault. I also had the feeling that this would be accompanied by an airdrop.

Though the enemy assault had come to something of a standstill, we continued to be shelled and bombed throughout the night and suffered some minor casualties to both equipment and personnel as a result. But the damage that we suffered was slight compared to what we had done to the enemy that first day.

As expected, at the crack of dawn the following morning, heavy rifle fire broke out all along the defensive position, and the battle was again joined. About ten o'clock, Conga Six called to inform me that his left flank was receiving heavy pressure and that one of his company strong points had been driven out of its defensive position.

"How bad is it?" I asked Dammer. "Do you think you can contain it?"

"Well, we are holding in our other positions, and I have started a reserve force of about a half company to counterattack on our left, so the situation isn't too critical at the moment. I just thought you should know that we are getting heavy pressure and that it looks as though the main effort may be coming this way. I'll keep you posted."

"Right, Herm. Thanks. Saint told me a moment ago that nothing spectacular was going on in his area and that it looked like you were getting all of the action so far. I'll alert a part of my reserve just in case you get into trouble. Stay in touch." Dammer wasn't one to get overly excited, and I knew that when he thought he was about to get into trouble he would warn me. But I decided to be prepared for any eventuality, so I instructed my operations officer to have the reserve prepared to move on a moment's notice.

"Jerry, I just received word from Dammer that he has a pretty good fight going on over there and that the enemy may be making his principal effort on our left flank. Will you do two things, please? First, get hold of the fire-control center and ask them to contact the 2nd Battalion — maybe they can give them some additional fire (artillery and mortar). Next, please have a part of my reserve ready to move on five minutes notice. Tell the commander that his mission will be to restore our left-flank positions. I just want him ready to go in case Dammer gets into real trouble."

"Yes, sir. I'm talking to the artillery commander right now, and he tells me that they are shifting some fires over to increase the support of the 2nd Battalion."

"Good — Chick, any news about the airdrop?" I had asked Childs to stay on top of any reports of transport aircraft in the area, for we knew that this would be a good time for that operation to be launched.

"No, sir, nothing yet. But conditions are certainly in their favor — no wind, bluebird sky — they may not have a better chance for the rest of the maneuver."

"That's certainly the truth."

"Sir, General Sibert wishes to speak with you," the Sergeant Major said as he handed me the telephone.

"Fantastic Six here."

"This is Fox Six. I wanted to inform you that my headquarters is withdrawing from the battle area, and that you are now, as of this moment, in command of all Aggressor ground forces. Good luck and happy hunting."

There had been no indication in the original directive or the "Play of the Exercise," that Sibert's headquarters would "retire" from the battlefield leaving the 65th responsible for all Aggressor ground operations. But there it was; we had work to do, and fast.

The staff was notified at once of this sudden change in the situation and set to work planning to meet it. My immediate concern was to establish communications with all of the other troops originally under Sibert's command and now under my control. I needed to know their

of the hill in front of us, but I was able to see the sky overhead. It was soon filled with ballooning white parachutes that appeared to be the size of handkerchiefs with puppet-sized figures dangling from the ends. Following closely in the wake of these descending figurines were the bright red- and orange-colored chutes carrying the paratroopers' supplies and equipment, such as mortars and machine guns; it was a beautiful sight. The blue and red pastel-tinted sky formed a perfect picture background for what seemed like a children's miniature show but would soon turn into a "bloody" battle when the enemy hit the ground.

The drop reminded me somewhat of the one made just a few miles inland from St. Tropez on the southern shores of France, just prior to the beach landings in Operation Anvil. In that operation, however, the air force made a navigational error and dropped the paratroops right on top of a German regiment of infantry. A rifle-wielding, bayonet-jabbing, hand-to-hand melee followed, which our men won fortunately.

This drop, however, was different in several respects. To begin with, it was made on a very level, unobstructed piece of terrain where there was little or no chance that any of the parachutists would be injured, instead of in the DZs in the rear where they would have been made in actual combat. Secondly, the maneuver director had selected this particular drop zone where the many spectators could see the entire show without having to move from the bleacher seats which had been erected for their comfort.

At the precise moment that the paratroopers hit the ground, our preplanned artillery and mortar barrages (simulated) descended upon them. Like a beach assault, the most vulnerable time for these forces is when they hit the ground: they are disorganized; not assembled into a fighting unit; have not gathered up their heavy weapons and other necessary supplies; and, most importantly, are out of communication with one another.

Following this barrage, we ordered our reserve battalion to hit them before they could recover from the artillery bombardment, and the results were disastrous for them. It was fortunate for me that I had not ordered the reserve battalion to move to Dammer's assistance, for this mission was of a higher priority. Later, I was advised by the senior umpire that the parachutists had suffered 50 percent casualties as a result of our attack, but these figures did not include those who had been impaled on our pikes in the DZs. This accounted for another 10 percent.

As it turned out, however, it was the 40 percent who escaped us that did the real damage. Unfortunately, too, we did not capture the battalion commander, who happened to be one of the most aggressive paratroop commanders in the army at the time, Lieutenant Colonel ("Little Joe") Stilwell, son of the famous General ("Vinegar Joe") Stilwell of the China-India-Burma theater of operations during World War II. It was Stilwell and his small force which, later that evening and early the following morning, managed to penetrate St. Clair's position and eventually drive him back from the high ground overlooking the beaches on our right.

But on the morning of the second day of operations, the steam of the attacking forces seemed to be petering out, and Dammer was able to hold his position for the time being. We heard later that this slow up in the action was because both the senior ground and naval commanders had been declared casualties.

The ground commander had come ashore sometime during the morning of the second day to take personal command, and he was accompanied by the senior naval commander who wished to observe the action. Both had been met by one of the natives of the island, a Puerto Rican soldier in *jibero* working clothes, who had handed the ground commander a small gift as a token of appreciation for their liberation. When the General opened the package in the presence of the admiral and a prebriefed umpire, a small puff of smoke came out of the box. Inside was a note which said, "This is a booby trap — you are now dead." This idea, which had originated with Eddie Sibert, may seem to some a rather childish trick, but it was intended to demonstrate forcefully the cunning means to which the enemy will go to catch the unwary, including generals.

Because of the delay in the appointment of new ground and naval commanders, it was late on the afternoon of D plus three before the enemy regained his original momentum in the assault on Dammer's position. In the meantime, we were able to contain Stilwell's attack on our right flank.

Dammer's position was somewhat more vulnerable than St. Clair's because it was not on as dominant terrain. The enemy, with his superior strength there, was soon able to roll Dammer back. Additionally, with this rapid build-up, we would probably find it increasingly difficult to make a determined stand and would soon have to assume a more mobile posture — which is another way of saying it would not be long before we would have to run like hell for our next defensive position in the rear.

Though our forced withdrawal was not a surprise, several things had to be done, and done quickly. I called the staff together and issued the necessary instructions to implement the plans that we had laid for just such a contingency.

"Chick, will you please start the move of our CP to the rear. It now appears as though the enemy has gathered his strength, and we are going to have to be quick on our feet if we are to escape complete defeat.

"Jerry, we need another reserve force we can use to influence the action when that time comes. As a matter of fact, whenever I use what reserve we have, you might take that as your signal to automatically constitute another one, OK?"

"Yes, sir. Our original reserve battalion has been pulled back from the drop zone, but it is going to need some reinforcements and additional equipment before it will be ready to fight. They suffered about 30 percent casualties."

"Right — I suspected that they would — at any rate, get me one that I can use immediately."

"Yes, sir."

"And don't touch Carno's battalion yet. I want to save him for the final go-around."

I had directed Major Ramirez, my supply officer, to organize a provisional battalion made up of truck drivers, cooks, KPs, and other odds and ends of personnel and to train them for use as a reserve in a last-ditch situation. When finally put together, this battalion consisted of about five hundred and fifty men, quite a formidable force. We had used this bobtail outfit once during one of our practice counterattacks, and it had proved to be quite effective in a "clutch" situation.

I asked my S-2 (intelligence officer) to step up the timing on the reports of the enemy. We had one small liaison plane that could be used for reconnaissance. Instead of waiting for the ground observers and others to give us telephone reports, I wanted to have the pilot and observer in the plane give us radio reports on the enemy's dispositions. If any reports were too confidential or detailed, he was to make a fly-over and drop a written message. I wanted to be able to react quickly to any enemy action. I didn't expect to use Carno's battalion much before D plus five, at the earliest. I told him in the meantime to keep his supplies on the trucks and mobile.

A retrograde movement, while engaged with the enemy, is a tricky business, and moving a headquarters at the same time only complicates an already difficult maneuver. Security and communications are the two principal problems in moving a large headquarters. There isn't too much that can be done about the former except to disperse the vehicles as they make the move. But many things can be done to insure noninterruption of communications. During the preparation of our deliberate defenses, we had laid telephone wire to each of the successive CPs; reconnoitered new routes from there to each of the battalion defensive positions; found new locations for the reserve forces and laid telephone wires to them from my new command posts; kept my jeep radio in constant communication with all of the units of my command, so when I moved I would be in instant contact with my commanders.

Furthermore, it is not unusual during such operations for the tactical situation to become critical, and this one was no exception. As we began our move to the rear, the enemy began to increase his pressure on our left flank once more. But instead of reinforcing Dammer with troops, we decided to hit the enemy with the concentrated fires of all our artillery and mortars. This proved to be very effective. It gave us the necessary breathing space to complete our retrograde movement and prevented the enemy from getting in behind us. The umpires gave us credit for wiping out one entire enemy company and about a third of another one. This amounted to over three hundred effectives, and the enemy couldn't afford many more losses of that magnitude.

But even this large number of casualties did not stop our attacker, for with the approach of daylight on D plus four he hit our right flank, and for a few hours it looked as though we were in real trouble there as well. I sent in the Reserve Battalion, which Allen had constituted, to relieve the situation and withdrew St. Clair. But this did not stop the momentum of their attack, and we were forced to continue our withdrawal without halting at our second defensive position. There was only one course of action open to us: that was to go into a completely mobile defense — run, stop and fight, and run again. By a series of counterattacks, shifting of artillery and mortar fires and some good footwork we were able to avoid disaster and stay alive.

Even so, by the morning of D plus five, we were getting awfully close to the far side of the island and the water's edge. When we finally reached our last defensive position, we still had two more days before the maneuver would be over. If we could just hold on until then, we could at least claim that the mighty 3rd Division had not defeated us. Possibly this was a technicality, but it would be a feather in our cap nevertheless and a blow to the prestige of one U.S. Army division.

With all of the counterattacking that we had been doing, we had managed to keep the enemy off balance, but it had also been hard on the troops; they were dog tired. All of these moves had been made on foot, but the men had not complained even once. As a matter of fact, they seemed to gain new life with each setback of the enemy. They knew that the 65th was making a good showing, and they worked like Trojans. I had never seen troops with as much enthusiasm and will to win.

But there comes an end to any man's endurance, and our troops had just about reached that point. Now was the time for the Provisional Battalion to get into the act. Just as I started to call for Ramirez, he was right in front of me.

"Carno, I was just going to ask Jerry to alert you for action."

"We're ready, sir," he said.

"Yes, sir, Carno started his organization last night, and they are ready to go," Allen said. "We have briefed him on the situation, and he has dumped his supplies because we have no other place to go; we knew that you would approve," he continued.

"Right, Jerry, I got so wound up in trying to stay out of trouble, I almost forgot about you, Carno. Now here's the dope. We have been looking over the situation, and we believe that with the build-up going on in front of our right flank, the enemy intends to try the *coup de grâce* there, probably by tomorrow morning, D plus six. That will give him all day and night to clean up the battlefield before the maneuver is halted by the umpires. We figure that if you hit him just as he starts his attack, we may have a chance to stop him and save the day. What do you think?"

"Sounds good to me, sir. We're ready to go any time, sir."

"Good, Carno. Now tell me briefly what you plan to do."

"Well, sir, we have six tanks that are operational, and Jerry has attached them to me, and this is the way I plan on attacking. I plan on starting out in a column of companies and hitting their left flank. We have arranged with the artillery to give us a heavy barrage, which they will lift on call. Then I want the infantry troops to develop the situation before I commit the tanks. I'll hold one infantry company in reserve and not use it until I am forced to. That's about it, sir."

"Very good, Carno, you are not only one helluva fine supply staff officer but a good tactician as well."

Jerry and Chick approved the plan wholeheartedly.

About midafternoon a swarm of visitors descended upon us. The newspaper and radio people, the brass from the Pentagon, navy, air force, and army, and more importantly, Generals Sibert and Porter. All were curious about the Puerto Ricans who had obviously stopped the famed 3rd Division and had not yet been driven into the sea, as had been expected. Everyone was very complimentary of the regiment, particularly Sibert and Porter, although neither of them seemed at all surprised at the results of the maneuver up to this point. They had, of course, seen the Puerto Ricans in action before and knew what they could do when they put their minds to it. I had not had that experience before, and I was enjoying it for the first time.

The night of D plus six passed quietly enough, ominously so, I thought, for this was the eve of the final big battle which would determine the outcome for us, either defeat or the sweet taste of victory. Whether the Puerto Ricans had the staying power to continue to slug it out against overwhelming odds was still a question that had to be answered; the following day would do that.

It was like the night before the last game of the World Series. The commanders and I, like the manager and his coaches, had a series of telephone conferences during the night to insure that we had not forgotten even the slightest detail of our plans. And when I hit the sack about two in the morning, the staff was still mumbling in quiet tones.

The next sounds I heard were at first light, and they were just like those on the first day of the maneuver — one continuous roar of thunder as the navy and air force opened up on us. It brought me out of my bunk to my field desk in one leap; the time for action had arrived.

"Jerry, check the battalions, will you, and find out if you can see where it looks like the main effort is being made."

While Allen made the calls, I listened to his side of the conversation with each commander, and it sounded as though the enemy was making his final drive on our right flank. When he had finished, he confirmed this, but I held back and did not pass the word for Ramirez to start his attack until I could talk to the battalion commander who had taken over St. Clair's position. He knew our plan, and since he had a fine sense of timing, I knew that he would signal me just when such an attack would have the best chance for success.

Within minutes that call came in, and it was time for Ramirez to get under way. I wished him well and then sat down to chew on my finger-nails and await the outcome — our last bolt had been launched, and there was little that I could do from then on, except worry.

We were lucky, I guess, for just as I gave the order for Ramirez to commence his attack, the chief umpire, who was in my CP at the time, called off the maneuver and told me that the counterattacking battalion would not have to move. At least we received credit for launching the attack, even though the outcome was doubtful in my mind. On the other hand, I am quite sure that it would have come as a surprise to the enemy, and that in itself would have given us some advantage.

There was considerable excitement around the headquarters when everyone learned that the maneuver had ended. I would describe the attitude of the personnel as one of wide-eyed, happy disbelief as to what had happened; we all felt that we had at least achieved a partial victory. We couldn't say that we had won the maneuver, but we sure could brag about the fact that the 3rd Division had not driven us off the island, which the script had clearly indicated would be the final outcome.

A few minutes after the exercise ended, I was notified that there would be a critique and that all senior commanders were to assemble at a specific location immediately after lunch. Apparently only the very high-level brass from the Pentagon were to make any comments. I hoped this might cut down on the time we would have to listen to a rehash of everything that had taken place in the six days of the maneuver, which was the usual procedure in most critiques.

As I made my way through the hundreds of observers and umpires at the designated assembly point, I received many compliments about the Puerto Rican troops, particularly about their hard work and skill in constructing the defensive fortifications and their staying power, which enabled them to continue the fight against overwhelming odds. One senior general stopped me to compliment us on our mobile defensive tactics and the surprising end to the maneuver. Instead of being a ragtag, disorganized, and fleeing bunch of Puerto Ricans, as had been expected, we had added insult to injury by staging a counterattack which, had it been allowed to continue, would have knocked the surprised enemy back onto his heels.

The critique itself did not take much time, primarily because there were some embarrassed senior army officers who probably thought that the less said the better. At least that is the impression I gained listening to the speakers and the conversations going on around me. The umpires did levy some strong criticism on both sides, but again it seemed to me that when we sorted out all of the platitudes, or bromides, the 3rd Division received the brunt of the censure.

I was particularly interested in the side comments of the audience. The looks on their faces were expressing shock, amazement, disbelief, or downright glee, depending upon what part each had played in the maneuver. The reporters from the newspapers and radio were particularly hilarious as they wrote their stories about the final outcome of the maneuver.

Many of these news releases were given to me after we had returned to Puerto Rico. Almost without exception each of them described how the underdog Puerto Ricans had chewed the tail of the "Paper Tiger" — the best that the Department of Defense could put into the field. As one reporter wrote, "The 65th RCT [Regimental Combat Team] also took matters seriously in other respects; ordered to set up beach defenses, they built concrete-log bunkers so well-sited, so thoroughly dug-in, that the marine umpires perceived that the landing forces would be cut to pieces. They ruled about half the block houses blown up, supposedly as a result of naval gun fire. Now, it is very doubtful that naval gun fire would have destroyed those bunkers or aerial bombing either."

Another one wrote, "that the attacking forces had pushed inland from a beach that they did not win, and not all of the paratroopers had been able to join the landing forces for the simple reason that they had been killed or captured when they were dropped." He further expressed the view that some of the assaulting commanders thought that their plans had fallen into the hands of the enemy, which of course they had not. The plain truth of the matter was that the Puerto Rican troops had just beaten the hell out of our supposedly best-trained assault forces.

Several weeks later we received the following communications which was heady praise for what I had originally considered "rum and Coca Cola" troops.

New York, NY
20 March 1950

ACP 201.22
Subject: Letter of Commendation
To: Commanding Officer
          65th Infantry Regiment
          Losey Field, P.R.

I wish to commend you and the officers and men of the 65th Infantry Regiment for your outstanding performance of duty in connection with Operation PORTREX.

The regiment provided the backbone of the ground defenses of Vieques. Much careful planning, sound military knowledge and plain hard work was necessary to adequately organize the terrain for the defense. The final results of your efforts appeared on D-Day when the invader established a beachhead through umpire indulgence. Throughout the tactical phase of the operation, the 65th Infantry Regiment proved itself a well-trained, skillful organization at least the equal of the best that the invader brought against him. The ensuing conflict against heavy odds brought me great pride and satisfaction in that our troops earned for themselves an enviable reputation for enthusiasm, "know-how" and serious devotion to duty.

I wish to take this opportunity to state that the 65th Infantry Regiment during Operation PORTREX lived up to the finest traditions of the service. Please accept for yourself and pass to each officer and man of the regiment my sincere thanks for their loyal effective support and my congratulations upon a splendid performance of duty.

[Signed] EDWIN L. SIBERT
BRIGADIER GENERAL, U.S. ARMY COMMANDING

Then, a few days later I received the following additional letter from General Sibert.

AG 201 - Harris, W. W. (0)
Subject: Letter of Commendation
To: Colonel W. W. Harris, 018170
         Commanding Officer
         Fort Brooke, Puerto Rico

I wish to commend you for your superior performance of duty as Commanding Officer, 65th Infantry Regiment during Operation PORTREX.

Your drive and enthusiasm as well as your professional knowledge were important factors in successfully preparing the major tactical positions for the defense of Vieques. In the tactical phase of the exercise you employed your troops skillfully and effectively. Throughout the exercise you demonstrated the initiative, imagination and the sound judgment of the best type of senior officer. The confidence I felt upon turning the field command over to you on D plus 2 was fully justified by the command ability which you demonstrated from then until the end of the maneuver.

Please accept my sincere thanks for your loyal effective support as my major subordinate commander and accept as well my congratulations on a duty well performed. A copy of this communication will be made a part of your 201 file.

[Signed] EDWIN L. SIBERT
BRIGADIER GENERAL, U.S. ARMY COMMANDING

Vieques Maneuvers. Building a command post to withstand naval and air bombings.

Antipersonnel mines and booby traps were planted in the tangled mass.

The paratroopers arrive. Defense alerted.

Palm trees felled before being interlaced and wired together with barbed wire.

Happy faces at conclusion of Vieques maneuvers. Major E.G. Allen, Brig. Gen. Edwin L. Sibert, Col. W.W. Harris, Maj. Gen. Ray E. Porter, Lt. Col. G.W. Childs in the background.

Men of the 65th crowd the deck of the U.S.S. *Marine Lynx* en route to Korea, 23 August 1950. U.S. ARMY PHOTO

Training aboard the U.S.S. *Marine Lynx*, 16 September 1950. U.S. ARMY PHOTO

3

NEW MOVEMENT ORDERS: DESTINATION UNKNOWN

The maneuver was over. The dust had settled. The sea gulls had returned. The flagstaffs and the standards had been lowered and cased, and the mighty 3rd Division had departed quietly. And we had relished, savored, rehashed, refought, and rewon the "war" many times over.

But now we were faced with the uninteresting prospect of cleaning up the playground. This meant filling in hundreds of holes in the ground and cleaning the beaches of the half-cut coconut trees. Mile after mile of telephone wire had to be collected, repaired and rereeled onto signal corps drums. Most cantankerous of all, we had to unthread the unthreadable tons of barbed wire we had used and then rewind it onto spools so that it could be used again.

But we had plenty of time, or so I thought. We should be able to do all of this at a rather leisurely pace — do some exploring of this old Caribbean-pirate hideaway; get in some fishing a la Ramos-Vargas style; visit St. Thomas and St. Croix, two other islands in the Greater Antilles chain; and maybe just do nothing but some plain and fancy loafing. We did manage to do some of these things — for exactly two days.

Once again, the unexpected came in the form of a Department of Defense document. This time, it directed the close-out of all but three of the existing army posts in Puerto Rico and reduced the strength of the already understrengthed 65th. And even more of an affront, we were humiliated by being told that the regiment was to be relegated to the level of a mere caretaking establishment. Hereafter, our principal mission would be to paint and repair government buildings, cut grass, capture stray dogs, and chase Latin lovers if they encroached upon the sacred grounds of the moth-balled military reservations.

The effects of this ill-advised directive were traumatic; the doom and gloom were apparent everywhere.

We had been hailed as the conquering heroes, the saviors of the cause, the redeemers, the liberators, the emancipators, and the jack-at-a-pinch winners, figuratively speaking that is, in a lopsided maneuver. And now this. A fine reward for our efforts. Someone in the Pentagon had failed to get the word, and our pride had been struck another blow. Or was it envy this time? Well, we didn't really know, except that the reason given was fiscal — but why us?

Although I didn't say so, I thought to hell with it. We had already done more than I hoped we would do in that first half year. The administration of the regiment was functioning properly. We had made more than a creditable showing on our training tests. I had had my chance to command a regiment in maneuvers, and we had done well. There really wasn't much left to prove, except to take the regiment off to war somewhere, but there wasn't any war.

So we went about our chores of dismantling the battlefield, closing out installations, setting up caretaking teams, and reducing strengths. The most difficult of all of these duties was finding quarters for the service families. There was no problem for the 2nd Battalion, since it would stay at Henry Barracks. The 1st Battalion from Losey Field and my headquarters was something else. The 1st was headed for Fort Buchanan, on the opposite side of San Juan from Fort Brooke, where my headquarters and headquarters company would move. Buchanan had some housing facilities but not many. Neither did Fort Brooke (El Moro Castle), so many of the families, particularly those of the enlisted men, had to find accommodations to rent in the San Juan area, where they were both scarce and expensive.

While all of these projects were under way, we also had another exercise to perform that was much more pleasant. It just happened that the regiment's fifty-first anniversary and Armed Forces Day fell on the same date, May 20, 1950. We planned a large reception, parade, exhibit of arms and equipment, and a general open house. Governor Munoz-Marin, Doña Felicia, mayoress of San Juan, and many other dignitaries were there, and it turned out to be a very pleasant affair. I think that the very large attendance was due in part to the publicity of our success in the maneuver — although no real excuse was ever necessary for the people of Puerto Rico to pay homage to their beloved 65th Infantry.

exact dispositions, strengths, and supply status, and we had to integrate them into our plans for future ground action, which had been Sibert's responsibility up to this turn in events.

But while these mechanics were being worked out, we still had to "fight the war." The most critical event yet to come was the parachute drop. Unless we repulsed that operation successfully, we could be in real trouble. Then, while I was reviewing and checking on our planned reception for the paratroopers, my telephone rang again, and the action began to get even hotter.

"Fantastic Six here."

"Conga Six again, sir. Our left flank is now getting heavier pressure, sir. I have committed part of my reserve, but it looks like we are going to need help real soon. I thought that I had better alert you to the possibility of some trouble here."

Knowing that Dammer would need help very soon, some action on my part was indicated immediately. "Thanks, Herm. I'll have my reserve alerted to move in your direction. Keep in touch. And by the way, have you seen or heard any sign of transport aircraft?"

"No, sir, I haven't. But there are certainly one helluva lot of landing craft headed this way. Looks like they are bringing in the division tail." (Supply and other follow-up troops, like heavy artillery.)

This news confirmed our estimate that the enemy probably had sufficient ground troops ashore to mount a coordinated attack, and with it the parachute drop. This can disrupt an entire defensive force, even though in itself it may not be divisive, and this caused me concern. During the time of the famous Bulge, around Bastogne during World War II, just the rumor that the German Commando Otto Shorzeny and his paratroopers had landed behind the American lines was enough to send chills up the backs of some officers of our high command. But whatever the invading force was up to, we did not have long to wait before we found out.

Within an hour after my conversation with Dammer, the enemy hit him with the full force of at least half the 3rd Division, and more were on their way. St. Clair, on the other hand, received only slight probing actions against his lines. There was no doubt about it now, the enemy's main effort would be directed at rolling up our left flank and attempting to get in behind our positions from that direction.

Then as we had anticipated, the heavy hum of the low-flying "boxcars" could be heard in the distance — right on time. I asked Allen to set our counterattack plans in motion immediately to combat this threat. Then I walked out of my CP to watch the show. I could not see the DZs because

One of the very kind messages which was read at the parade ceremonies at Armed Forces Day was the following:

HEADQUARTERS
UNITED STATES FORCES ANTILLES
Office of the Commanding General

New York, N.Y.
APO 851, Postmaster

AG 006   17 May 1950

Subject: Organization Day of the 65th Infantry Regiment
          and Armed Forces Day.
To: Commanding Officer
          65th Infantry Regiment
          Fort Brooke, Puerto Rico

1. The 51st Anniversaryof the 65th Infantry Regiment which coincides with Armed Forces Day, Saturday 20 May 1950, provides an opportunity for me to congratulate the officers and men of this splendid requirement for the regiment's record of fifty-one years of outstanding achievement.

2. The deeds of the officers and men of the 65th Infantry Regiment have been gloriously written in the pages of history. The regiment has always responded in the finest military tradition to the call of the nation in the time of need. The peacetime standards and the combat readiness of the 65th Infantry Regiment are at an all time high today. The performance of the regiment during Operation PORTREX recently held on the island of Vieques, Puerto Rico, attests this fact. The praise and commendation showered on the regiment by high-ranking officers of the Armed Forces during the PORTREX critique were tributes to the leadership and soldierly proficiency of the 65th Infantry.

3. The citizens of our country can well be proud of this superbly trained, high-spirited organization which is a vital part of our defense team in the Caribbean and one of the outstanding units of the United States Army today.

[Signed] EDWIN L. SIBERT
BRIG. GENERAL, U.S. ARMY COMMANDING

The future looked good for fishing. In fact, I was in the throes of preparation for a three-day fishing venture in the briny deep with Eddie Sibert when the telephone rang — it was about ten minutes before Sibert was to pick me up.

"That's probably Sibert's aide calling to tell me that he is on his way and should be here any minute," I remarked to my assembled well-wishers as I walked into the house to answer what I thought was a routine call.

"Harris, here."

"Eddie Sibert, Bill. I guess that our fishing trip is going to be delayed for a spell," Sibert said rather gloomily. "I have just been notified that you and I are wanted on a three-way teleconference with Panama and the Pentagon. Meet me at the telecon room in twenty minutes."

"Yes, sir."

I made my way thoughtfully back to the front porch to break the news that the fishing trip was cancelled. It was a mystery to me, I thought, as I walked over to the headquarters and up the steps to the "classified room." War in Korea had broken out on June 24, but we couldn't be going there. The army had just completed our reduction in force, and after all, this was still the all-Puerto Rican 65th United States Infantry Regiment. But the more that I thought about it, the more I realized that a reduction in force, a small thing like a regiment not having even half of its personnel and practically none of its authorized equipment was not going to make any difference to the Pentagon brass when it came time to order it into combat. As I look back on the situation now, the whole picture reminds me of the tales told by Cornelius Ryan in his beautifully written book *The Last Battle*. Shortly before the end came, when the little Austrian corporal had personal command of the OKH — the German Army High Command — he had ordered divisions moved here, there, and elsewhere, with no knowledge or possibly indifference to the fact that those very units existed only on paper — even though his staff had very carefully pinned their divisional symbols on the situation map.

Yes, that had to be it. I could think of no other reason why the Pentagon brass would want to talk to me, although a number of the senior officers there were good friends of mine and were still serving on a tour of duty that had started about the same time that mine had in 1945. Well, I'll soon know, I thought.

Without going into the details of the operation, the visible portion of the teleconference equipment consists of a typewriter and a large white screen — like the one used in showing home movies — and an operator. The messages, both those dispatched and received, appear on the screen in clear text just as they appear on this page. When a conferee wishes to send a message to another conferee on the other end of the line, he writes the message out in longhand and gives it to the operator, who then types it out on his typewriter; the equipment does the rest. The message is automatically coded or sent in the clear, depending upon the classification given it by the sender.

At precisely one minute before the scheduled time for the conference to begin, Eddie Sibert walked in. He smiled and said, "You know, I have been thinking about a reason for this conference, and the only logical conclusion that I can reach is that the 65th is headed for Korea. What do you think?"

"That's about the size of it," I replied. "I can think of no other good reason." And then the screen began to type out the names of the conferees in the Pentagon. As I had suspected, I knew most of them. Panama was silent and so was Eddie Sibert as the conference progressed, for though the orders were technically being transmitted through Panama and the Antilles Command, I was the principal recipient of the glad tidings that were to follow.

"The very fact that this conference is being held and everything that follows is classified as secret."

"You are directed to prepare the 65th Infantry Regiment for an overseas assignment. Destination: Unknown (secret)."

I liked that part about "the 65th Infantry Regiment," as though we were three thousand strong instead of being more like the half-strength British Light Brigade which had been dashed into antiquity at Tripoli.

"The plan is," the teletype continued to clatter out, "for the 65th Infantry to move to an unknown destination overseas, there to join up with the 3rd United States Infantry Division and go through a cycle of basic training before onward movement to your final destination (secret)."

"That can't be possible," I yelled. I turned to Sibert. "Can't you see the reception that we will get after our little *pas de deux* with them at Vieques. We'll be about as welcome as the country cousins who dropped in unexpectedly on their city relatives for Sunday dinner."

But it was true.

"The 30th Infantry Regiment at Fort Benning will be stripped of most of its personnel as fillers for the other regiments of the 3rd Division, and the 65th United States Infantry Regiment will replace it (secret)."

"The 65th will take all of its athletic equipment (secret)" was the next startling statement that appeared on the screen.

"You will be prepared to sail within ten days time on the following three Liberty Ships . . . secret." and the people in the Pentagon named them. The only one that I remember at the moment was the rocking, rolling *Marine Lynx,* which was assigned to lift the personnel of the 65th to its unknown destination.

"The 3rd Battalion, 33rd Infantry in Panama is hereby detached from that organization and assigned to the 65th United States Infantry Regiment (secret)."

This was the same battalion that had been assigned to us for the Vieques maneuver, and I welcomed that. At least we would have three battalions. But what about fillers for the 65th and some overstrength to replace the initial casualties until trained replacements were sent to us. I had gathered from the plan that we would join up with the 3rd Division in Japan and train together for several months before going on to Korea. But I knew, as sure as God made little green apples, that this would never happen. The situation in Korea was deteriorating rapidly, and it had been my experience during the war in Europe that reinforcements were often rushed in to plug the holes with little regard for such niceties as trained fillers and overstrengths. I decided to ask some questions if the Pentagon would give me an opportunity to do so.

"The 3rd Battalion, 33rd Infantry will sail on the 3—M and equipment of the entire regiment will be lifted by the 3—M (secret)," the teletype clacked out.

This meant that we would be out-loaded administratively and not combat-loaded; this worried me. Once we were on the water headed for the Far East, anything could happen and more than likely would. To be administratively loaded means that the troops sail on separate ships, without their heavy equipment. If trouble is expected at the other end of the voyage, troops should be combat-loaded, with their equipment on board the same ship they are on; then they are ready to fight.

I would have to question this decision, too, I thought. We would never stop in Japan.

When the Pentagon conferees completed their instructions, they asked if I had any questions. I did, lots of them.

"Question: Request 65th Infantry be allowed to combat-load (secret)" was the first. There was silence for approximately ten minutes, while the Pentagon planners kicked that one around among themselves and then the reply.

"Negative — desire you load as originally directed (secret)."

The term *negative* when translated from militarese to layman's language means, "Look, soldier, leave the planning to us. All you have to do is implement the orders."

Since I did not have all of the facts, I felt that it would be useless to pursue the question further, though I felt sure I would later regret that I hadn't pressed the point. So I passed to the next question.

"Question: Foreseen here, possibility 65th will proceed direct to final destination without intermediate stop and receive "on-the-job" training. Request therefore, that regiment not be required to take athletic equipment. End of question (secret)."

Again there was a lengthy pause and then the reply.

"Negative."

I didn't seem to be doing very well with my requests, so on to the next.

"Question: Request authorization to recruit personnel with at least six months PS [previous service] to bring regiment to full strength plus 10 percent overstrength. End of question (secret)."

The pause was shorter this time and the answer was:

"Approved."

Good, I thought, we are getting someplace.

"Question: 65th short items, personal and organizational equipment. Request authorization to send lists of shortages by TWX and that equipment be married up with regiment at final destination. End of question (secret)."

I had purposely designated "final destination" in hopes that the conferees on the other end would admit the possibility of our going directly to Korea without a stop. And, the answer:

"Approved. Desire you list shortages by class and service to expedite delivery (confidential)."

I was particularly concerned that we had no mortars and that our vehicles were old and almost worn out, but I held out little hope that the latter would be replaced.

My questions continued, covering details of sailing, personnel matters and so forth. Finally, the telecon was completed. All we had to do now was implement.

When I walked into my headquarters, I was greeted by a chorus from my staff, "When do we leave for Korea?" This was an indication of how fast information traveled on the island. I had not called my office to advise anyone that the fishing trip had been canceled, nor that I was going to a teleconference, yet they had the news before I could get back. This reminded me of what some friends had said about their service in the Philippines; they had better communications than Western Union, they had the "bamboo telegraph."

The incident also proved once more the futility of classifying military information which everyone recognizes as relatively unimportant. I have never understood why we classify certain military matters such as movement to an "unknown destination"; unless, of course, the commitment of the 65th United States Infantry Regiment might shake the very foundations of Peking and cause the Chinese to intervene in Korea.

There was no question that everyone in my headquarters and elsewhere knew what was afoot, for a kind of carnival air prevailed — like an amusement show that travels from place to place with its ferris wheel and merry-go-rounds. And when we asked the radio broadcasters to announce that we were opening up recruitment in the 65th and needed men with six months or more previous service, the results were astounding.

We said that we would enlist some two thousand men and that all who were interested should report to Fort Buchanan the following morning. When I drove there to see the response to our announcement, I found the streets and sidewalks leading up to the post jammed with men waiting to get in. We could have recruited fifty thousand, if we had needed that many. I must admit that initially I was somewhat dubious about the possibility of getting that large a number of volunteers, but we literally turned them away in droves after we reached our quota.

Now that recruitment was underway, we had other problems needing attention before our sailing. Generally, they were in the usual areas, personnel and supply. I decided to send Major Allen by air to St. Louis with allotment and insurance papers for hand delivery to the finance officer there. He would mail the supply lists from St. Louis to the Pentagon and rejoin us in Panama. Despite Allen's efforts, some dependents did not receive their allotments from their husband's pay, so my wife had to make a personal appeal to the Finance Center in their behalf.

Our ship, the *Marine Lynx,* had limited facilities, so we had to improvise a lot. Bed space had to be shared on a shift basis because we had too many men for the number of bunks available. Messing was also a problem requiring detailed scheduling to insure three hot meals daily for each man. Consequently, mess lines operated from breakfast in early morning to dinner in the late evening. The men would alternate from bunk or mess line to topside. The time spent topside would be devoted to training except for necessary relaxation time.

We decided that the training schedule aboard ship would include basic instruction in the care and cleaning, stripping and assembling of both individual and crew-served weapons; dry-run reviews of marksmanship; bayonet training; the tactics and techniques of the employment of the squad and platoon — essentially the same subjects which had been included on our tests the year before. Then, we had to organize and train our mortar company in the use of the 4.2-inch mortars, and the medical company would have to review their instruction in field expedients. With these general outlines agreed upon, Jerry Allen set about drawing up the schedules to implement our decisions.

Later, at sea, we watched the medical corpsmen use regular litters, and some that they improvised, to carry mock casualties from "battlefield" to "battalion aid stations". Some humor was added to this grim business by their having to carry the "wounded" around and through the narrow companionways and up and down the steep stairwells, sometimes unceremoniously dropping their passengers on their heads. They also practiced making arm and leg splints from discarded fruit crates, and pitched first-aid tents on deck using nails for tent pins. I am sure the ship's captain would have scalped us if he had seen that procedure, but we were desperate for time. We expected to be in combat in one month.

It may seem ludicrous in retrospect to remember Lt. Ammon's mortar company training off the fantail of the ship while at sea, but this was the only real practice they had, so it was invaluable. Within three hours of our arrival in Korea we were in a bloody fire fight, so the rest of their training was on the job, as it was for the rest of the troops.

Just before our sailing we received two excellent officers, Maj. William Friedman and Lt. Charles Boyle, both of whom were to perform distinguished services in the regiment in the months ahead.

The morning of our sailing a departing ceremony at Fort Buchanan was held which included speeches by Governor Munoz-Marin and General Sibert. No families were to be allowed at the formation, but still there were hundreds of spectators blocking the gates to the port. Our "secret" movement orders were apparently no secret to the local populace.

When the time came, both Sibert and Munoz-Marin gave us an inspiring send off and wished us good luck. I responded by saying, "While I did not know what the 65th would be called upon to do in the coming months, whatever it was, I felt quite sure that the regiment would give a good account of itself."

From there we marched to the dock and began loading aboard the *Marine Lynx*. Though it had been estimated by the Antilles transportation officer that this would not require more than six hours to complete, it took twelve. He had failed to take into account the narrow passageways and stairwells of the *Marine Lynx*. By the time the men squeezed and tugged their barracks bags, Spanish guitars, mandolins, bull fiddles, and themselves through these to the troop quarters in the lower decks and everyone was aboard, it was 0300 hours 23 August 1950 before we were under way.

Later, I received several letters from Antilles headquarters, and in one of them a friend had written that we looked like an old Spanish galleon when we sailed out of the port. The men had filled the decks, the railings, the lifeboats, and even the superstructure of the ship, including the ladder to the crow's nest, in order to get a last glimpse of their beloved island. The other two communications I received at that time were official letters from Generals Sibert and Porter (see Appendix).

For the most part, the men were silent as we sailed out of San Juan

Harbor. I had hoped that we would pass close to Fort Brooke, for I knew that the men's families would still be waiting and watching for us, but it was still too dark to make them out, and I could only see the faint silhouette of El Moro Castle as it blended into the early morning sky. But I knew that they were there.

As I stood at the railing, I wondered how well these men would fight when they were committed to combat. A commander never really knows until after the first battle what his troops are going to do, and this unknown quantity, the human factor, can mean the difference between defeat and victory.

But I had work to do. Our final destination was something like twenty-nine days and twenty-three hours away. During our preliminary planning, we had discussed the many problems inherent with just living aboard ship for that period of time, but we had really only settled on a general routine of sleep, head, chow, topside, chow, topside, chow, sleep, head, etcetera, etcetera — leaving the details of each to be worked out during the voyage. Now the time for implementation was at hand.

When we got down to the task of scheduling and related problems, we decided to set up the general guidelines and let Allen, our S-3, and his staff, do the detailed work. There was one problem that is usually connected with training that did not confront us this time, however, and that was stimulating interest in the subject matter. No one believed we would be permitted the time to engage in any extended training program at an interim location, like Japan, as had been indicated in the Washington teleconference. Everyone was convinced that our first landing would be in Korea.

Within a few days the ship was teeming with activity twenty-four hours a day. It was like a city that never slept; a poem of people; a land of make-believe. If you were looking for a friend or a man for a certain job, you had only to stand in one place, for he was sure to pass by sometime between one sunrise and the next.

In addition to regularly scheduled instruction, we published a training bulletin that carried matters we wished to stress as well as noteworthy news about the conduct of the war in Korea. These pertained particularly to the guerrilla-type warfare that the North Koreans employed and that was not too well known by American troops. In each case, we commented on the lessons to be learned. As an example, we published accounts of how American soldiers had been ambushed by so-called refugees fleeing south from the North Koreans. Willy-nilly, our troops would march down the road and pay little or no attention to the seemingly harmless, baggy-drawered men, women, and children until suddenly some of them whipped out burp guns, pistols, and hand grenades and dry-gulched our soldiers. We repeatedly told our men to trust no one, and this lesson paid dividends later.

A military man can make many mistakes, such as attacking in the wrong direction, defending in the wrong direction, defending when he should be attacking, or doing nothing when he should be taking some military action. And there could be a logical explanation for his actions. But being taken by surprise did not fall in that category, for it was completely unwarranted, unexplainable, and unacceptable. We demonstrated every means of trickery that we could conjure up to train our men to be alert. We drilled them repeatedly in the principles of scouting and patrolling. We warned them to be leery of booby traps, to survey and observe their surroundings constantly, but, above all, not to trust anyone.

One of the most fatal mistakes that American soldiers made in those early days was to trust and depend upon the South Korean soldiers. When the latter were integrated into the American units, our people would assign them heavy-duty jobs such as hauling supplies, digging foxholes, or carrying the heavy mortars and ammunition. Then, when the military situation became sticky or critical, our troops would look around for their guns and ammunition, and the South Korean soldiers would have disappeared over the hill, probably to the North.

Another military axiom we drilled into our men was the wisdom of controlling the dominant terrain in battle. Our ancestors had learned this lesson the hard way when they fought the American Indians during the frontier days. But we seem to forget history, for most of our men in World War II had to relearn it, and the same was true in Korea. Vietnam proved to be no different. In Korea we never permitted the enemy the luxury of controlling the high ground, whether we were in a defensive position for the night or attacking. We didn't have helicopters to lift the troops and equipment; we moved on foot, and sometimes we had to scratch and crawl on both feet and both hands to make our way to the tops of the mountains, particularly in the rugged Taebaek Range.

In addition to this formal training, we reestablished the weekly meeting with the senior noncommissioned officers that had been started the first day in Puerto Rico. The purpose of these conferences was to obtain their views or complaints on matters of general interest to everyone in the regiment, as well as to constantly remind them of their responsibility within the chain of command.

Many worthwhile suggestions came from these meetings. One I particularly remember was that we select a battle name for the 65th. The final selection, generally agreed by all to be the best, was the Borinqueneers.

This was the name of the more peaceful of the two original Indian tribes that inhabited the island of Puerto Rico, and many of the men were direct descendants of that industrious race of people. Later, in Korea, the name Borinqueneers became well known, even to the Chinese. We also used it as the name of our daily training bulletin, which we then converted to more of a newspaper and which carried all types of news, including personal items; it subsequently became quite a morale factor in the life of the men, and was as much in demand as any paper published in Puerto Rico.

Time passed. I noted in my diary when we had traveled some 1,949 miles with only 5,918 more to go; that was September 10. We were at latitude 20 degrees 12 minutes N and longitude 108 degrees 21 minutes W, with a course of 249.8 degrees and making about 17.28 knots per hour toward Seattle, Washington. From there we were to follow the Great Circle Route to the Japanese Islands.

It was on that day, too, we heard the news that the Secretary of Defense, Mr. Johnson, had resigned, and that the president had appointed General George C. Marshall to replace him. To us, this was good news. It seemed to be a sign that our government was willing to admit that the diplomats and the politicians had failed to keep the peace, and that the military had been called upon to restore it. We would at least be given the manpower and the other wherewithal to do the job. In general, this did happen, but the administration was never willing to admit that we were at war and continued to refer to the action and deal with it as the "Korean Conflict," or the "Korean Incident," or the "Korean Unpleasantness." I am quite sure that none of us who were there would have called it anything but a war, and the worst kind, for the armed forces were called upon to protect the country and the lives of a people battling among themselves.

However, the other news we heard was not so good. The 24th United States Infantry Division, which had been rushed from Japan to stem the tide of the attacking North Koreans, had been completely overrun, and the division commander, Maj. Gen. William Dean, had been captured. This was sad news for all of us, particularly for his son-in-law, who was a member of the 65th. The dribs and drabs of troops being committed to combat piecemeal were being chewed up by the enemy about as fast as they arrived in Korea. The politicians had systematically and methodically reduced the armed forces of the United States to an ineffective number, and equipped these poorly. It was now hoped that with General Marshall as Secretary of Defense the problem of the military would be understood.

Then, to top off that day's excitement, we ran into a hurricane, and all the lights and power aboard ship went out. We pitched and rolled out of control for about four hours with none of us knowing what was going to happen next. When I stopped one of the merchant seamen to ask him how we were doing on the repairs, his reply was something to the effect that this happens all the time — we would get under way pretty soon — not much consolation for a bunch of foot soldiers.

Later that same night I made a note in my diary that we had crossed the International Date Line and had lost one day as a result. Then four days later we sighted land. I was standing on the top deck in the late afternoon when the man in the crow's nest bellowed out, "Land ahoy, off the port bow." I was a bit startled at his outcry, for I thought that with our knowledge of electronics we would have a much more sophisticated way of sighting land, but I guess that in the navy, like the other services, some things just do not change. At any rate, there it was, a faint but distinguishable thin, gray line on the horizon. We thought it was probably the coast of Japan.

All work stopped immediately as everyone came topside to get his first view of land in several weeks. But we were still a long way from port, wherever it was, and we went to bed that night still wondering whether we were going to disembark here or somewhere else.

Early morning cleared up that question, however. Shortly after breakfast, a cablegram was received ordering both the ship's captain and me to send a representative ashore for new orders. We had now identified the shoreline as the port of Sasebo, Japan.

I told Childs that he had better get ready to go ashore and while ashore to see if there was any news of either the equipment ship or our other battalion from Panama. We were going to be needing both of them before too many hours passed. I also suggested he ask about the situation in Korea.

I certainly wished now that I had harassed those people in the Pentagon to let us combat-load. If I had persisted, or maybe had General Porter or General Sibert intervene — but it was too late to worry about it now; the die was cast. Childs left in the captain's boat and returned two hours later.

"You were right, Colonel. Our orders direct that we proceed at once to Pusan," Childs reported.

"I knew it. What else did you find out?"

"Do you remember Col. Edgar Hume who was with us in Civil Affairs?"

"Sure do, why?"

"Well, I ran into him in port. He is the GHQ representative in Sasebo and the one who handed me our new orders. He said to tell you hello, and wished us the best of luck. It seems as though things are a bit sticky in Korea. Eighth Army headquarters is located in a building right on the dock — seems like they have no place else to go except back here."

That sounded bad. Chick continued.

"He also told me that our battalion from Panama would be delayed — their ship broke down in mid-Pacific, and they had to go back to Hawaii and reload on another ship. They won't get into Korea for another week or ten days."

"Damn, what else can happen to make this more difficult?"

"That isn't all of the bad news yet, Colonel. Our equipment ship has also been delayed, and it is about four days behind us."

"Oh, no."

"Yes, sir. I don't know too much more about the situation except that we are due to sail immediately and expected to arrive off Pusan by early morning. There is no information as to how or where we are to be committed to action, but Hume seemed to feel that we wouldn't have far to go in any direction before we were in a fight. One of General Walker's personal representatives will meet us at the dock in Pusan and give further orders."

"I see. Well, there's no use worrying about it now. There's nothing much we can do about it at this stage of the game."

"That's right, sir. Oh, one other thing Hume told me. He said that we had been scheduled to make an amphibious landing at Inchon — I don't know exactly where that is except that it is somewhere near Seoul, on the northwest coast of South Korea. The X Corps, under command of Maj. Gen. Edward M. Almond landed there a few days ago and apparently caught the North Koreans with their pants down. We had been scheduled to go in with them, but when we were delayed, they changed our orders to Pusan."

Within the hour we set sail for Korea. Great Britain's wartime Prime Minister, Sir Winston Churchill, had once described Russia as "a mystery wrapped up in an enigma." The same could be said of most of the countries of the Far East — most certainly Korea. The peninsula of Korea extends out from the underbelly of the mainland of China for some six hundred miles and splits the subaractic Sea of Japan from the Yellow Sea. Even though it lies in about the same latitude as the state of Kentucky, the temperatures range from over one hundred degrees Fahrenheit in the South during the summer months to well below minus forty degrees Fahrenheit in the rugged mountains to the north. Later we were to fight in both these extremes of temperature.

The land mass of the peninsula is divided by the steep, precipitous, and almost impassable Taebaek Range of mountains that runs north to south along the coastline of the Sea of Japan. In the north, the ridges of these mountains reach some six thousand feet. Combined with the extreme cold and the heavy snowdrifts and winds from the steppes of

China and Manchuria, military operations in that part of the country are extremely difficult and hazardous. Only the natives, the Chinese, and the little donkeys and goats that inhabit the place can even exist there.

The southern portion of the peninsula, though just as desolate, was the breadbasket of the entire country; which is why the North Koreans wanted it and one of the reasons the Russians were helping them try to take it.

I knew some of the history of the country and how it had become divided as a result of World War II, but this was of little consequence at the moment. The important factor was that only an artificial, geographical line at the 38th Parallel divided the two parts of the country. North or South, the people themselves, to my mind, were the same.

The longer that we were in the country, the less we trusted any of them —North or South Korean. Some people may describe them as "hospitable, docile, gentle folk, and potentially fine soldiers," but we never found them so at the "grassroots level" at which we operated. I do not question for one moment that they can adapt themselves to any specific environment or conditions and behave like human beings, but I saw some dreadful things, such as barbaric executions without trial. I really found our policy hard to understand.

4

GO THAT WAY

Early in the morning of 20 September 1950, our ship inched into the dock at Pusan in that God-forsaken country. In the distance, we could see the bleak-looking hills and gentle sloping valleys that were dotted with rice paddies which the farmers were plowing with water buffalo. Perched on small knolls every mile or so were small clusters of eight or ten straw-roofed adobe huts which we were to learn later was about the normal size of a local farm community, usually consisting of one family. By custom and tradition, this included grandparents, their sons and daughters, the grandchildren, and sometimes even the great-grandchildren. All of them made up one independent community completely loyal to one person, the "Old One," or the patriarch of the family. These clusters were more or less self-sufficient in the production of both food and fiber, and we were to learn later that they had few, if any, feelings of national pride or homogeneity. They could not care less who controlled their country.

From what we could see of it, the city itself was no more than a larger collection of the same size and type of adobe huts, for there could not have been more than six buildings taller than one story, and they looked as if they had been built about the time of Genghis Khan. There appeared to be few paved streets or sidewalks, and the only form of transportation I could see, other than the U.S. Army vehicles, were the two-wheeled bicycles the Koreans rode in about the same manner as the French do theirs — like maniacs.

I have no idea of the number of people living in Pusan at that time, but I am quite sure that regardless of their number, there was neither sufficient bed nor board to accommodate them. We could see hundreds of people just wandering aimlessly along the dusty streets or standing and talking or squatting along the roadside cooking their meager supply of food over a small fire. No doubt the invasion by the NKPA (North Korean People's Army) had sent thousands of them scurrying to the towns and villages in the South seeking security and protection from the Communist regime of North Korea. Later, we were to see columns of them that stretched as far as the eye could see, plodding along carrying most of their worldly possessions on their backs. Only occasionally would we see a family with a small pony or a water buffalo staggering down the road carrying an unbelievably heavy load that probably represented the total worth of four generations.

On the dock below us the chatter and clatter of the stevedores was much the same as in any other port with one difference — the Old Ones. They stood apart from the laborers, standing or squatting in groups of twos and threes, talking to one another and doing nothing else. There was no mistaking their position in life, for they wore long, flowing white robes instead of the workingman's baggy cotton britches and padded jacket, and instead of the usual wide-brimmed straw hat, they wore stovepipes of horsehair which were tied with string chin straps.

Then, to add to this bizarre scene, as our ship eased into dock, the United States Army Band ashore struck up a loud and brassy rendition of the famous old tune, "The Sidewalks of New York." It did not take long to determine who selected the music for this occasion, for as I walked down the gangplank, the first two people I saw were old friends from the early war days in Washington, D.C.: Brig. Gen. Crump Garvin and Col. Ray G. Stanton. Garvin was the commander of the Pusan Base Section, and Stanton was his deputy.

After a bit of reminiscing, they led me to a reception committee composed of President Syngman Rhee's cabinet officers and introduced me to each of them. The last one in the line, a lady minister, handed me a large bouquet of flowers, which I quickly passed to Colonel Childs. And then, to the delight of the men, Childs strolled off nonchalantly, carrying them like a June bride.

Garvin had told me that the Eighth Army commander, Lt. Gen. Walton H. Walker, wanted to see me as soon as possible. While Childs took command of the unloading and the drawing of two hundred rounds of rifle ammunition per man we had been allocated, I made my way to his headquarters, not more than two hundred yards away.

Again I was met by an old friend, Col. Eugene M. Landrum, General Walker's deputy chief of staff. While we waited for the army commander to see me, Landrum brought me up to date on the military situation. Among other things I learned that the Inchon Landing had been highly successful and X Corps had caught the North Koreans completely by surprise. This success had in turn greatly relieved the pressure on the Eighth Army, which had been fighting to hold its own within the Pusan perimeter.

General Walker looked just as I had pictured him: short, slightly on the stocky side, with thinning gray hair and a pleasant-looking face. I soon learned, however, that his reputation for abruptness and short, clipped sentences was well founded. Within seconds after I had sat down, he asked me if I thought that the Puerto Rican soldiers would fight.

I minced no words in answering him in equally abrupt terms. I told him that I thought they were the best soldiers that I had ever seen. Then I briefly sketched my own original apprehensions about serving with the 65th and how they had performed in Operation Portrex. When I finished, General Walker quite correctly remarked that a maneuver was one thing and actual combat something else, to which I agreed. I then told him that, like most commanders going into combat with their regiment for the first time, I could not be completely sure how my troops would react in their first engagement, but if determination, pride and state-of-training had anything to do with it, I had no worries about the Puerto Ricans' fighting ability or their courage; further, I was prepared to go with them to do battle with anybody. This was pretty strong language to be using in speaking to the army commander, but I meant every word of it. I was anxious to head off any opinion he might formulate in his own mind as a result of statements made by others.

General Walker appeared satisfied with my answers, or he may have felt that the natural course of events would soon provide the answers, for he stood up and motioned for me to follow him to the large window behind his desk. There, pointing down to a number of passenger trains in the marshaling yards, he said, "Bill, do you see those trains?"

I nodded.

"Get on them and go that way," he said, pointing north.

Very short, simple, succinct, and to the point. As a matter of fact, my orders were not quite, but almost, as brief as those issued by Admiral David Farragut at Mobile Bay on August 5, 1864, when he ordered his fleet to attack Confederate forces gathered there. His words, now immortal in the annals of the United States Navy, were, "Damn the torpedoes, straight ahead."

I knew from the briefing I had received from Gene Landrum that the situation around the Pusan perimeter was still a bit fluid and that the most pressing problem was for us to get under way. Therefore I asked no questions or for further clarification of my orders, as I would have under normal circumstances. I bid General Walker and Gene Landrum goodbye and headed for the troop ship, knowing that more specific instructions would be issued in due time.

As a matter of fact, I had hardly stepped out of the Eighth Army Headquarters Building when I saw the first elements of the regiment marching toward the rail yards. Childs had already received instructions as to where we were to go, a small village called Samnonjin, about twenty or thirty miles to the north. We were to detrain there and await further orders.

Loading was completed in something less than an hour, and since the engines had already built up a good head of steam, we were soon chug-a-lugging off down the rails. And chug-a-lug it was, for the coaches and the engines, though built in the United States, were replicas of those used by Col. "Buffalo" Bill Cody when he was hunting prairie cows on the plains of the West during the late nineteenth century.

We lurched and staggered down the tracks while the South Korean, who might jokingly have been called the engineer, alternately stopped and started the train and then blew his whistle, as though he were signaling someone; I am convinced that he was.

Though his antics may have been purely coincidental, they brought results, of a sort that is. The lead train, on which I was riding with elements of the 2nd Battalion, had not gone more than ten miles from Pusan when we suddenly heard sporadic rifle fire ahead and on our flanks. It did not take long for us to determine that we were the target. The crash of the splintering glass and the thud of the bullets as they struck the inside of the car were all the proof we needed as we all hit the deck and scurried for cover, flat on the floor, under the seats, and even in the toilets — which were actually worse than the possibility of being hit by a bullet.

We had spent an awful lot of time training our men to be alert and avoid being taken by surprise. Now here we were, within a few hours after landing in Korea, being dry-gulched. I must admit that I was a bit chagrined.

We had just entered a large cut through a hill where the embankments on both sides were high and steep when the first bullets began to zing and splat inside of our car. It was at this same moment precisely that the engineer also decided to slap the brakes on and bring the train to a screech-

ing halt. In discussing the incident later, we concluded that another lesson
had been added to our indoctrination on how to fight guerrillas: even
in supposedly controlled areas, they could and did operate boldly and
effectively; this was a practical demonstration of that capability.

When the first shock of the attack was over, our troops went into
immediate action. Since it was Dammer's battalion, I made no attempt
to direct the firefight. It was his problem, and he was perfectly capable
of dealing with it. He first organized a base of fire within the cars in
order to keep the enemy engaged and force them to keep their heads
down. Then he led other troops of his unit out the rear end of the last
car and attacked those on the right side of the train. Under the protection of that base of fire and the train itself, he was able to quickly drive
off that force; and then, just as skillfully and effectively, he led an attack
on the other side of the train. The entire episode did not last more than
thirty or forty minutes, but even in that short period of time, one could
see that the Puerto Ricans had no fear whatsoever. They took to that
little skirmish like ducks to water.

Our first encounter with the enemy won without any casualties on
our side, we continued to rattle on without further incident, down the
tracks about four bumps per cycle of each square wheel until we reached
Samnonjin at dusk. Unloading was accomplished in jig time, and we
then set about organizing a 360-degree, wagon-wheel type defense. Each
unit was assigned a specific sector; pup tents were pitched, and individual
and crew-served weapons positions were dug immediately. The idea for
this circular defense was another of the lessons we had taken from the
history of the early settlers as they moved westward across the plains
of Colorado, Oregon, and beyond. When they halted for the night, they
pulled their wagons into a tight circle as a barricade; then the animals
and the people were placed on the inside of the circle.

Since we had no kitchen or other equipment for that matter our first
meal on Korean soil consisted of those delicious and delectable C rations
that World War II GIs learned to love so well. And as expected, we were
soon surrounded by most of the curious people of the village. Equally
unsurprising, our men started to give out food and candy, particularly
to the children. However, since we had already had one lesson in guerrilla
tactics, I did not care to see another, at least not on the same day. So
harsh as it may seem, we put an immediate stop to what could have
become a local relief project or worse, a bad habit which could get us
into serious trouble at some later date.

Having finished eating and assuring myself of the security of our
positions, I headed for my bedroll under my jeep. As I lay there that
first night trying to sleep, I again thought of my teleconference with

the Pentagon and my request to combat-load. Though I did not know what else the future had in store for us, it was reasonable to assume from our recent encounter that the enemy was all around us and that we would probably see plenty of action before many hours had passed.

There was also something else that bothered me as I lay there trying my best to close my eyes and get some sleep — a strangely familiar odor permeated the air where we had set up camp. Pungent and penetrating, the smell seemed to be suspended in the still, humid atmosphere that hung over us like an invisible cover. Though I tried my best to identify it from the many barnyard smells I knew, the sandman caught up with me, and it was morning before I was able to solve the mystery. We had bivouacked in a field of garlic.

Early morning also brought me a better view of the dour, sandy, scrubby-looking countryside, as well as a closer look at the village of Samnonjin. It was like all of the others we had seen during the trip from Pusan: one large cluster of eight or ten thatch-roofed adobe huts with mud chimneys, four or five water buffalo standing peacefully nearby chewing on their cud, dozens of small fry scampering about as mama-san prepared the first meal of the day over an open fire in front of the hut while the smell of charcoal smoke, cabbage, and garlic drifted in our direction. We were later to learn that the native dish was called *kimchi,* and we came to like it; that is, some of us did.

It was here, too, that we had our first close look at the Korean people themselves. Generally speaking, they were a small, lean, and wiry-looking people, with deeply sun-tanned and wrinkled skin. All of them, men and women, were dressed alike. On their feet they wore low-cut, thin, rubber, moccasin-type slippers, which we were later to see the people in North Korea wear even during the coldest weather when the temperature was well below freezing and the snow at least four feet deep. But small, lean, and wiry looking as they were, they each had the strength of an ox.

While several of us stood there watching, one Korean man walked over to an embankment about four feet high where a large abandoned truck motor was lying. While we watched, he strapped a wooden-frame type of a contraption to the motor, then squatted down and fitted the entire assembly to his back, tied the rope straps across his chest, straightened his legs, and walked off down the road carrying what must have been at least two hundred pounds of metal. I do not believe that any three or four of us there, all together, could have lifted that motor two inches off the ground, to say nothing of carrying it on our backs. It had to be seen to be believed.

Having witnessed this demonstration, we were curious about the wooden frame he had used; so we examined one. It looked just like the capital letter A, and for that reason it is called an A-frame. It was fitted with rope straps that could be tied around an object and loops that could be slipped over the arms and onto the shoulders.

But we had more serious problems facing us than deciphering the mechanics of Korean weightlifting, for it was now getting on toward midday, when we should have received movement orders. The early morning news had carried quite an account of the Inchon Landing and compared it to the other successful amphibious operations which General MacArthur had launched during the war in the Pacific. We heard how the X Corps, consisting of the United States 7th Infantry and 1st Marine Divisions, had taken the enemy by complete surprise and had now begun an assault on his stronghold in Seoul. While doing so, they were sitting astride enemy lines of communication that extended all the way to the vicinity of Pusan. No doubt the enemy in our area also heard the same news. By this time their commanders would probably be trying to do one of several things: beat their way back to the North and the sanctuary of their own areas; dispose of their uniforms and equipment and melt into the South Korean population; scatter and employ small-unit, guerrilla tactics until they could be reorganized and supplied from the North; or commence an all-out kamikaze attack against us. No one knew, of course, which method they would employ — probably a combination of several of the alternatives. But regardless of the enemy's intentions, I was anxious to get under way and not be caught trying to defend ourselves on the low ground around Samnonjin.

Earlier in the morning, Childs had told me that he had received a call from Eighth Army headquarters to the effect that we had originally been held in GHQ reserve (General MacArthur's headquarters), but upon our arrival in Pusan, we had been released to Eighth Army control. Further, we were being assigned that day to IX Corps under command of Maj. Gen. J. B. Coulter and that we would probably be hearing from him shortly. This change in our command assignment from operational control of GHQ to Eighth Army and then to IX Corps was what had taken the time and explained the delay in our receipt of orders.

But whatever these were to be, we knew that we were going to become involved in the break-out of the Pusan perimeter, which General Walker had informed me was in progress in conjunction with the X Corps landing at Inchon. And our guess wasn't too far wrong, as we found out later, for the Eighth Army had positioned us right in the middle of where two NKPA (North Korean Peoples Army) divisions had been sighted. It was probably a good thing for our own peace of mind that we did not know we were sitting in such a precarious spot, for two infantry battalions with no mortars, artillery or tanks might have quite a time battling two enemy divisions, even though they might be employed in smaller-unit size. What was it that Thomas Gray had said? "Where ignorance is bliss, tis folly to be wise."

As I was mulling all this over, I was called to my command radio — the IX Corps operations people wanted to speak with me. This time it was Col. William B. Kunzig, a friend of many years, who informed me that — having been released by Eighth Army to IX Corps — headquarters was assigning us to the 2nd United States Infantry Division and that we would receive our operational orders from that unit. This must have set some kind of a military record, for within a period of twenty-four hours we had been under the operational control of four different levels of command.

Kunzig also told me that the 2nd Division was under command of Maj. Gen. Lawrence B. Keiser, and he probably would be in touch with me shortly. In the meantime, it was suggested that we get ready to roll, for IX Corps anticipated that Keiser would employ us somewhere close to our present location. When Kunzig said that, he in effect confirmed our information that Eighth Army had dropped us off smack in the middle of the two North Korean divisions; but when I challenged him on the point, he refused to admit it; he just chuckled.

But it was obvious that we were not too far from where the action was taking place, for not too far away we could hear somebody's heavy artillery pounding away, and occasionally the chatter of automatic weapons could be heard in between the explosions of artillery shells.

Then, within minutes of my conversation with Kunzig, the sergeant major handed me a radio message from General Keiser which stated that he was sending his light plane, an L-19, to pick me up and bring me to his headquarters. This was it — it wouldn't be long now until I would know how the men of the 65th would stand up against an enemy.

The flight to 2nd Division headquarters required only about ten minutes and about another two minutes for a jeep to get me to the operations tent where General Keiser was waiting. We reminisced for a few moments, for he had been my tactical officer at West Point, and then we got down to the details of our employment in conjunction with his other operations.

Though I hadn't realized it until I had seen the area from the air, we were bivouacked almost within a stone's throw of the Naktong River, and this I learned was the same general area in which the 2nd was heavily engaged. Keiser's 9th, 23rd, and 38th Regimental Combat Teams were operating more or less independently in seeking out and destroying the NKPA units that were now withdrawing from the Pusan area back along the river. I gathered too that the large organized units of the NKPA had pretty well come apart at the seams in their haste to beat their way back to the North. As a result, they had broken up into guerrilla bands and had taken to the hills. From there, they were harassing our formations, destroying our truck convoys, and playing hit-and-run tactics rather than meeting our forces in an open battle. And, unless I am terribly mistaken, I also gathered the impression from that briefing that there were some fifty or sixty thousand of them still in the area. That is one helluva lot of enemy, disorganized or otherwise, in one area, particularly when you are sitting in the middle of it.

After some additional briefing, General Keiser gave me our missions, which I later recorded in my diary for posterity. Having initially been given a rather general mission to "Go that way," we were now being assigned a multiplicity of odd jobs:

A. Send one battalion to Hill 409 to relieve a battalion of the 9th Infantry there.

B. Destroy what remained of the 10th NKPA Infantry Division in the vicinity of Hill 409.

C. Move one battalion to a village named Yuga-myon and secure the bridge in that area which controlled the 2nd Division's main supply route (MSR) to Pusan.

D. Locate my headquarters and Headquarters and Service Companies near the village of Changyong, which as I remember is about eight or ten miles from the junction of the Nam and Naktong rivers.

E. Conduct aggressive patrolling in all areas and locate and destroy all enemy encountered within the area bounded by Hill 409, Yuga-myon, and Changyong — a total of about forty square miles.

In assigning these missions, General Keiser had emphasized that he wanted us to send out combat-sized patrols which would be large enough to engage the enemy where and when we found him. The situation was very fluid, with the NKPA units constantly on the move, employing their hit-and-run tactics. Therefore, if we had to wait for small reconnaissance patrols to report their locations, the enemy would probably have moved before we could mount a large enough force to engage them. I noted that the 2nd Division was using battalions for these patrols, but since we had only two such units, we decided to employ companies of about two hundred and twenty men for these missions. Later, however, when the 1st Provisional Philippine Battalion was attached to us, we were able to increase these patrols to about two-company size.

By the time I returned to my headquarters, I found that the 2nd Division had already sent trucks, which they had promised me, to assist us in the moves to our new locations. Unfortunately, there were not enough of them to lift even one battalion, so priority for their use was given to the 2nd Battalion, since we had assigned Dammer the most urgent of the missions, the relief of the 9th Infantry Battalion on Hill 409 — the hot spot.

The 1st Battalion was given the mission of holding the village of Yuga-myon and securing the bridge located there. As had been directed, my headquarters and the Headquarters and Service Companies were to move to Changyong. But because of the shortage of transportation, our moves were not completed until about a week later; my diary shows that my headquarters and Headquarters and Service Companies closed into Changyong at 1530 hours, 28 September 1950.

It was very apparent by now that the situation was changing by the hour, for we had no more than reached Changyong than we received orders to continue on to Hyopchon, about ten miles farther east. It seemed as though every unit in Eighth Army was on the move, for we had been in constant competition with most of them for use of the roads. We had crisscrossed with so many other troop convoys that I was concerned one of our 2nd Division drivers might absentmindedly follow one, and then the rest of the trucks behind him would hook onto his tail and follow like a string of elephants in the circus. It would have taken hours, maybe even days, before we could have located our wandering warriors and returned them to the fold. All of this frenzied activity was, of course, due to General Walker's desire to catch every NKPA soldier in South Korea before he could escape to the North. It was like a game of hare and hounds.

I soon learned, again through the intelligence grapevine, that the reason for positioning us at Hyopchon was to concentrate the regiment right in the middle of five NKPA divisions; the ante was going up. I often challenged such estimates of enemy strength, as I did this one, but I really had no way of disproving their accuracy, and I was too scared not to believe it. Whatever the estimates of their number, within a few days we found a big nest of them.

If ever we needed the rest of our troops it was now. We were due to have a battalion of artillery, a company of tanks, a company of engineers, and some ordnance and signal personnel and equipment, in addition to our 3rd Battalion assigned to us; but we had no current information as to when any of them would arrive. When I called Eighth Army to inquire about these units, I was told that our 3rd Battalion probably wouldn't arrive in Pusan before the first week in October. As for the other units, they were to come from the 3rd Infantry Division, which was still in the United States; no firm date had been set for its arrival in Japan, and the plan was for it to train there for several months before being sent on to Korea. It was, in other words, anyone's guess when those units would arrive.

Then, to my absolute disgust, the following morning 1,150 South Korean (ROK) soldiers arrived at my CP with orders from Eighth Army assigning them to us. Having 1,150 ROKs, or even 50, to watch in addition to our other problems, was all that we needed. If they had been NKPAs, I would have known what to do with them, but ROKs I wanted no part of.

I heard later from some officers who had served in Korea during 1952 and 1953 that the ROKs eventually turned out to be pretty good combat troops, after they had been trained and equipped. But in the early days they were not to be trusted. Then to add insult to injury, Eighth Army also advised me that we had no disciplinary power over them. If we had any problems, said the Eighth Army staff, we were to refer the cases to the ROK Army headquarters in Pusan. I could just visualize the administrative problems this would cause us, in addition to guarding those who required it while awaiting ROK Army disposition. We would probably need half of our troops for guard duty alone.

As far as I was concerned there was only one solution to the problem, and we used it. We assigned one ROK soldier to each of our ten-man squads. Then I knew where he was and what he was up to. With nine of our men watching him all of the time, he couldn't do much damage. When one of them committed an offense requiring disciplinary action, and this was frequent, our procedure was to relieve him of his weapons, ammunition, and equipment (all U.S. property), lead him out to the road, point in the direction of Pusan, and motion for him to start walking. Within three month's time we had reduced our quota of 1,150 to about 40 or 50 whom our men felt that they could trust, although I never did.

While my headquarters and the other two units moved toward Hyopchon, I jeeped to the locations of our two battalions and went over their combat patrol plans with each of the battalion commanders. Later I assigned our I and R (Intelligence and Reconnaissance) Platoon the responsibility for reconnoitering areas which these battalions could not cover within our zone.

Since this platoon had only thirty-eight men, it was not strong enough to operate as a combat patrol against the large numbers of enemy that were reported in our area. I therefore instructed the S-2 to insure that the platoon leader, Lieutenant Caban, understood that his mission was one of reconnaissance only. He was not to engage in a firefight but to limit his activities to verifying the information that a particular area along the Naktong River was "swarming with NKPAs," as had been reported to us. Since it was an NKPA tactic to hide out during daylight hours and then to attack at night, it was our plan to have the I and R Platoon locate these reported enemy concentrations and then keep them under surveillance until we could move a large enough force into the area to engage them.

I had great confidence in Caban and his platoon sergeant, M. Sgt. Federico Pagani, Jr., so I had no hesitancy about sending them on this rather hazardous mission. And as I expected, they found the enemy but not without some serious consequences.

From what I was able to piece together from Pagani's after-action report, as well as conversations with other members of the platoon, they found the enemy just where Eighth Army had reported they were — and about a thousand strong. They were bivouacked along a deep creekbed that branched off from the main river, but one which was relatively dry and had sufficient foliage and underbrush to conceal them from air observation.

The platoon had been able to keep the enemy under observation until about dusk without being discovered, at which time I had directed the platoon leader to withdraw to a cover position within our perimeter defense. They were also instructed to leave a small patrol of several men to maintain contact with the enemy. But when Caban started to lead his men away from the riverbed, his jeep struck a land mine and blew up with a thunderous explosion that set the vehicle on fire and seriously wounded him and three others — Lieutenant O'Neal, Corporal Rodriquez, and Private First Class Herrera.

Immediately following the noise and flash of the explosion, the platoon was subjected to a withering hail of rifle and mortar fire, and it was only due to the quick reaction, presence of mind, and bravery of Pagani that the remainder of the platoon was able to escape without further casualties. With complete disregard for his own safety, he pulled the injured men from the flaming jeep and beat out the fire which had already consumed their clothing and seared more than 90 percent of the skin. He then gave each of the wounded men a morphine pill in the hope that it would reduce their pain and prevent them from going into shock until he could get them back to the Medical Company for proper treatment.

Then, even though they were still under fire from the enemy and still in the middle of the minefield, Pagani quickly reorganized the platoon and led it and the wounded men back to the headquarters without further mishap. There the wounded were given immediate emergency medical assistance and later evacuated to a base hospital in the rear area. But several days later we were informed that they had died; we had lost some good friends who were outstanding soldiers and brave men, our first casualties of the Korean War.

Had it not been for the quick thinking and heroic actions of Pagani, we probably would have lost the entire I and R Platoon. For these courageous actions, he was recommended for and received one of the highest decorations that can be awarded a man in the service — the Soldiers Medal. Later I recommended him for a battlefield promotion to the grade of lieutenant and made him the commander of the I and R Platoon, where he served with distinction for the remainder of the war. It was in this capacity that he was also decorated with the third highest award for bravery that the United States government bestows upon an individual in combat — the Silver Star.

Two other men who had assisted Sergeant Pagani, Sergeant Arguinzoni, and Corporal Vega, were also decorated for bravery.

Combat soon became almost routine, and few days passed that did not find us in a fight. Within the first ten days of October my headquarters made three moves: from Hyopchon to Sonju, then to Waegwan, and finally to Kumchon. With each new movement order we were told that the situation was more critical than the last and that we should move as fast as possible. This urgency was borne out; the situation did get more critical, and an even larger concentration of the enemy was found at each new location. By the third week in October, we had been officially credited with capturing 829 prisoners and killing 215 others. During the same period we lost 23 men killed and 17 wounded.

On October 3 we received orders to go to the assistance of one of IX Corps' isolated radio relay stations that was under attack. Because there were so few American units, and these were so widely dispersed, it had become necessary for senior headquarters (corps and divisions) to locate a series of radio relay stations on high terrain in order to maintain communications and hence command control of their subordinate units. But because of the shortage of troops, these stations were not given the infantry protection they needed. Left to their own devices, the only possible hope they had for survival was to find a position on the high ground and pray that the enemy would not find them. In many ways, the signal corps troops were the unsung heroes of the Korean War, as they have been in most wars.

The IX Corps unit in need of help was not too far from Hill 409, where the 2nd Battalion was located, so I assigned the mission to Dammer. At the time, he was busy beating the bushes for the remnants of the 10th

NKPA Division, but he was able to spare two platoons. We both hoped that they would be sufficient to do the job. As he later reported to me, the two platoons arrived just in the nick of time, for they found the besieged men fighting desperately to beat off what looked like a final, all-out enemy attempt to destroy them. The action didn't last long, for Dammer's men quickly deployed along the base of the hill and engaged the enemy from their rear. Caught between two fires, they surrendered without firing another shot. That operation netted us fifteen prisoners, with no losses on our side.

On October 4 we received orders to relieve the British 27th Brigade, in addition to our other missions, and found ourselves in still another hot spot. I do not suppose that there were really any cool ones anyplace in those early days, but it did seem that wherever the action was, the 65th was sure to be found.

It was on that date, too, or the following day that one of Dammer's patrols brought in a Korean who said he had been hiding an American officer for several months. He produced the officer's dog tags to prove it. They belonged to a Lieutenant Hicks of the 24th U.S. Infantry Division, which had been cut to ribbons shortly after its arrival in Korea.

As the record will show, General MacArthur had not been responsible for Korea prior to the outbreak of war there. Although we had some American troops in Korea acting as advisers to the Korean Army, they were under the control of the U.S. State Department. Then when the NKPA invaded the country, our president gave the responsibility for defending it to General MacArthur. With barely enough troops to occupy Japan and, more important, keep the Russians from taking it over, General MacArthur was forced to deploy his small forces to Korea in piecemeal fashion in order to buy time until other units could be shipped from the continental United States.

This was a prime example of how the State Department and other politicians failed in their job of keeping the peace and then quickly turned the problem over to the military to solve. It was also another classic example of our inadequate national strategy (national policy), for we failed to make adequate plans and preparations for such a contingency. If we were going to accept the responsibility for rehabilitating South Korea, we should have been prepared militarily to defend it, for we knew that both the North Koreans and the Russians had designs on it.

One of our Japanese interpreters had barely finished translating the Korean's statements when Lieutenant Hicks himself walked into the CP. He had followed the Korean at a sufficiently safe distance to make sure that he was not walking into a North Korean unit. When he saw that we were American troops, he came in himself. Though Hicks was still dressed in his military fatigues, with his six-inch beard and long hair he looked more like one of our hippies than an army officer. This was soon remedied however, for within a few minutes after his arrival, we arranged for him to take a much-needed bath and get a shave, and we found some clean fatigue clothes that came close to fitting him, though not quite. At any rate, when he reappeared about an hour later he looked like an entirely different man.

He told us how he had been flown into Korea with the first group from the 24th and that they had been committed to action immediately, somewhere in the vicinity of Taejon. So far as he knew, he was the only member of his platoon who had not been either captured or killed in the bitter and bloody fighting that followed. The NKPA outnumbered them by about ten to one. He said that he and his platoon had become separated from the remainder of the company when it was overrun by at least one battalion of the enemy. During the melee that followed, he had been able to beat off one or two would-be killers in hand-to-hand combat. He said that he shot one with his carbine and then hit the other one on the head with the butt of his gun. Then he and two of his men made their escape by jumping into a shallow creek and following it downstream for several hundred yards until it branched out. There they became separated from one another, and he never saw them again.

He said that he hid under a wooden bridge for three days without either food or water while the enemy searched for him and his two companions. On the third day, he saw some Koreans working their rice paddies nearby, but since the NKPA were still in the area, he was afraid to ask for help for fear the farmers would turn him in to save their own skins. But when the enemy moved out on the morning of the fourth day, Hicks said he walked out into the fields and by a combination of sign language and some pidgin Japanese, he identified himself as an American and asked for something to eat. One of the South Koreans took him to his hut in the village, gave him food, and allowed him to stay with him and his family for nearly two months.

He told us that his Korean friend and his wife had fed him well, but that he had had some initial difficulty learning to like their bland, meatless diet. But he said that he soon became used to it and that he was now quite fond of it. Nevertheless, I noticed later that he had no trouble readjusting to American food, even though it was canned C rations.

There was no question that Hicks had been one of the more fortunate ones who had escaped from the NKPA, for they had very effective ways of wheedling information out of the natives of any country, including their own — like beating them or breaking their arms or legs or sometimes just plain executing them if they refused to talk.

Hicks stayed with us several days while our doctors gave him a good physical examination and rebuilt his strength with food and rest. Then at the end of the short period, Eighth Army ordered him flown to Tokyo where he was hospitalized and subsequently returned to the United States. On about October 6 our battalion from Panama arrived and with it, the biggest surprise of all — a company of engineers, a company of tanks, and a battalion of artillery, all from the 3rd Division. Their arrival was most welcome. The company of tanks and the artillery battalion were composed of black soldiers from the Continental United States. These units fought superbly during the entire year that they were attached to the regiment.

The artillery battalion was commanded by Lt. Col. Harry M. Stella, an all-American football player at West Point, who turned out to be one of the finest artillery commanders ever to serve with us in Korea. Later when we joined the 3rd Division, it appeared that the artillery commander of that division, Brig. Gen. Roland M. Shugg, did not agree with my opinion of Stella, for he relieved him from his command. In my view, however, his replacement was never quite able to demonstrate the same know-how or control that Stella had during those wild and woolly days before the 3rd Division arrived in Korea.

Several years later, when I was on duty at the Pentagon, I received a letter from Stella to the effect that he had received a very poor efficiency report from Shugg and as a result he had been passed over for promotion to the grade of colonel. He asked if I would write a letter for the record stating my opinion of his capability as a combat commander, which I was glad to do. Subsequently he informed me that a new promotion board had recommended him for advancement, and I was glad that I had had an opportunity to rectify a serious injustice to a very fine soldier.

The Panama battalion was commanded by Lt. Col. John Gavin, but shortly after his arrival he was promoted and therefore had to be reassigned out of the regiment. I then selected Major Allen, our S-3, for that post. In due course he was promoted to the grade of lieutenant colonel. In turn, Maj. William Friedman was made the regimental operations officer to replace Allen, and both of these officers served with distinction during the remainder of my tour of duty with the 65th.

Almost concurrently with the arrival of these troops, the 1st Philippine Provisional Battalion was attached to us. Initially it was an ineffective fighting unit, which I soon decided was due to the attitude of the battalion commander. He was more of a complainer than a doer, and I finally asked that he be relieved of his command. His replacement, Lt. Col. Dionisio Ojeda, a very fine and capable officer, quickly rekindled the spirit and fighting capability of the Filipino soldiers. The battalion soon gained a reputation as one of the best fighting units in Korea, much to General MacArthur's complete delight.

As our equipment and these reinforcements began to arrive, we soon became quite a formidable fighting force. We were also quickly learning the techniques employed by these guerrilla fighters and, more importantly, learning how to beat them at their own game. They knew the terrain and had been well trained in hit-and-run tactics which they employed most effectively at night. We learned, on the other hand, that our most effective technique was to hunt out and destroy them during the daylight hours and then go into an all-around, wagon-wheel, defensive position on the high ground at night. We also learned to remain in those defensive positions no matter how many of the enemy attacked us.

Their technique was to try to slip up on us at night, usually during the early morning hours. Then when they were discovered, they would blow bugles and whistles and give bloodcurdling yells as they attacked, in hopes that they could scare hell out of us. They succeeded in doing this only once. Our men quickly learned to hold their ground, regardless of the number of yelling, screaming enemy that hit us. The Puerto Ricans calmly took aim and fired their weapons with deadly effect. Many times with the arrival of daylight, the bodies of the dead NKPA soldiers (and later, the Chinese) would be stacked up in front of our positions like so much cordwood.

But it was the moonless nights that gave me the most worry, for the success of their guerrilla tactics depended in large measure on their ability to slip up on us without being detected. One system we devised to light up the battlefield was to fill a large number of fifty-gallon oil drums with a combination of gasoline, oil, and cotton waste like that used by mechanics in a machine shop. Then we would place these fused drums around our positions. When our outposts discovered the enemy moving in on us, they would set these cans on fire with tracer ammunition and light up the entire countryside. We also used artillery star shells for the same purpose, when we had them.

Our increased strength and improved techniques were now beginning to pay dividends. On 9 October, the I and R Platoon and a patrol from E Company hit the jackpot. Sergeant Pagani and his platoon found a concentration of approximately two thousand NKPAs in the vicinity of the village of Waegwan, and the E Company patrol, under command of M. Sgt. Acevaso Adguanas, and second-in-command Sgt. Rafael Rivers, found a cache of Russian-made artillery pieces and enough ammunition to equip an entire battalion and keep it firing for at least a week.

While we laid plans to attack the enemy force near Waegwan, we took immediate steps to dig the artillery cache out of the sandy creek bottom where it had been buried. It was our guess that it had all been carried, piece by piece, to this location by the North Koreans before they ever invaded the South. It would have been comparatively easy for them to transport the components down from the North in their two-wheeled carts or to carry them on their backs, as we had seen the man do with the eight-cylinder gasoline motor strapped to an A-frame. I doubt whether any South Koreans would have taken notice of such an operation, and even if they had, they probably wouldn't have reported it to anyone for fear of reprisals by the Communists.

As for the enemy concentration near Waegwan, we laid plans to box them in on three sides with our battalions and to use the Naktong River as a barrier on the fourth side. Then, if the enemy attempted to swim across the river, it would be like shooting fish in a rain barrel, which is what it turned out to be. At one time, when our supply personnel attempted to draw water from the Naktong for drinking purposes, they had to move several miles upstream before they could back their trucks down to the water's edge because of the large number of dead bodies that were either floating in the river or beached along the banks. Of course, any water we used for drinking or cooking purposes was always treated with purification tablets.

The operations we set in motion in and around Waegwan to eliminate the two thousand enemy lasted until almost the end of the month and ranged over an area of some fifty miles or more. Some specific accounts of the fighting during this period by both large and small units is worthy of detailed description for they gave further proof that the men of the 65th were cool, determined, self-reliant, and effective combat soldiers. They were fearless.

The first incident that comes to mind involved a combat patrol of thirty men from C Company, which engaged the enemy near the village of Hwaggan. This little collection of adobe huts was in the approximate center of the zone of operation we had assigned to the 1st Battalion, and St. Clair planned to attack the enemy there with two companies abreast, holding the third in reserve.

Company C, the left assault company, had sent out a patrol as an advance party to make physical contact with the right flank of the enemy. Because the ground was so open — with little or no vegetation or other form of cover or concealment — the patrol leader had to move his unit with great caution to keep it from being discovered. Directing his lead man, or "point," toward the east, he deployed his unit in a diamond-shaped formation so that there were approximately one hundred yards between men in order to disperse them and to provide all-around protection for the entire group. He then directed them to move out cautiously

around the lower slopes of the hill on their left. From there he hoped
to enter a draw which led to the position where the enemy had been
sighted.

Moving carefully and cautiously, the patrol succeeded in getting within
about five hundred yards of the enemy's known position when suddenly
a machine gun opened fire, pinning every man to the ground. The gun
and its crew had been so cleverly concealed in a hole in the ground that
the first indication the men on patrol had of it was when they heard its
unmistakable rat-a-tat chatter and saw and felt the dirt and gravel being
kicked up all around them.

The enemy fire was so accurately placed that it seemed to the patrol
leader and his men that it was only a question of time, and not too much
of that, before every one of them would be killed. It was still a little
cloudy, for the morning sun had not burned off the ground haze, and
the patrol leader had trouble trying to pinpoint the gun's location. Every
move he made to improve his vision brought down a hail of bullets. He
tried to crawl backwards, thinking that he could retrace his steps and get
out of the enemy's line of direct fire, but that didn't work. The NKPAs
had let the patrol move to a point of no return before they opened fire,
and he and his men were caught. To add to his problems, there was little
hope of any help from the rest of the company, or the battalion either,
for at least another hour or maybe more. In that length of time the
patrol would surely be wiped out. If he could just get some of his men,
or even one man, who could fire at the machine-gun crew, it might make
them keep their heads down long enough for the patrol to make a rush
for a safer position, but it was beginning to look hopeless.

But it is in times such as these, when the battle appears to be lost, that
one man, or sometimes several, rises to the occasion and a new hero
is born. This was one of those times. On this occasion, that man was Cpl.
Catalino Aruz-Perez.

Corporal Aruz-Perez, an automatic rifleman with the patrol, seeing
that the other men were helplessly pinned to the ground and unable to
return the enemy's fire, jumped to his feet and, with complete disregard
for the murderous hail of fire directed at him, ran and crawled across
an open field to a position from which he could fire his weapon at the
enemy crew. Now this takes some doing, just physically, for a Browning
automatic rifle weighs from twelve to fifteen pounds, and it is an un-
wieldly weapon to handle. With eight or ten clips of ammunition weighing another six pounds or so, plus the weight of the rest of an infantryman's equipment, he has trouble just trying to march at a normal ca-
dence. To run, and at the same time try to keep from being shot, takes a

strong man, physically and mentally. Aruz-Perez accomplished all this. The other men of the patrol could hardly believe their eyes. All of them were sure that Aruz-Perez would be killed before he could take another step. But he continued, alternately running in a zigzag pattern, then hitting the ground and firing, then jumping to his feet and running again until he was able to find a relatively safe position. From there, he delivered such a steady deadly stream of fire that within several minutes he had killed the enemy crew and silenced the weapon. For his bravery and initiative, Corporal Aruz-Perez was awarded the nation's third highest decoration, the Silver Star.

The discovery of the patrol of course alerted the enemy, who immediately staged a counterattack against St. Clair's entire battalion. At one phase of these actions, the enemy was able to cut off one of Saint's platoons and isolate it so completely that for a time it was feared that every man in that unit would be either captured or killed.

This platoon happened to be the right flank unit of the 1st Battalion. When the enemy counterattacked in that direction, it became separated from the remainder of the company. The platoon leader quickly realized his predicament and organized his unit into an all-around, perimeter defense on the top of a small hill and prepared to fight it out.

From that position, the platoon leader and his men could see the battle raging all around them. They knew that they could expect no help, for the time being at any rate, from the remainder of the battalion, for it was almost completely surrounded by hundreds of NKPAs, and more were coming.

Determined that they would never surrender, the men of the platoon prepared for a long siege. While half of them burrowed into the ground for cover, the other half beat off repeated enemy attacks. Though the battle raged all through the night, the platoon was able to hold its position until the battalion was able to send help, and the enemy was driven off.

When it was all over, it was obvious that the platoon had suffered some severe casualties. Had it not been for the heroic efforts of Cpl. Guadalupe Ortiz, Medical Corps, many of those who had been wounded would have died. In the midst of some of the heaviest fighting, Corporal Ortiz had made his way about the assaulted area while under heavy enemy fire, constantly exposing himself to extreme danger in order to administer first aid to the wounded. He then worked throughout the night giving aid and carrying the wounded to a central point where he armed himself with the weapons of some of the wounded and stood guard over them until the battalion relief force arrived. For his gallantry and courage and for saving the lives of many of his comrades, Corporal Ortiz was awarded the Silver Star.

Though we continued to tighten the noose on the enemy we had bottled up along the Naktong, they just as stubbornly counterattacked our nighttime, defensive positions at every opportunity. During one of these attacks, a large enemy force hit the perimeter defenses and the outlying security posts of E Company. One of these outposts was a roadblock that Lieutenant Carsley, the company commander, had set up to prevent the enemy from infiltrating to his main company position through a narrow pass.

About 2 A.M. the enemy tried his usual tactic of slipping up on the platoon guarding the roadblock, but the men on guard heard them and opened fire, which immediately brought the rest of the platoon into action. One of the men fired into the fifty-gallon drums that had been placed around their positions, lighting up the sky as if it were daylight. As soon as the NKPAs realized that they had been discovered, they charged the platoon, screaming and yelling like banshees.

These Comanche-type yells and bugle calls could put the fear of the devil himself into a man's soul, but our men had become accustomed to them, and they just stood their ground, calmly mowing down the enemy as he sent wave after wave in. We had learned, too, that many times the NKPAs initially sent two or three waves of troops in to just scream and yell, which was about all they could do for they were not armed with anything but clubs or hand grenades. They were supposed to scare us, and when we started to run, the better-armed enemy ranks in the rear would then move in for the kill. Several prisoners whom we had taken within the first few days indicated to us that it was just about as safe for them to charge us unarmed as it was to hold back, for they would have been killed anyway.

It was during some of the heaviest fighting at that roadblock, however, when defeat or victory hung in the balance, that the platoon commander was seriously wounded. It is precisely at such critical stages of combat that the commander's active control is most needed. The individuals of such a unit often become so intent upon fighting their own little war that they sometimes fail to notice the other action going on around them. They may not take advantage of a particular situation that could be turned in their favor, or they may fail to observe a breakthrough by the enemy at a certain point and not shift their fires to stop it. This is when the leader of the unit, who should not be involved in individual combat unless it is absolutely necessary, must take the necessary steps to influence the action; that is, exert his authority at that crucial psychological moment which is usually the turning point of the battle.

Again, as was to happen many times, the initiative, know-how, and bravery of one man saved the day. Pfc. Pedro Morales, a natural-born leader, seeing that the platoon commander was wounded and out of action, immediately assumed command. Knowing that the outcome of the battle depended in large measure on the men of the platoon holding their positions despite repeated attempts to drive them out, Private First Class Morales began to move from man to man, quietly reassuring each one that they would win the fight if everyone stayed in his foxhole and continued the deadly fire on the enemy.

Time after time he crawled or ran across the open ground that was swept by hostile rifle and automatic fire to direct the fire of the men where it would be the most effective. When he was finally satisfied that the members of the platoon had settled down and were holding off the enemy's vicious attacks, he moved to a position where he could bring the large volume of fire of his own automatic weapon to bear on them.

Though he was in a completely exposed position, he remained there continuing to pour a deadly volume of fire on the enemy, killing twenty-one of them and capturing another five.

There was no question that the outstanding initiative and inspiring leadership and courage displayed by Morales was the final motivating force which turned the tide of that battle and saved the platoon from complete annihilation. For his heroic actions, Private First Class Morales was awarded the Silver Star.

As soon as the firing broke out, Lieutenant Carsley heard it immediately and started to send one of his other platoons to assist the besieged outpost, but just as it started out, another large enemy force hit his main position.

This attack also began with the usual Comanche yells, bugles and whistle blowing, and a heavy volume of rifle and automatic-rifle fire. But within seconds after it started, they also began to receive some very heavy mortar fire, and these were different.

Carsley had been shelled by mortars before, but these had a deeper, heavier whine as they came out of the tube. The noise of the explosion as they hit and the hole that they dug in the ground were both at least twice that of any others that he had either heard or seen before. Several days later, when we captured some of these new weapons, we found them to be Russian-made, 90-mm mortars with a base plate as big as a jeep. They were vicious.

Then not long after these mortars began to fall on his position, Carsley received a report from the platoon leader of his 1st Platoon that they were receiving a heavy volume of enfilade fire that was coming from a machine gun located on a hill off to their right. Quickly realizing that this flanking fire might soon wipe out that entire platoon, he immediately selected several of his best riflemen and personally led them to a position from which they could engage the gun. He then stood up in full view of the enemy in order to draw their fire, which in turn would reveal their location. Once his men saw the muzzle blast, they immediately started to fire at that location. Within minutes they had put that gun out of action.

But Carsley still had his work cut out for him. His troubles had only begun, for at the same time that he was working on the enemy machine gun, several NKPAs managed to penetrate another platoon position and began to infiltrate into the very center of his company defenses. From here they could have inflicted great damage, possibly even causing the men to panic, had they not been discovered in time.

Fortunately, however, Private Cruz-Alicea arrived on the scene at about the same time that the enemy riflemen reached the center of the company position. Yelling at the top of his voice to give the alarm, he immediately charged straight into a group of three North Korean soldiers, firing at them as he ran. But as he did so, other enemy soldiers began to appear over the crest of the hill and attack the position. Even though Cruz-Alicea had alerted his comrades and his courageous assault on the enemy did temporarily stop the infiltration, it appeared for several minutes as though the company position would be completely overrun.

Carsley, in the meantime, had heard Cruz-Alicea give the alarm and had quickly gathered up a dozen or more of his headquarters personnel. They, too, charged into the thick of the fight, with Carsley leading them. Within seconds there was a grand melee of individual hand-to-hand combat, with Carsley and his men pressing such a vicious bayonet attack on the enemy that those who were still alive on top of the hill soon surrendered.

With the integrity of his position once more restored, Carsley set about reorganizing his platoons, relocating his rifle and automatic riflemen, and at the same time directing the fight against the enemy still trying to assault the hill from below. When dawn finally arrived, the enemy broke off the attack and withdrew, leaving seventy-eight of their men dead and another sixty-four as prisoners.

Both Carsley and Cruz-Alicea were later awarded the Silver Star for their quick thinking, initiative, and outstanding courage and bravery. Cruz-Alicea's award was made posthumously, for he was mortally wounded during the fight and died several days later.

It was about the same time, 17 October, when one of the companies of the 1st Battalion also ran into trouble. Like the others, St. Clair had kept constant pressure on the enemy in his area, and I guess that the NKPAs were beginning to feel the heat. At any rate, they hit his right assault company with a very strong counterattack. The initial information he received from the company commander came in a rather garbled message to the effect that they were about to be overrun. Since he was in the process of leading an assault on the enemy's right flank with the battalion reserve, Saint called for an officer volunteer who would go to the besieged company and radio him more accurate information of the conditions there: should he send immediate relief or could the company hold out until the battalion engaged the enemy's flank, which should relieve the pressure on them?

First Lieutenant Horan of Company B immediately volunteered to lead the motorized patrol consisting of five jeeps and twenty men, not a very large force because its mission was one of reconnaissance and not combat. En route, and not far from the little village of Tommalik-tong, Horan and his men ran into a small enemy force that opened fire on them, causing the patrol to disperse and take cover. Though small, this enemy group had chosen a commanding position on top of a small hill which controlled the road and the approaches to the besieged company.

Horan had only two alternatives: either to fight it out with the enemy on the hill and try to eliminate them or to abandon his vehicles and try to make his way on foot some two miles around the small enemy detachment that was holding him up — neither of these choices was very attractive as far as Horan was concerned. If he stopped to fight, he would be wasting time as far as the accomplishment of his original mission was concerned, and there was always the possibility that the enemy could hold him off indefinitely. On the other hand, if he gave up his jeeps and tried to go cross-country on foot, he probably wouldn't reach his objective on time either.

Quickly considering his dilemma, Horan decided to fight. This was precisely what anyone knowing him would have said he would do; he was just the kind of an individual who would run in only one direction when there was a fight around — straight for the enemy.

Ordering his men to dismount, he deployed them as skirmishers and began his rush toward the enemy position. So vicious was this attack that the NKPAs pulled back from the hill and commenced a delaying action, fighting all the way, as they headed back for the security of their own supporting troops. However, Horan immediately took up the pursuit and was personally leading his men in the chase when he was suddenly struck by an enemy rifle bullet and mortally wounded.

Though in critical condition and in need of immediate medical attention, he continued to press the advance on the enemy and so inspired his men that they captured three prisoners and dispersed the remainder.

Though his patrol was small in number, when they finally joined up with the men of the company, Horan felt that they could hold out until the remainder of the battalion arrived. He so radioed St. Clair. Acting upon this advice, Saint continued his attack, relieved the pressure on his company, and over the next several days captured two hundred enemy and killed another seventy-five.

Though Lieutenant Horan was given medical attention as soon as possible, he died the following morning. For his outstanding initiative, aggressive leadership, and extraordinary courage and heroism, all of which were in keeping with the highest traditions of the military service, Lieutenant Horan was awarded the Silver Star posthumously.

By now the 65th was beginning to gain something of a reputation as a fighting unit, and we started to have a number of high-ranking visitors. Though no one said so, I suspected that they wanted to find out what made the Puerto Ricans tick. No question about it, we had been lucky in the number of enemy that we were given official credit for either killing or capturing compared with so few losses of our own. So the visitors started arriving, and they were very complimentary of the fighting ability and courage of the Puerto Ricans.

The first two to visit us were Maj. Gen. Lawrence B. Keiser, commanding general of the 2nd U.S. Infantry Division, under whose command we had served since our arrival. The other was Maj. Gen. William B. Kean, commander of the 25th U.S. Infantry Division. Then, shortly after they had arrived and we had discussed the Puerto Rican soldiers, I learned that we were being assigned to the operational control of Kean's division, and that the shift was effective immediately.

Though I had expected this new assignment to bring with it some new missions and probably another move or two, it did not work out that way. We were to continue just what we had been doing, rounding up the large enemy force that we had boxed in along the Naktong River.

And we had them boxed in, but good. So well in fact that they now stopped trying to run and dug in for a fight to the finish. We had overlooked one very important military principle, that of always allowing your enemy at least one avenue of escape; then when he tries to do that, you can clobber him as he streams out. But we had hemmed them in completely, and they became desperate. When men become desperate, they sometimes become fanatical. This was what was beginning to happen with the NKPAs we had cornered, who now appeared to prefer death to capture; this could mean many more casualties for us.

To combat this new situation, we decided to let them die, but hopefully without having to sacrifice our men in accomplishing the job. We decided to move our tanks in to chew them up. As the tanks moved through the area they called for our artillery to pulverize those whom they could not destroy. Then along with this massive firepower, we asked the air force to do some controlled bombing within the area. By this time they had developed a napalm bomb containing a jellied substance that exploded into one large sheet of flame as it hit the ground. Due to the force with which it hit it would then roll across the area in a ball of scorching fire that burned everything in its path to a frizzle.

We did not stop our attacks completely, however, for we continued to close the noose on the enemy's throat even though the tanks, artillery, and air force napalming pounded away at them. But in so doing, we almost slipped the rope around the neck of Colonel Allen and his 3rd Battalion. He had originally been assigned the responsibility of sweeping along the Naktong from the south, with his right flank resting on the left (west) bank of the river. When we decided to continue our infantry attacks, Allen moved out in that same direction and with the same mission. However, they had hardly gotten under way when his left assault company came under heavy small-arms and mortar fire which stopped the entire company except the company commander and five or six men belonging to his headquarters group.

When Allen received the radio report from that company commander as to what was happening to him, he realized at once that this attack could pose an even more serious problem than having the one company pinned to the ground. If the enemy were successful in rolling up his left flank, that would push him and the rest of the battalion into the water. Then instead of the enemy having to swim the Naktong, Allen and his men might be faced with that bleak prospect.

As soon as we received a report on the situation, we immediately ordered the tanks, the artillery, and the air force to concentrate on the area where the enemy was closing in on Allen's left assault company. With that help Allen was finally able to consolidate his forces, extract the one company, and completely clean out the enemy in that area.

The 3rd Battalion had no more than finished destroying that nest of guerrillas, however, when we heard rumors to the effect that we were again going to receive new orders. This time we were to be assigned to the X Corps, commanded by Maj. Gen. Ned Almond, who had commanded it when they made the landing at Inchon. I had no details about what we were to do or where we were to go, but I did receive instructions that we were to break off contact with the enemy along the Naktong within several days and be ready to move immediately thereafter.

I must admit that at the time I had little or no reluctance about breaking off contact with the enemy along the river, although I would have gladly finished off the job had we been allowed to stay there. But I was ready to go on to some other task, and I think that the men were too.

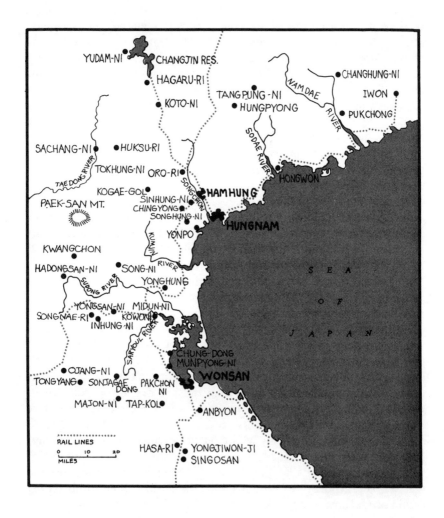

Area of Operations Winter Campaign

5

THE CHINESE VOLUNTEERS

We were now headed for the "Big Game" of the season — like the traditional Missouri-Kansas rivalry in the Big Eight Conference or the Texas-Texas Aggies in the Southwestern League. Up to this point, we had been playing practice games or scrimmaging or doing on-the-job training, as it might have been called. At any rate, it was to be different — quite different in fact. Instead of our fighting only two thousand North Koreans, the 65th — along with the 7th U.S. Infantry and the 1st Marine Division — was to come face to face, even eyeball to eyeball, with about two hundred thousand Chinese volunteers. And the word *volunteers* should be cleared up at once before it gives an erroneous impression. They were the type of volunteer who had two choices: to go with the Chinese People's Army into Korea or have their heads cut off.

But this is getting ahead of the story, and perhaps we should begin with the beginning of this new phase in our operations. It all started during a lull in the action along the Naktong River. I was ordered to report to Eighth Army headquarters which had moved from Pusan to a village named Taegu about thirty or forty miles from where we were located. It was there that I learned about a new operation that was being planned and in which we were to participate.

Word had been received from GHQ that the 65th was to be relieved from the operational control of the 25th U.S. Infantry Division and the IX Corps and assigned to the X Corps. I understood that shortly after the latter unit had made its landing at Inchon, it had been pulled back to Pusan, where it was preparing to out-load by ship to northeastern Korea, to a place called Wonsan on the Sea of Japan. The unit was to stage another of General MacArthur's amphibious runs around behind the enemy, this time farther to the north than any American troops in Korea had gone to date. Since we were to be a part of this new operation, I was advised before I left Eighth Army headquarters to have the regiment prepared to move immediately upon receipt of orders — within several days.

But by the time I returned to my own headquarters, the staff had already received the official word, for I was greeted by Childs.

"Well, here we go again, Colonel."

He had received a call from Army G-3 (operations) that we were to start our move to Pusan on the twenty-eighth. Today was the twenty-seventh.

G-3 also said that I was to proceed to Pusan ahead of the rest. General Almond wanted me to report to Wonsan immediately and was sending his light plane down to Pusan for me.

"What did army say about trucks to move us to Pusan?" I asked Chick.

"Trucks are on the way, sir. I'd guess that they'll be here by late afternoon today."

"I see. Well, I don't have to tell you that breaking off contact with the enemy is a dangerous operation anytime, and trying to do it in broad daylight is really taking a chance. I suggest that we ask the battalion commanders where they want us to spot the trucks and let them handle their own move back to an assembly point somewhere near here. Then you can move the whole outfit as a unit. OK?"

"Yes, sir."

"How many trucks did they give us, Chick?"

"Three companies, sir."

"Then let's allocate one to each of the battalions and have the commanders tell us where they want them spotted.

"One other thing, Chick, better have S-3 alert the Filipino Battalion to be ready to lend a hand if any of our men run into trouble trying to break off contact."

"Right, sir. I'll have the staff arrange the move of the battalions, and I'll get Ojeda in here and go over some emergency plans with him."

"Good. The NKPA are just liable to try something funny when they see our battalions start to pull out, so it's a pretty good idea to be ready for them."

"Right, sir. When you figure on leaving, Colonel?"

"Well, to tell you the truth, Chick. I'm not too keen about moving around on that road at night, so I guess I'll be on my way as soon as I can get something to eat. I'll get in touch with you after I get to Pusan. If I can get any additional information, I'll call you by radio."

Then as quickly as I could, I asked Ramos to have Vargas and my radio operator pack up, eat, and be ready to roll within an hour. I also told him that he and the others were to wait in Pusan for the arrival of the regiment and report to Colonel Childs.

Though we had about a three-hour trip to Pusan, we arrived there well before dark, and I was glad that we had. Roads at night anywhere in Korea were about like running the gauntlet between two lines of Indian braves who are intent on hacking hell out of your skull as you run between them. Actually the gauntlet might have been a better gamble than driving through that guerrilla-infested country.

We didn't let any grass grow under the wheels of that jeep, I can assure you, and we reached our destination without mishap. For a lack of something better to think about en route, I tried to figure out the relationship between X Corps, Eighth Army, and GHQ — General MacArthur's headquarters. As nearly as I could calculate, X Corps was operating as an independent unit within Eighth Army's area of responsibility and was subject only to the direct, personal orders of General MacArthur himself. Then, to further complicate the matter, General Almond, the X Corps commander, had retained his title as General MacArthur's chief of staff, which he had been prior to assuming command of the troops in the Inchon Operation. I have never heard of a similar command set up in the entire history of the U.S. Army. It was indeed unique, but it worked — although rumor had it that General Walker was furious. Later, in North Korea, coordination between the two commands was a bit tenuous, too, for the 65th had the assignment, and I had some difficulties which will be related in due course.

Pusan had not changed since we had seen it a month earlier. It was still the same dirty, dusty town as before, except that the weather had become cooler in the evening.

By the time I located General Almond's pilot it was after dark. Because the airport had no lights, he recommended that we wait until morning to fly to Wonsan, which we did. After a good night's rest and an early breakfast, we took off up the eastern shoreline, and I had my first view of the rugged Taebaek Mountain Range, which we were to see the hard way many times later. From our altitude, I guessed that in some places the peaks of that range reached at least six thousand feet above sea level and looked every bit as treacherous as our Rocky Mountains do in Colorado and equally as hard to climb or cross. We were to have plenty of experience doing both before the end of the year.

Starting in the steppes of southern Manchuria, the Taebaek Range extends all the way down the eastern coast of the Korean peninsula and forms a very definite barrier for any east-west military operation, as we were to learn before many months. Only the natives and their small ponies ever seemed to be able to negotiate it with any ease. One of the few passes through it, I discovered, is located at Wonsan, which was probably one of the principal reasons our operations were to be based from there, as protection for our back door as we continued our move to the far north, where one unit of the 7th U.S. Infantry Division even reached the Yalu River. I also discovered after we arrived there that a village named Yonghung was another terminus of an east-west passage through the Taebaek Range.

Other than the mountains, I saw little of the countryside to the west. I did see many fishermen along the coast, with their little sampans bobbing up and down in the water and their small adobe huts hanging from the cliffs like so many wasps' nests. In fact, I wondered how anything but a bird or a billy goat could ever get back and forth from them to the water's edge, but apparently these people did.

The flight to X Corps took about two hours. When we arrived, a jeep was waiting to take me from the airstrip to the headquarters, which was located in what had been a North Korean Navy headquarters building. From what I have read, I suspect that was the same one where the men from the captured U.S.S. *Pueblo* were held at one time.

General Almond was out on an inspection trip when I arrived, but I was told that he would return by dark and would see me then. In the meantime, I discovered that one of my closest friends and classmates from West Point, Col. Aubrey D. Smith, was General Almond's G-4 (staff officer-supply), and he took me in hand.

Smitty had been born and raised in a little town in Missouri named Boonville. He and I had entered the United States Military Academy at the same time. We had become rather close friends during those years at West Point, and we became even more closely associated when we served together as second lieutenants at our first army post — Jefferson Barracks, Missouri. It was there, too, that he met and married Dorothy Krueger, the daughter of then Col. Walter Krueger, who later gained fame as General MacArthur's 8th Army commander in the Pacific campaigns.

Many people in the army considered Smitty a terrible braggart, although I never did. It was true that he did brag of what he could do, but he could do whatever he said he could, and I respected his ability and his intelligence. I guess if I had to fault Smitty, I would say that he was probably the most outspoken army officer I ever knew. He had little patience with lazy or indifferent officers, and the army had some; and the stupid he could not tolerate, and we had some of those too. I always had a feeling that, having been the son-in-law of such a famous four-star general, he had few inhibitions around officers of very senior rank. As a result, he had no hesitancy about giving his opinion on any subject, whether or not that opinion clashed radically with anyone else's present, senior general or otherwise.

Smitty and I spent several hours in the operations room where he pointed out the locations of our troops and those of the enemy on the situation map. The latter far outnumbered the former. He also told me what missions were to be assigned the 65th by General Almond, and they were enough to make my hair stand on end. He cautioned me not to indicate in any way that he had briefed me on these details, for if it became known, there would be hell to pay. So when the staff and General Almond briefed me later in the evening, I accepted what they told me without asking for additional details. I already knew them too well.

When Smitty and I finished talking in the operations room, I made some hasty calculations and came out with an estimate something like this. The 65th was to move to a village named Yonghung, about sixty miles to the north. From there we were to head west, make contact with the right flank of Eighth Army (1st Cavalry Division), which was supposed to be about sixty or seventy miles west of Yonghung. While doing this, we were to meet, make contact (physical) with the enemy force coming from the North, and "develop that situation."

Now on the face of it, that didn't sound too bad. But when he said that the enemy force consisted of two Chinese armies and that no one really knew even the approximate location of Eighth Army's right flank, those two factors made quite a difference.

To begin with, the two Chinese armies probably consisted of six corps, each having three infantry divisions, and each of those having about ten thousand men. Roughly then, the enemy force consisted of about two hundred thousand Chinese. With the strength of the 65th at about six thousand men, that would make the odds about thirty-three to one in favor of the Chinese. Somewhat jokingly, but with a nervous twitch, I told Smitty that in past operations we had been credited with either capturing or killing about thirty enemy for every man that we lost, and these odds were not too bad. The only trouble with this current operation, however, was that there would be no survivors to figure the statistics or to tell the story.

The part of the mission where we were to "develop the situation"

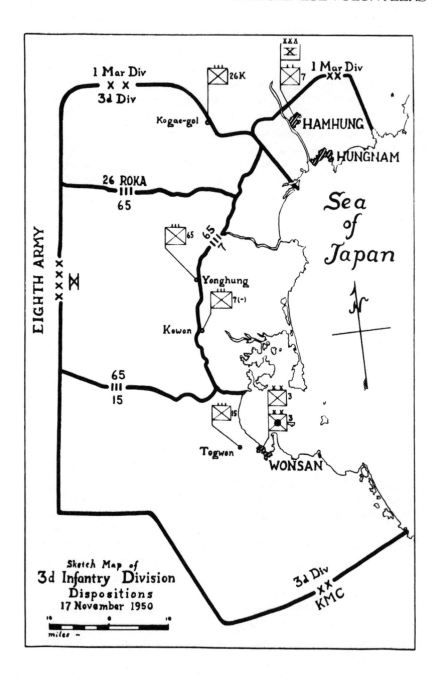

Sketch Map of
3d Infantry Division
Dispositions
17 November 1950

with the two hundred thousand Chinese coming down from the North resembled something that Jonathan Swift might have written. I felt myself in the fictional regions of Lilliput, Brobdingnag, Laputa, or the land of Houhynhnms. I could just see the 65th tearing into two hundred thousand Chinese. More than likely they could run over us without knowing that they had hit anything.

The final straw was the mission to make contact with the right flank of the Eighth Army, when no one was sure just how far they were to the west of Yonghung. That operation had all of the earmarks of playing Russian roulette with a six-shooter loaded with six live rounds and no blanks, instead of five blanks and one round of ammunition.

Though I was in a state of trauma and fidgets the rest of the day as a result of what Smitty had told me, I did manage to keep my cool at dinner that evening. Maj. Gen. Clark N. ("Nick") Ruffner, the corps chief of staff, had invited me to have my meals in the commanding general's mess. When I arrived there that first night, I found myself sitting at Almond's table, just to his right — definitely a position of honor above the salt; or, as I thought later, a privilege only accorded some character being granted his last wish just prior to being sacrificed to an Aztec deity. Smitty sat just to my right.

Although it is generally the custom in a large headquarters like a corps or a division, to have a briefing for the commanding general after dinner in the evening, usually the conversation at that meal also gets around to the day's happenings, the situation in general, and the individual experiences of the various staff officers during the past twenty-four hours. This becomes a sort of preview of what is to follow in the detailed briefing later. This one took a little different turn, however. I had no sooner sat down after being greeted by General Almond than Smitty let fly.

"Bill, I wouldn't go where you are being sent unless the corps commander gave me written orders to do so and at least four infantry divisions."

Although his remarks were directed at me, there was no question that everyone in the room heard exactly what he had said, including General Almond. There was a stunned silence, as if a bolt of lightning had hit the place, while we all waited for General Almond to hit the roof and probably tell Smitty that he was relieved from his assignment to X Corps and ordered back to Tokyo. But nothing happened. General Almond went right on eating as if nothing had been said.

Not to be content with his first bombshell, Smitty added, "Unless you are crazier than I think you are, if you go out of here on those missions, they'll eat you alive."

I was so dumbfounded, I couldn't say a word. General Almond just acted as nonchalant and composed as if Smitty didn't exist, which was just about what happened, for I heard later that he was ordered back to GHQ in Tokyo.

"Tell me about the Puerto Ricans," General Almond said, trying to cut off any further conversation about the unpleasant aspects of our missions.

In response to his question, I told him about the same things I had said to General Walker and then brought him up to date on our activities since we had been in Korea. But while I tried my best to limit the conversation to a discussion about the men of the 65th, Smitty would have no part of it and continued to elaborate on his original statements.

"Bill, you're nuts — if you think for one minute that your whole damned outfit will come out alive, you've got another think coming." And so it went. When everyone rose to go to the briefing, I heaved a sigh of relief, but that feeling didn't last very long.

After the staff had reviewed the enemy situation, which, by the way, included no numbers (just a big bunch of red symbols on the map denoting enemy), the G-3 (operations officer) proceeded to outline the missions of the 7th Infantry and the 1st Marine Division and, finally, the 65th Regimental Combat Team. At one point, when the briefing officer discussed our moving to the west to make contact with the right flank of Eighth Army, Maj. Gen. O.P. Smith (not to be confused with *Colonel* Smith, my classmate), the division commander of the 1st Marine Division, looked over at me and said, "Bill, think you'll need any help?"

In reply, I just smiled as though this was old stuff as far as the 65th was concerned. Actually I was in a cold sweat and afraid I would reveal my concern if I opened my mouth.

When the staff had completed its portion of the briefing, General Almond rose to make a few remarks, mainly emphasizing that as soon as the 65th landed in Wonsan, we were to head out to the north for Yonghung and from there extend ourselves to the west and do two things: make contact with Eighth Army and develop the enemy situation in that area.

It was three days before the regiment landed. During that interval, Smitty continued to warn me to the point that I couldn't sleep at night — all I could think about were the hordes of Chinese we were about to face.

During the day, however, I found some solace in wandering around the headquarters trying to gain additional useful information by talking with the staff and studying the enemy position as it was posted on the situation map from time to time. I did several other things as well —

one of which was to later make the difference between life and death for every man in the 2nd Battalion, including me.

I believe it was on the morning of the second day after my arrival at X Corps, and I was meandering around outside the headquarters building when I saw what looked like a large radio truck standing idle. The two operators and the driver were sitting in the shade under the truck playing cards. I have no idea to this day what prompted me to do it, but I walked over to the truck and started a conversation with the men. As nearly as I can remember, it went something like this:

"Good morning."

"Good morning, sir," from all three of them.

"I'm Colonel Harris, the regimental commander of the Puerto Rican outfit, the 65th."

"Oh, we've heard of that outfit, sir," one of them said.

"Yes, sir, we sure have," said another.

"They must be some fighters," said the third. "We hear most of the radio conversations all over Korea, and we've heard about your men."

That was interesting, I thought. "What are you men doing?"

"Nothing, sir. Just waiting for someone to tell us what to do."

"You mean that you don't have a job?"

"No, sir."

"Hmm, how would you like to go with us?"

"Great, sir. We've been waiting for someone to give us something to do. Where you headed, sir?"

"Well, General Almond just gave us the mission of going to a place called Yonghung. From there, we are to head out west and make contact with some enemy coming down from the North."

"Oh, we've been listening to radio reports about them, sir. So you got that job," said one. "OK, I'm ready."

"So am I," said the other two.

"Fine. Now I'll tell you what we'll do. My regiment is supposed to land here in about two or three days, and when it does, I'll come by here and pick you up. How's that?"

"That's OK with us, sir. We'll be glad to get to work."

"By the way, what kind of a radio is this?" I asked.

"Come here, sir, and I'll show you," said one of them who seemed to be in charge. And with that, he opened the rear panel door of the truck and showed me a piece of equipment that had the power to send a message anywhere in Korea and even as far away as Japan.

This was a real find, I thought. I only hoped that no one discovered that I was stealing it from the corps or that someone suddenly decided to give the operators a mission that would prevent them from going with me. And so it was all set. I stayed around for a few more minutes talking with my newly purloined recruits, but I was afraid to stay too long for fear some enterprising young second lieutenant of the signal corps would spot me and discover what I was up to.

Since General Almond had been heckling me every time I saw him to waste no time in getting to Yonghung and beyond once my troops landed, I organized a small beach party from some of the corps headquarters personnel who volunteered to help me expedite the troop unloading. While talking to these officers, I discovered that one of them had an ANGRC-9 radio mounted on his jeep, the same kind that I had on mine. This solved my problem of communicating with Childs while the troops were still afloat. With the permission of the officer, I had his operator change the crystal setting on his radio so that he could get into my command net. I was all set.

As I recall, it was at the evening briefing on the third day that I learned the 65th would pull into Wonsan about three o'clock the following morning.

"Are you all set, Harris?" General Almond asked me.

"Yes, sir." And when I replied, I hoped that he would not ask me for any details or that the staff would not prolong the meeting too long. I wanted to get out of there before someone, just by chance maybe, said, "Say, about that radio truck — sorry; we have other plans for it." But no one did, and the meeting broke up with Smitty still telling me that I was out of my head.

Shortly after midnight, I assembled my beach party and headed out for the Wonsan Harbor. En route, I called Childs on the radio and found that the lead ship was approaching the breakwater around the harbor and that they expected to dock within the next hour to hour and a half.

"Monarch Six calling Monarch Five. Monarch Six calling Monarch Five," I repeated into the radio microphone. Then within less than two minutes, Chick answered. He had apparently been expecting my call and had not been too far away from my jeep on the top deck.

"Monarch Six calling Monarch Five. Chick, what time do you estimate your arrival here?"

"Monarch Five to Six. I was just told that we should be in there within the next hour to hour and a half; over."

"Monarch Six to Five. Great. We're all set here. Will you have Henry Six [Colonel Dammer, commander of the 2nd Battalion] get on the horn with you. I want him to come off first, followed by Losey Six and then Amador. How do you read me? Over."

"Monarch Five to Six. I read you five by five, how me? Over."

"Monarch Six to Five. I read you five by five; over."

"Henry Six here; over."

"Monarch Six to Henry Six. Will you please prepare to unload first. Mission necessitates immediate departure after unloading. Meet me at the bottom of the gangplank and I'll give you the details. How do you read me? Over."

"Henry Six to Monarch Six. I read you five by five. Roger. Will do, over."

Normally we would have spoken in code, but there was no real necessity to do so at this particular time, at least I didn't think so. We had used code names to designate the commanders rather than calling them by name. But even if we had named names, I did not believe that the enemy would be monitoring our conversations at that time of the morning, and they couldn't have identified us even if they had.

Though I did not know it at the time, instead of the rest of the regiment following immediately behind the 2nd Battalion, General Almond had diverted the other two battalions and attached them to the 1st Marine Division, which had been ordered initially to move to the west from Wonsan. I would have known about this change sooner except that we were busily engaged with the enemy that night and part of the next day, and it never occurred to me to ask just where they were. I assumed that Chick was following my instructions, and that they would arrive there any minute.

I never did learn, however, whether General Almond had ordered this as a last minute change in his plans or whether he had had it in mind all along. I saw him at the dock shortly before the troop ships dropped anchor, but he didn't say anything about it at that time. He merely inquired if everything was all right and then asked how soon we were leaving for Yonghung. I assured him that things were in hand and that I was going to move with the 2nd Battalion as soon as it unloaded. And that was all that was said until I saw him again the following afternoon at my headquarters in Yonghung.

Unloading the 2nd Battalion was a simple matter since we would be using X Corps trucks to transport us, and I had not planned on taking my tank company or the artillery battalion because the unloading of those units would have delayed us. Besides, Childs would be following along shortly, and we would have them and the other battalions by at least noon the following day, or so I thought.

As the gangplanks were lowered, Childs and all three of the battalion commanders led the column of troops onto the dock where I quickly brought them up to date on the situation and our missions.

With everyone all set, I headed for the X Corps headquarters building and my radio truck, hoping at the same time that no one would see me make the turn to the left instead of continuing straight ahead from the beach toward Yonghung. To my complete delight, all three of the men were standing alongside their truck waiting for me.

"All set?" I yelled.

"Yes, sir — ready to go," they answered almost in chorus.

"OK, follow me," and I indicated for Vargas to head back toward the dock area and join Dammer's truck column which was already on the road.

It had been dark when we pulled out of Wonsan, but now the sun was coming up over the horizon, and we could see some of the country around us. It was not too much different from other places in Korea where we had been except that we were now headed into higher country than we had been before. The terrain was still as sandy and loamy looking as ever, with little or no vegetation except the usual rice paddies, which were now turning green instead of looking like a series of pig wallows. From my map and the curve of the road ahead it appeared that we were more or less headed up a deep valley formed by two separate chains of the Taebaek Range. I didn't like the idea of being on low ground, but there wasn't anything that either Dammer or I could do about it. Since we were mounted in two-and-a-half-ton trucks that could not get a footing in the deep rice paddies or travel over the narrow dikes that separated them, we were — through no choice of our own — road bound. This was a perfect setup for an ambush because we were strung out in one column, with high ground on both sides and in front of us.

However, Dammer had taken the necessary precautions by putting scouts well out to our flanks and to the front and rear of our column, and although he did not have as much information as I did about the possible number of enemy ahead, he knew that we were in virgin territory and that anything could happen — and did.

We had not been on the road very long — about an hour I'd say — when all four of us became hungry and Ramos broke out the C rations. We had pineapple juice, crackers, and cold canned beans — not exactly a feast or what I would have chosen for breakfast if I'd had my druthers, but good nevertheless. And while we are on the subject of food, I should mention now, before I forget, that we were really to eat high on the hog before too many days passed. We discovered among other edibles in

Korea that the place was literally infested with Chinese ringnecked pheasants. I never had such good shooting and, more important, good eating in all my hunting days. Firearms and gunpowder had long been denied the Korean civilians. As a result the pheasants had become as numerous and thickly populated as chickens in a barnyard — and just about as tame. When any of the four of us spotted a bird or two, or maybe a dozen in one place, we would deploy like skirmishers on the battlefield and shoot them with our carbines. When we brought the first bag of them in for the cook to prepare, I discovered to my amazement that none of the officers of my headquarters mess would eat them, so Ramos and Vargas and I really had a feast.

But to get back to our march toward Yunghung, Ramos had no more than handed us our rations when that old familiar, whompf-whompf of incoming mortar fire sent us scrambling out of our jeep — pineapple juice, beans and all — into the ditch alongside the road. All up and down the line of trucks, everyone else was doing the same thing, looking for a hole in the ground. Whompf-whompf-whompf-whompf. They now had the range and began to pour it on us, called — in artillerymen's lingo — "firing for effect." The worst part about mortars is that you do not know where they are headed until they explode, and then it may be too late. Direct-fire weapons, on the other hand, like the guns in the artillery, can be heard when the round is fired. The whine of the projectile can also be heard while it is rotating in its flight to the target. If you can hear it in coming, you can head for cover. But the first time you know that mortars are headed in your direction is when they hit the ground and explode, and that takes all of the fun out of it.

Then shortly after the mortars registered on us, we could hear the chatter of automatic weapons. Their fire was incoming, too, for we could see the bullets kicking up the dust around several of our men. From where I lay in the ditch alongside the road, it looked like the enemy had taken position on the small knoll straight ahead of us.

There couldn't have been more than a dozen of them altogether, but they were in several groups, each armed with both rifles and automatic weapons; and they were looking right down our throats from their higher elevation. Dammer would have to drive them off before we could make any further move toward our objective. While he was occupied with that problem, I crawled over to my jeep and gave Childs a call on the radio.

"Monarch Six calling Monarch Five, come in please."

"Monarch Six calling Monarch Five, come in please," I repeated several times before Chick finally answered.

"Monarch Five to Six; I read you loud and clear; over."

"Monarch Six to Five. Henry has run into some opposition ahead. Looks like he can handle without much problem but wondered about your progress; over."

"Monarch Five to Six. We're on the road with Losey in the lead and Amador coming off ship behind him; over."

"Monarch Six to Five. Roger. I'll stay in touch. Just wanted to know your location in case Henry needs help; over." And me, too, I thought.

"Monarch Five to Six. Roger; over."

"Monarch Six to Five. Nothing further here; over and out."

"Monarch Five to Six; over and out."

Though I didn't anticipate that Dammer would have any trouble driving the enemy back, I wanted to make sure that our other battalions were available should they be needed. As mentioned earlier, Childs still had not been given any indication that the rest of the regiment was going to be diverted by Almond. When Dammer did clear out the enemy hold-up and we continued our march toward Yonghung, I felt fairly secure in the knowledge that Chick and the rest of the men were not too far behind. Happiness is being ignorant of what the future holds; happiness is walking into the Lions' Den, thinking that the lions are not at home; happiness, in this case, was the feeling of false security.

Off we went. I would guess that it took us another three hours before we reached Yonghung. It was just starting to get dark. The sun was still hanging on top of the mountains, but it wouldn't be there long. It had taken Dammer's men several hours to chase the enemy off and then another half hour or so before he got his troops back into the trucks. All told it had taken us most of the day to travel just sixty miles or a little more.

As we came in sight of our objective, Dammer halted the column for his men to take a look around before we entered the town. I'd say that there were three or four thousand houses there, so it wasn't a small village. It was certainly large enough for a sizable enemy force to hide out in, but everything looked normal from what I could see. The farmers were still busy in the fields, and the villagers were moving about as though it were just another day. When Dammer's scouts signaled all clear, he started the column forward.

"OK, Vargas, let's catch up with Colonel Dammer."

"Yes, sir," and with that he pulled out of the column and speeded up until we came alongside Dammer's vehicle.

"Herm, this place looks too damned peaceful to me."

"I was just thinking the same thing, sir. I don't like the looks of it."

"Tell you what we'd better do. See that high ground just on the west edge of the town?"

"Yes, sir."

"Suppose you head for that and get into a perimeter defense before it gets dark. I didn't mention it to you before, but General Almond told me that an artillery battalion would meet us here. I believe he said it was the 999th or the 666th Field Artillery. I don't know who it belongs to or how it got here. Anyway, I'll take a look for it while you are getting into position for the night."

"Right, sir."

"OK, Vargas, let's go. Head on through town, and Ramos —"

"Yes, sir."

"Suppose you two [referring to him and the radio operator] face around to the rear and keep your eyes and ears open." They could do this by hanging their feet over the back of the jeep and riding shotgun fashion like the guards on the stagecoaches in the old days — not a very comfortable way to ride in a jeep but certainly one way to give us an all-around look-see at what was going on. This had become SOP whenever we traveled alone in the jeep and was to save our necks on more than one occasion.

"Looks quiet enough here," I remarked to Vargas as we drove through Yonghung.

"Yes, sir — looks OK, sir."

"Well, let's keep a sharp eye open. I don't trust any of these—"

"Yes, sir."

"And I don't see any artillery battalion either, do you?"

"No, sir, I don't see one either, sir."

"See that low ground off there to the right of town?"

"Yes, sir."

"Let's head off in that direction. Maybe they bedded down in that little streambed for the night."

And we hadn't gone more than two or three hundred yards before we could see that that was just exactly what they had done.

"Holy Hanna. Will you look at that. There they are, on the lowest ground in the entire area. Let's get over there as fast as we can."

I only hoped that they had not settled too well and that I could get them moved to our position on top of the hill before dark. But by the time I found the battalion commander, it was too late; darkness had caught up with us. He also told me that he had dropped off the artillery pieces from their prime movers and had the guns surveyed in for firing. I didn't figure that he would be able to do that in the darkness if I moved him. Then we would also be running the chance of having them ambushed if we tried to move in the dark, so I decided to let him stay put and only hoped that nothing would happen before morning when I would get him tucked in on top of the hill with me.

Before I left him, however, I gave him the frequency of my command radio net and had his operator set their frequency so that we would be in communication with one another. I also directed him to start a wire party from his end. I would do the same from the other end, so that we would also be in communication by telephone as well. I wasn't happy with his position, but there wasn't anything that I could do about it before morning, so I wished him luck and headed up the road to where Dammer had taken position.

As Vargas drove up the hill, we could see that someone had already dug foxholes all around the top, giving us as good a perimeter defense as we could have made for ourselves.

"Let's find Colonel Dammer, Vargas."

"Right, sir."

"Well, how about that, Herm? Looks like someone has done our work for us," I remarked when we found him in one of the adobe huts on top of the hill.

"Yeah, how about that. I'll set up my CP in here, sir."

"Good. I'll find a spot to light on too. I'll let you know where I am after I get there."

"OK, sir."

Perhaps this is as good a time as any to explain that I did not at any time try to command the individual battalions because I believed that my commanders were perfectly capable of running them without my interference. Had I believed otherwise, they would not have remained in command very long. So with that thought in mind, I found an empty foxhole and put my bedroll in it. Ramos and the others found similar accommodations nearby where they, too, set up light housekeeping for the duration of our stay there.

"Charlie" [This was Lt. Charles E. Boyle whom I had brought along as a one-man staff].

"Yes, sir."

"Would you mind telling Colonel Dammer that I have set up my CP here in this foxhole?"

"Right, sir."

"And Charlie —"

"Yes, sir."

"Where is our radio operator?"

"He's right here, sir. Sitting over under that big tree."

"Good. If you will, after you have told Colonel Dammer where we are, will you ask the operator to make contact with corps headquarters and stay in contact with them throughout the night?"

"Right, sir."

As has been mentioned, I will never know what prompted me to talk to those men at corps and to bring them along. Though I am not a deeply religious man, I am sure that it was Divine Guidance which led me there, for we had no means of our own to communicate with corps headquarters. Our ANGRC-9s were not powerful enough to carry that distance. Without the stolen radio, we would have been out of touch with everyone.

While I waited for Boyle to return, I thought how lucky we had been in finding a complete all-round defensive position made to order for us; we would have been hours preparing one ourselves. I wondered why the enemy had allowed us to move into them, and then I remembered that Dammer had kept pressure on their line of out-guards and continued to move forward aggressively until we reached Yonghung. That pressure had probably prevented the enemy main body from getting all set before we arrived, I thought.

When Boyle finally returned from the missions I had given him, our little group prepared to settle down for the night. We had our usual cold C rations, opened up our bedrolls and put them in the small foxholes prepared for us by courtesy of the enemy, and then hunched down into our nests like a hutch of rabbits. There wasn't much conversation after that, and soon we were all in the land of Nod . . .

Whompf — whompf — whompf — whompf. There was that noise again, and following close behind it was the also familiar zing — zing — zing — zing of in-coming rifle fire. But it was the whompf that I didn't like; I was never able to accommodate myself to mortar fire, and neither was anyone else to my knowledge.

Why, I do not know, but when the first round hit, I looked at my wrist watch and noted that it was exactly 1:45 in the morning — just about four or five hours after we had settled down for the night and just long enough for the enemy to think that we were asleep, happy in the thoughts that we had driven off the opposition and had nothing to worry about.

Within a few minutes I also noted that the enemy rifle fire was creeping around our perimeter and had now almost closed the circuit. It had started on the west side of our position and had then moved slowly around to the south, then the east, and was now coming from the north; there were apparently enough enemy troops that they had our position completely surrounded. Later, we estimated that about two enemy regiments had attacked us — that would be something in the neighborhood of about three thousand enemy.

Our men immediately took up the challenge and started to fire their rifles at the creepy, shadowy figures that were trying to sneak up on our positions, but we did not have the capability of returning their mortar fire. In our haste to get on toward our objective, I had frankly overlooked the attachment of the Regimental Mortar Company to the 2nd Battalion; it would certainly have come in handy right about now. There are times in combat when a commander wonders just why he did or did not take some particular action, and this was one of those times for me.

I would guess that the battle had been going on for about an hour or an hour and a half, when it occurred to me that if the fight continued at that pace for many more hours, there was a good possibility that we might get low on ammunition, so I sent word to Dammer to let me know the status of his supply.

"Charlie."

"Yes, sir."

"Will you find out from Colonel Dammer what his ammunition supply amounts to? It looks to me like he may run kind of short if his men keep up at the rate they're going. It's only about 3:30 A.M., and it's a long time till daylight. Ask him if he will let me know right away what his estimate is."

"Right, sir."

But even with the arrival of daylight, we probably wouldn't be in any better shape, I thought. We still didn't know how many enemy there were, and they might be in sufficient force to overrun us just by the weight of sheer numbers. I must admit that it was a rather hairy situation. Though I knew that the Puerto Ricans would give a damn good account of themselves in any hand-to-hand combat, if it got down to that (and I hoped that it wouldn't), just the thought of dying like a hero was not one bit of consolation. Just to emphasize the point — again the whompf — whompf — whompf — whompf. They were registered in on us and beginning to fire that dream of all artillerymen — fire for effect. They had recorded the range and were letting us have it.

It took Dammer some time to get the word back to me about the status of his ammunition, for it was about 4:00 A.M. before Boyle returned.

"Sir, Colonel Dammer had to talk to each of his company commanders before he could give me the answer. He said that if the firing kept at this rate, he would be out of ammunition by about 8:00 A.M."

"I was afraid of that. I wish now that I had taken a little more time before we started out. I forgot to bring the mortar company and forgot to ask Dammer if he had a "full load." (Called a "basic load" for a battalion, this amounted to about 250 rounds of ball ammunition per man and other equivalents.)

"Yes, sir, but if you had, that would have delayed us at least another hour."

"I know, Charlie, but at least we wouldn't be about to run out of ammo."

"Yes, sir."

"Where did you say that radio truck is?"

"Right there, sir, under the tree."

"OK, tell you what we're going to do. I heard there at corps that the quartermaster in GHQ was working on airdrops of ammunition and supplies, and they have been working with the Air Force Transport Command in Tokyo. Here, give me that book of message forms."

I wrote out an operational priority message to General Almond at X Corps headquarters which went something like this:

Operational Priority

From Harris to Almond

Under attack by enemy force estimated at two repeat two regiments. Estimate 2nd Battalion will be out of ammunition by 0800 hours. Request emergency airdrop of basic load rifle ammunition comma medical supplies comma and C rations period signed Harris.

"Here, Charlie, have the operator send this in the clear so that it won't take an hour to encode and decode the damn thing. The enemy already knows that we're here, so no use to send it classified."

"Yes, sir. Here's the radio operator now, sir."

"Good, and Charlie — have him note that I have marked it "Operational priority." This is the speediest classification that can be given a radio message — time was of the essence. I knew that the corps staff would have to go to Tokyo for the airdrop, and I estimated that they could do that in short order. Then if we were lucky and several aircraft were available, we just might get that airdrop before it was too late, though I would not have bet on it at the time. At any rate, there was nothing more that I could do now except wait, and worry, and hope that we didn't run out of ammunition before 8:00 A.M.

In battle, there are few things more wearing on a commander's nerves than not knowing what is going on — what the situation is like. Are we holding the enemy? Are they breaking through anyplace — and a thousand and one other worries. But I had decided not to bother Dammer.

Though I was a bit sanguine about our chances of escaping alive — in "good heart" as they say — I knew that everything now rested on the airdrop. Unless the enemy received some more reinforcements, I felt that we could hold them — that is, if we received the airdrop. If we didn't, that would be another story. But I'll admit right now that I fully expected we would be taken prisoner before the day was over. And from what I had heard about their treatment of prisoners, the next few hours were among the longest of my life.

Earlier during the night I had talked to the artillery commander over my radio, and he seemed to be OK. His position was not under attack, but when he heard the firing in our area, he had alerted his entire battalion and they were ready in case the enemy did hit them. I had not asked him to give Dammer any artillery support because he would have been dropping his rounds right in on top of us if he did. I did alert him to this possibility, however, and if we were overrun, he was to shoot his preplanned fires right on us.

The very thought that the situation would get to that point was a bit disconcerting, to say the least. As a matter of fact, I spent the next few hours hunkered down in my foxhole worrying myself into a nervous sweat. I thought of the warning which Smitty had given me; I worried over whether we would run out of ammunition before our resupply arrived; and with each new and strange noise, I would query Charlie Boyle whether he thought it sounded like airplanes.

Shortly before daybreak, the earth shook and trembled and my foxhole gulped. The sky lit up with the white glow of a blast furnace, and a gray black mushroom cloud billowed out above us. I could clearly smell the pungent odor of ozone, and to this day I do not remember exactly what I thought had happened. It looked and sounded like the world had come to an end, and it scared the living daylights out of me. If I recollect, the most logical thought which passed through my mind was that the Chinese had hit us with a thermonuclear warhead and that we had had it.

When I finally recovered my composure and my bones had ceased to rattle, I realized that whatever it was, it had hit the artillery battalion and I knew that it had wiped out every man in it. I tried but could not reach the commander by either the telephone or the radio. The worst part was that we were completely surrounded by the enemy, and there was no chance for any of us to go to the battalion's assistance. I had to be content with waiting for further developments.

I was fairly sure in my own mind, however, that not one single man would walk out of that explosion alive.

"Good God in heaven, Charlie, what was that?" I yelled at the top of my voice.

"I don't know, sir, but whatever it was, it was one helluva big bang."

"You can say that again."

"No doubt that it hit the entire artillery battalion, sir. Probably killed every man there."

"I don't doubt it one minute. Keep trying on that radio of ours will you, Charlie, and see if you can rouse anybody."

"Yes, sir."

"And, Charlie, while you're doing that I'm going to slip over to Dammer's CP and see how he is doing." I had withstood the temptation about as long as I could, and now I had to find out what was happening.

"Right, sir."

"Herm, did you hear that explosion?"

"I sure did, sir — what in hell was it?"

"Damned if I know. Only thing that I do know is that it probably got every man in that artillery battalion."

"That's for sure. I don't see how anyone could have lived through that explosion."

"Well, there isn't anything that I can do about it at the moment. How's your situation here?"

"I've just been talking to my company commanders. We're sure getting low on ammunition. Have you heard anything from corps? Charlie told me that you had sent an operational priority radio request for a basic load. Hope they come along pretty soon. One of my company positions was just driven back, and we're trying to retake it now. And by the way I'll have at least one recommendation for a Silver Star for one of my officers."

"Oh, who is that?"

"Lieutenant Latoney, sir. I'm sure you remember him. He's in H Company."

"Yes, I remember him very well. Write it up and I'll send it to our board."

"The report that reached me was that Latoney had really saved the day where the enemy managed to punch a hole in our lines. His mortar platoon (60-mm) was right behind the point where the enemy came through, and if it hadn't been for his quick thinking they might have infiltrated all the way into our positions. He got up on a piece of high ground where he could get a clear view of the enemy and from there he directed such intense fire on them that it stopped the attack. They also tell me that it looked like every enemy soldier on that side of the hill was firing at him and that he just stood there directing his platoon as if they were all on the practice range. That takes real guts, you know, Colonel.''

"I agree, Herm. Write up the citation and let me have it.''

"Right, sir. I'll probably have several more before this is over.''

"I wouldn't be surprised — well, let me have any of them that you think are worthy of consideration.''

Dammer did submit several other recommendations for award of the Silver Star, but Latoney was the only one decorated as a result of the action there at Yonghung that first day. I know that our Awards and Decorations Board favorably considered the others, but we never heard what happened to them. I suspect that they were lost somewhere in higher headquarters, which is not at all unusual.

"I'll be getting back to my own hole in the ground, Herm. I've got Charlie trying to make contact with the artillery battalion, and I'd like to find out if he's contacted them — though I don't see how anyone could have survived that blast. If we just get that airdrop, maybe we could bust out of here and get to them.''

"Yes, sir. Let me know what you hear about the drop, will you, Colonel? We're getting pretty damn low.''

"OK, Herm, will do.''

By the time that I crawled back into my foxhole, the sky was beginning to light up, and we had a better view of our surroundings. This would also make it easier for our men to pick out their targets. It had been somewhat overcast during the night and, with no moon, every faintly distinguishable object could be seen as an enemy soldier creeping up the hill. I am quite sure that a great deal of our ammunition had been fired at just such illusions, but I couldn't blame the men. I would have done the same thing.

"Make any contact with the artillery, Charlie?''

"Yes, sir. I got hold of the Colonel's radio operator, but the colonel wasn't around so I didn't talk to him. It seems that an enemy mortar round lit right in the middle of their ammunition dump and blew it sky high.''

"How many men did they lose, Charlie?'' I was almost afraid to ask the question for fear of hearing the worst.

"Sir, believe it or not, they lost only one man killed, and several others slightly wounded. They lost most of their ammunition but only one gun. The operator told me that they had two ammunition dumps and that the mortars only hit one.''

"They really were lucky — glad to hear that they still have some ammo.

We can probably use them when it gets light enough for us to direct the fire.''

"The operator also told me that the enemy never did attack them with troops, just pasted hell out of them with mortars.''

"Charlie, listen a minute — do you hear what I hear?''

"Planes, sir — hot damn — sounds like several of them, sir.''

"It sure does. Let's see if we can spot them.''

"Right over there,'' Charlie yelled. "See them, sir? They're circling the artillery right now sir — and coming in low — wow, what a sight.''

Seven C-47s were coming right in over our positions, and out came the merchandise tied onto parachutes that billowed in the soft breeze and headed straight for our mountain top — right on target. With the first sight of the drop, a mighty cheer went up from the troops as they scrambled out of their foxholes to grab the chutes and keep them from dragging our ammunition off down the hill and into the hands of the enemy.

What a sight that was — beautiful. I've never seen anything so welcome in my entire life. As our men ran to retrieve the boxes, they yelled, *maná del cielo,* "pennies from heaven," and they certainly were. We were now prepared to fight it out on the top of that mountain until doomsday, or at least until we could get our other battalions up with us.

Other things began to happen now as well. The enemy gave us several more blasts of mortars and then broke off contact and high tailed it off in the thin woods to the south.

Shortly after the enemy stopped shelling us, up the hill and into our position walked a man I never expected to see alive again — the colonel commanding the artillery battalion.

"Man alive, what happened over there this morning — I never expected to see you again.''

"Tell you the truth, Colonel, I never expected to survive the night. The enemy hit us smack in our ammunition dump, and it looked like the whole world was coming to an end.''

"I know. It certainly scared hell out of us too. No joking, I thought you and your battalion had had it.''

"We thought so too. After the blast went off, I looked to see if I was all in one piece, and I can tell you that the whole thing was absolutely amazing. Why we weren't all blown to kingdom come is beyond me. And I only had one man killed and several wounded. They just happened to be near the dump when it went up, and the one man just disappeared; we didn't even find any shreds of his clothing. The two wounded men are not too bad off. I brought them up here to your aid station.''

"And I understand that you only lost one piece of your artillery.''

"Yes, sir, that's right. And we still have about half of our ammunition. I had split it into two dumps, and the mortars only caught one of them."

"Amazing — absolutely amazing. Well, sit down here and we'll make some coffee."

"Thank you, sir. I see you got an airdrop too."

"How about that? Right on the money. We were about to run out of ammunition and so I sent an operational priority message to corps." Then I told him the story about stealing the high-powered radio from X Corps. Without any question, that radio had saved the lives of all of us. Had we run out of ammunition, there was no telling what might have happened.

While we were sitting there discussing that unhappy prospect, Boyle came hurrying up to inform me that General Almond was also on his way into the CP. I walked over to the road leading into our position and waited there for the corps commander.

"Good morning, General. How did you get here so quickly?"

"Morning, Harris. As soon as it got light enough to see, we took off to find out what happened up here last night. You said in your radio that an estimated two or three regiments had hit you. Where are they?"

"They broke off contact when we got the airdrop, General. My battalion commander has a scouting party out right now trailing them so we don't lose contact."

"Unhuh. Good, let's take a look around. How many men did you lose?"

"None so far, General. The battalion commander is still checking, but so far as I know now, no one was killed; we did have several men pretty badly wounded though."

"Where are they now?"

"In the battalion aid station, sir."

"Let's walk over there."

"Right, sir," and with that I led the way.

While we walked to the aid station, General Almond said something to me to the effect that he didn't have much confidence in these colored troops. He said that he had had a bitter experience with them in Italy and that he didn't trust them. I knew that he had commanded the all-colored, 24th Infantry Division in Italy during the war, and I had heard that he had had some trouble, but I didn't know any of the details. At any rate, I didn't let Almond's statement go unchallenged.

"General, these troops are not colored. They are white — oh, I do have some colored Virgin Islanders and some colored Puerto Ricans — and my artillery battalion and tank company are colored, but the men of the 65th are white Puerto Ricans. And I might say that the colored troops have fought like real troopers. We haven't had any trouble with them.''

But apparently General Almond did not care to pursue the matter any further, for he had no more to say on the subject during the rest of the time he was in the CP. And neither did he say anything about diverting the rest of the regiment, either, for I did not find out about that until I talked to Childs on my command radio net later in the day.

After Almond left, I walked over to where Dammer was sitting, talking by radio to the patrol he had sent out to maintain contact with the enemy. When he finished his conversation, I learned what they had discovered.

"Sir, that patrol I sent out has just reported that they found the enemy holed up in a railroad tunnel about five or six miles south of here."

"The hell you say. Where's the patrol now?"

"Sitting up on a bluff overlooking the tunnel."

"Are the bastards still there?"

"Yes, sir. The patrol leader reports that they are. He says there are a few of them standing guard outside each entrance, and that the rest of them are still in there."

"Now's our chance. We ought to bottle them up in there."

"Right, sir. That's just what we're fixing to do. I told the patrol leader to stay there and keep an eye on them and that I would send some TNT down to him. He's going to blow in the mouth of the tunnel at each end."

"Great, good work, Herm. How does the patrol leader think he can slip up on them without being seen?"

"He doesn't, sir. He suggested that I send several platoons down there to drive the enemy into the tunnel and that his patrol can get above the mouth and loop the TNT charges into it. We just happened to have enough TNT left over from another job that we did in South Korea to blow each end of that tunnel to smithereens. I have one of my companies being assembled right now to send down there."

"Hot damn — go get 'em, Herm." And then I walked over to my little nest; I had some things that needed tending to, and I set about doing them. As a matter of fact, while I sat astride the latrine I had some time to think, and I couldn't help but chuckle at the fate of those SOBs who had attacked us. As far as I know, their bones are still there.

One other thing that I had on my mind was a very simple letter to His Honor the Mayor of Yonghung, if they had a mayor. If not, it was to go to the top banana of the town.

"Charlie, will you have a Nisei interpreter come over here right away.

I want him to write a translation of a message I am going to send." We had picked up several of these men from the intelligence section of Eighth Army shortly after our arrival in Korea, and they had been of great help to us in the interrogation of the North Korean prisoners. The Japanese had occupied Korea for so many years that the Koreans could speak and read Japanese just about as well as they could their own language.

While Boyle was getting the interpreter, I wrote the following message which I am sure is self-explanatory. It may not have been in complete accord with the Rules of Warfare set down in the Geneva Convention, but I am quite sure that it carried the meaning I intended. I kept a copy of the message for my own personal files, so the reproduction below is exact.

9 November 1950

To: The Mayor of Yonghung, Korea

If any North Korean soldiers or other Communist aggressors in this area are aided or abetted by the people of Yonghung, this city will be reduced to rubble forthwith.

Furthermore, if any movement of groups of people or large numbers of individuals are observed during the hours of darkness, the above action will be effected immediately.

[Signed] W. W. HARRIS
COLONEL, U.S. ARMY COMMANDING

Several days later, I received the following reply:

To: The Commanding Officer of the United Nations Forces in Yonghung:

In behalf of the entire populace of Yonghung Prefecture I wish to welcome you and your men to this city.

Words cannot express our joy and gratitude in receiving you and your forces here in Yonghung who are diligently and patiently showing us the democratic way of life.

We have resolved to cooperate wholeheartedly to you and your forces in all undertakings.

All the people in Yonghung pray for the health of you and your men.

Gratefully yours,
[Signed] CHUNG DONG PIL

I had come to the conclusion in South Korea that the loyalty of the people blew with the wind. If they saw an American unit passing, they would whip out the Stars and Stripes and wave it furiously. If it happened to be a North Korean outfit, they would no doubt do the same thing with *their* flag. Since I wanted to make sure that the people of Yonghung got the message, which they apparently did, I thought it best to warn them as to what would happen if they gave any help to the Communist forces. I can add here as a parenthetical note that we never had any further trouble in or around that village.

As a matter of fact, not long after that exchange of letters I received a written invitation from the mayor to come to a dinner that the city fathers wished to give in our honor. He invited me to bring as many of my officers as I wished, and that brought a laugh to several of us. To begin with, Childs was a finicky eater who would push his food (C rations) around on his plate and seemingly never eat enough to keep a bird alive. Then there was MacCaughey — I do not remember ever seeing him eat anything other than what was sent to him by his wife. I sometimes wondered what he did when the packages were delayed for one reason or another. And I could go on naming the rest of the staff who I knew would want no part of a dinner prepared by the people whom I had just threatened. But with some cajolery and arm twisting, I finally rounded up enough of them to attend and away we went on the appointed night.

The dinner was given at the Town Hall and served by the ladies of the PTA, I guess. At any rate it turned out to be one of the best meals I had in the entire time I was in Korea. They started with saki, and that flowed freely during the entire time we were there. This helped change the appetite of several of our group, for before the meal was over I noted that several of those who had appeared a bit squeamish at first were really lapping up the food and chasing it down with more saki. We were served the usual *kimchi,* rice, driedfish, salted rice, raw fish, and fish in about every form imaginable. But the hit of the evening was a small bird that had been stewed in brown gravy. The bird itself was not over two inches long, from its beak to its outstretched feet (all of which had been left intact), but it was one of the most delectable and delicious fowl I have ever eaten.

But to get back to the battle on the hill, shortly after midday I received a radio message from Childs that the other two battalions had been diverted to the 1st Marine Division in the vicinity of Wonsan; no explanation of how long they would be there or when they expected to arrive in Yonghung. This griped the hell out of me. If General Almond wanted us to head out toward the west and make contact with the Eighth Army and then "develop the situation" with the few hundred thousand Chinese who might be in the way, he'd better damn well let me have my other two battalions. I immediately mounted a harassment campaign on his staff to turn them loose and finally succeeded two days later.

Then, with the arrival of the rest of our force, we started extending our positions out to the west, gingerly at first — on tiptoe, so to speak. St. Clair's 1st Battalion was initially located in the general vicinity of a village named Kwangchon, about thirty miles from Yonghung (See sketch page 80). Allen's 3rd Battalion was positioned about fifteen miles west of Yonghung, and Dammer's 2nd Battalion was at Yonghung.

Facing possible numbers that were completely out of our league, our training at the Vieques maneuvers was now to stand us in good stead. To cope with a thirty-three to one odds, we had to be quick on our feet and alert to everything and everybody. The first indication of what was to come was the thousands of refugees that our battalions observed moving to the east and south. We had already learned that this was an ominous sign, for they always fled for their lives when they knew that the NKPA or the Chinese were coming. It was an accurate weather vane — the vanguard of the hordes from the north was not far behind.

This time we devised a slightly different variation to our system of mobile defense (i.e., run, stop, fight, run some more). We had the battalion commanders shift their defensive positions after dark each night. They would make much out of digging-in on a high piece of terrain and going into a perimeter defensive posture. They would be seen anyway if there were any enemy in the area, so they made no attempt to be secretive about it. Then an hour or so after dark, the battalion would move quietly down off that hill and dig in one nearby. We hoped by this bit of legerdemain to trick the enemy into attacking an empty hill. When this happened, our commanders would stage a counterattack while the enemy was trying to reorganize his force and get it under control. The battalion commanders also moved their companies around in the same checkerboard fashion, and the system worked several different times.

The first contact that we made with the enemy while we were in these extended formations occurred on 13 November when a motorized patrol from B Company, led by 1st Lt. Walter N. Higgins, encountered an OPLR (out post line of resistance) of about ten enemy entrenched on a commanding ridge in the vicinity of a village named Handongson. Lieutenant Higgins, riding in the lead jeep, saw the enemy at about the same time they observed him, but they were quicker in opening fire, and the patrol was forced to scramble from their vehicles and take cover in the ditches on either side of the road. Fully realizing that he would be a target for intense enemy fire and with complete disregard for his own safety, Higgins ran down the road toward the enemy and up the slope to a point from which he could fire his automatic weapon at them. So daring and unexpected was his attack and his fire so accurate that he killed two of the enemy, wounded several more, and caused the remainder to run for their lives. By these heroic and gallant actions, Higgins was able to extract his patrol from a serious situation and later lead his men back to the company where he reported the enemy encounter. However, during the time that Higgins was standing on the hill firing at the enemy he was struck by a bullet and mortally wounded. For his courageous action and exemplary display of leadership, Lieutenant Higgins was awarded the Silver Star posthumously.

It was about this same time, maybe a day or so earlier, that the 3rd Infantry Division Commander, Maj. Gen. Robert H. Soule (he had replaced General Clarkson shortly after the Vieques maneuver) arrived at my CP at Yonghung and informed me that the division would arrive at Wonsan within the next few days and that we would then become a part of his command. I had wondered ever since I had had the teleconference with the Pentagon just how the 3rd would receive the Puerto Ricans as members of their family after we had beaten hell out of them at Operation Portrex. With this news it appeared we would not have long to wait for the answer to that question.

With the arrival of the division in the area, X Corps soon assigned definite boundaries between the 7th Infantry, the 1st Marine, and the 3rd Infantry Divisions. These are shown on the sketch (page 86) of the 3rd Infantry Division dispositions as of 17 November. The 7th Infantry Division had the mission to head north from Hamhung, and they eventually reached the Yalu River.

But before relating that story and the action that followed our becoming a part of the 3rd United States Infantry Division, there are several interesting sidelights relating to our first night at Yonghung which should be told. The first of these had to do with the airdrop which had saved our lives. I knew that the commanding general of the Far East Combat Cargo Command, which had made the drop, was Maj. Gen. William H. Tunner, a friend of mine for many years; and I felt that the 65th owed him a letter of thanks, which I wrote. Then, several days later, I received the following:

Headquarters Far East Air Force
Combat Cargo Command

27 November 1950

Colonel W. W. Harris
Office of the Commanding Officer
65th Regimental Combat Team
APO 468

Dear Bill:

I just received your letter of 11 November this morning, and I cannot tell you how pleased and proud I was to receive it.

The airdropping of supplies may sometimes seem to us a fairly impersonal thing, and some of us may at times lose sight of the importance these drops have to a lot of individual soldiers on the ground. If we do ever lose sight of these things, letters such as yours bring us sharply back to the proper perspective.

We are, of course, watching the progress of the Ground Forces with most intense interest. I shall watch the progress of the 65th RCT with greater interest now since I know that you command them, and since my staff and I have been deeply touched by your letter of appreciation.

Should you get down to Ashiya Air Base (Japan), I shall be only too happy to lift a few with you and rehash Fort Benning Days.

Sincerest personal regards,

[Signed] BILL
WILLIAM H. TUNNER
MAJ. GEN. USAF COMMANDING

The Commanding General
Far East Air Forces
APO 929

25 November 1950

Dear Colonel Harris:

I have just finished reading a copy of your letter of 11 November to Major General William H. Tunner, my Commanding General Combat Cargo Command. I want you to know that the Far East Air Forces appreciates your written expression of gratitude for the airdrop made to your outfit.

Your letter will become a part of the Far East Air Forces historical records — for which we thank you.

We stand ready to assist again when and if the occasion arises. *Maná del Cielo* will arrive pronto.

Best regards and good luck.

Sincerely,

[Signed] GEORGE E. STRATEMEYER
LIEUTENANT GENERAL, U.S. AIR FORCE COMMANDING

General Stratemeyer had been an instructor of mine at West Point, but I had not seen him since my graduation in 1930, and General Tunner and I had served together at the Infantry School at Fort Benning, Georgia. He was the officer who had organized the U.S. Air Force Cargo Command that flew critical items of supply into the China-Burma-India theater of operations during the war. He had also organized and commanded the famous Berlin Airlift which supplied those people with the essentials of life during the Russian blockade of that city several years after World War II.

The second piece of memorabilia having to do with that night at Yonghung was the following dispatch which one of the X Corps public information officers, a Sergeant Moore of the U.S. Army Information Services, filed with his counterpart in GHQ, Tokyo:

Fm PIO GHQ CORPS
To PIO GHQ TOKYO

Moore Yonghung Stop Requote We got an airdrop of ammunition and believe me it was beautiful Para Requote These men of Sixty Fifth have done aye helluva good job here Stop Theyve done the kind of job that should make the islands proud of them Stop For many of them this was their first major action Stop Theyre making fine aggressive soldiers Unquote Para Colonel William W. Harris of St. Louis, Mo., commanding Sixty Fifth said Quote Men did aye damn fine job Unquote These men are good soliders End quote.

6

CHRISTMAS EVE:
EVACUATION FROM HUNGNAM

As I sit looking out the west window in my study this cold, blustery, snowy November day in Colorado I am reminded of that first winter in North Korea. The stark, desolate, mountainous wastes of that country are something to behold.

Then before my eyes are the names that shall remain imprinted on my mind — the Chosin Reservoir, the Yalu River, and that colossal enigma not too far to the north, China.

That period from about 17 November until Christmas 1950 was probably one of the most strange and unique times in American military history. Here were two senior commanders of two separate major forces operating independently of one another on the narrow peninsula of Korea. Both commanders were reporting to the supreme commander of the Allied Powers, General Douglas MacArthur, but neither bothered to coordinate his operations with the other.

The main force, of course, was the Eighth Army under command of Lt. Gen. Walton H. Walker, operating in the central and western zones of the peninsula. The other, the X Corps, under the command of Lt. Gen. E. M. Almond, was operating independently on the right flank of Eighth Army and along the eastern coast. And then, to make matters even worse, it was the scuttlebutt in X Corps headquarters that the two men were barely speaking, if at all.

Within this time frame both commanders were seesawing back and forth with a dual mission — each trying to force the NKPA to surrender and at the same time trying to drive the Chinese north of the Yalu River. It was also a time when the 1st Marine Division was snatched from an uncertain fate at the hands of hundreds of thousands of Chinese near the Chosin Reservoir. It was the time too when the 65th participated in the task-force rescue of the marines.

During this period the X Corps staged its now famous "amphibious operation in reverse" and evacuated the entire corps, along with its artillery, tanks, ammunition, transport, all of the supporting South Korean troops, along with all of the North Korean refugees who wanted to go back to Pusan. A completely successful evacuation of the following things and people: 105,000 American and South Korean troops, several hundred thousand tons of supplies, equipment and ammunition, approximately 17,000 corps and divisional vehicles, 91,000 North Korean refugees and most of their worldly possessions.

This truly extraordinary achievement displayed the highest form of military skill and boldness. Only one man could have planned and executed it, the supreme commander of the Allied Powers, General Douglas MacArthur.

As for the 65th RCT, our activities could be characterized by:

A. A marked increase in enemy activity as a result of the Chinese entering the war;

B. Fast-moving situations resulting from their overwhelming numbers;

C. The Puerto Rican soldiers fighting under the most severe weather conditions that they had ever encountered in their lives — at times the temperature reached as low as *minus* forty degrees Fahrenheit;

D. Assignment of a number of varied missions to the 65th RCT which included: (1) Offensive and defensive operations; (2) Continued reconnaissance in force to establish contact with approximately four Chinese armies, find the right flank of Eighth Army (X Corps headquarters did not have the foggiest idea where that flank was); (3) Daylight and nighttime withdrawals while still in contact with the enemy; (4) Providing the major portion of the troops for a "blocking force" through which the 1st Marine Division withdrew from the Chosin Reservoir; (5) Finally, holding a beachhead through which the X Corps staged its "amphibious operation in reverse," and all that went with it.

The above paragraphs, extracted from my written command reports and my diary, give only a brief description of what happened during those critical days. The details follow.

For those familiar with the various types of military operations, it can readily be seen that the only other major type of military action in which the 65th could have been involved would be what is called a "hostile river crossing," and we were to participate in at least one of these in the months to come as well. In that one we did not have the luxury of the conventional rubber rafts to make the crossing but had to do it the hard way — with hastily constructed log rafts and swimming against a forceful current under the direct fire of a battalion-sized unit of Chinese determined to prevent our crossing.

But back to North Korea, where the Puerto Ricans faced hordes of Chinese, eyeball to eyeball, and did not flinch — not even one eyelash. There is no question in my mind that before the end of that period, the Puerto Ricans had demonstrated to even the most skeptical of their critics that they were a force to be reckoned with. They were not easily pushed around, even when heavily outnumbered.

It was now about the middle of November and I received word that our parent unit, the 3rd (Marine) Division was due to open their CP at Wonsan on the eleventh.

On that same date, X Corps Operation Order (Opn. O.#6) was published. This order returned the 65th to the 3rd and assigned the Division a zone which extended from south of Singosan, a town twenty-two miles south of Wonsan, to Sachang-ni, about thirty-five miles northwest of Hamhung. The zone extended inland from the coast for a distance of about sixty thousand meters.

Opn. O. #6 also directed the division to relieve elements of the 1st Marine Division in zone, secure the Wonsan area, protect X Corps' western flank, prepare for offensive operations to the west, and station one infantry battalion in Hamhung as corps reserve. Division then issued its Opn. O. #1 in which the 65th was to continue operations in the west central portion of the division sector, with its main effort to be exerted on the Yonghung-Hadongsan axis. Hadongsan-ni, twenty-eight miles by air west of Yonghung, was roughly half again as far via the winding road which led to it.

With this new assignment the 65th's responsibility covered approximately nine hundred square miles (See sketch map page 80). In fact, our area was so large that there was no way really that we could patrol it, let alone defend it. And since our principal missions were still to make contact with Eighth Army as well as develop the "situation to the west," we continued our stretch out from Yonghung in that direction.

As a result of these extensions, our battalions were between thirty and forty miles apart, and visiting them each day posed a problem. It was suicide to drive the roads in a jeep, so I was given a small, two place L-19 aircraft to do the job. It was so lightweight and so slow that it could be landed on a country road without too much trouble, so landing strips were no problem. But it was big enough to make a good target for enemy snipers, as I soon found out. I had been shot at before, but this was my first experience at playing like a bird, getting his tail feathers dusted with buckshot.

With this continuing stretch out, the enemy activity began to increase, too, and the tension within the U.S. command began to mount in direct proportion. We knew that the main battle could be joined at any hour, or even at any minute. As a matter of fact, there were so many Chinese believed to be in the area that we were almost afraid to breathe out loud. Then to add to this nervous tension, the weather began to get really cold. We did not receive our winter clothing until late November, so we spent most of the nights trying to stay warm, and we continued our search for Eighth Army and the enemy during the day.

Our next contact with the enemy came during the early morning hours of the twenty-first when B Company was hit by an estimated three hundred enemy near the village of Packsan, while another large group struck their positions near Halmjong. Since we were continually moving our units around each twenty-four hours or so, and the battalion commanders would frequently split their companies into several groups in order to increase our chances of intercepting the enemy, B Company suffered these two separate attacks.

It is risky business for a commander to divide his forces in the face of such large numbers of enemy, but the whole venture was crazy to begin with. Creating this additional hazard was no nuttier than the rest of the operation.

The men at both B Company positions were ready when the enemy hit them, however. They were not surprised, but we almost lost all of them. The attack at Packsan came, as usual, during the early morning hours while our men were in their normal perimeter defensive position for the night. Located on the highest piece of ground in the area, they had a good view of the ground around them, but it was a moonless night, and the enemy was able to get up to the base of the hill before they were discovered. When they were, our troops opened fire and methodically began picking off the shadowy figures as they crept up the hillside. The firefight that followed was so heavy over the next few hours that the company commander realized it would not be too long before his men would be out of ammunition. It is difficult in times like these to enforce fire discipline — no moon, pitch dark, and every shadowy figure becomes an enemy. To avoid running out of ammunition, the company commander immediately asked for an airdrop which appeared to be the quickest way to get resupplied. This time, however, the process took considerably more time. By the time the company commander radioed through channels to me and we signaled division and they in turn notified Air Combat Cargo Command precious hours had passed. When the drop finally arrived, the enemy had started an all-out charge up the hill and were about to overrun our position.

However, with the airdrop our men gained new life and managed to beat off several other attacks before St. Clair was able to get reinforcements. It was a close call. We lost three men KIA (killed in action) and six wounded, but when the action was over there were twenty-five enemy bodies found and an equal number of prisoners were taken.

The situation at Halmjong was somewhat different. Here the B Company detachment was on the move, probing for the enemy, when it was hit. Moving along the top of a rather flat, sparsely wooded, scraggly and rocky ridge, the patrol leader knew that the enemy was there somewhere and that it would only be a matter of time until he found them. If there was any one thing certain in that bloody war, it was that the NKPA and CCF (Chinese Communist Forces) could always be counted upon to be on high ground. Since this was also our *modus operandi,* we almost always made contact if any enemy were around.

But on this occasion the B Company patrol leader came very near to being mouse-trapped, or what we call dry-gulched. Hiding behind the scrubby trees and large rocks, the Chinese allowed the patrol to move through a gap in their positions to a point where they almost had it surrounded before they opened fire. Our men immediately hit the ground and returned the fire, but the patrol leader could soon tell from the volume of incoming rounds that he was greatly outnumbered. Not wanting to wait until the situation got out of hand, the patrol leader did what all good leaders should do in such situations, he radioed his company commander for help. But as so often happens in combat, by the time St. Clair got the message, it was badly garbled. Realizing that the quickest way to find out the true situation was to go there, Saint jumped into his jeep and headed for the surrounded patrol. As he did so, he called for his reserve company to start moving in his direction.

Since the ridge was not more than a mile away, Saint was able to get there in a matter of minutes. When he finally scrambled to the top, he could see that his men were really in trouble. Calling for his reserve company to move up as fast as possible, he then moved forward about a hundred yards toward the patrol.

Somehow managing to survive the hail of bullets that swept the entire area, he was able to reach the patrol's general location. It took only a quick look for an old pro like Saint to realize that the men were too close together, too bunched up. Just one good burst of machine-gun fire could have killed them all. His first job then was to get them spread out, but still in a position where each man could fire most effectively. But this was going to take some doing. To do this, he first had to get their attention, and that wasn't going to be easy with all of the rifle fire and the other battlefield noises. But by yelling at each of them and signaling by hand he was able to get the job done. Of course all the time that he was doing this, he also made himself a prime target for the enemy's fire.

When the reserve company finally arrived, Saint ran to the far edge of the ridge to direct that unit's attack. With almost parade-ground precision and unbelievable calm, he then maneuvered his unit so that the enemy was caught in a crossfire. And that was the end of that fight. Those enemy soldiers who were still alive surrendered immediately. St. Clair really distinguished himself in that action.

About this same time the other two battalions were also heavily engaged. Dammer's 2nd Battalion was besieged by a numerically superior force near a village named Kowan, while Allen was attacking a large force near Song-ni. It was during the attack on the 2nd Battalion that one of our often unsung heroes of the 65th Medical Company proved to be the inspiration to the troops.

Dammer had his companies stretched out about five miles in a staggered line which ran more or less from northeast to southwest. Though each of them was in a perimeter-type defensive position, he fully expected an enemy attack from the west. But instead, the enemy tried to go around him and hit the position from the opposite direction. When they did, they collided with the right flank company to which Sgt. Luis M. Marrero was attached, and a vicious fight followed. The company stood its ground, however, and beat off repeated enemy assaults for about four hours until it became daylight. The enemy then broke contact and quickly took off for the hills to the west.

During the firefight, twelve of our men had been wounded, five of them seriously so. And in each case when the call *"Médico"* came, Sergeant Morrero responded without hesitation. Despite the freezing weather, his shortage of medical supplies, and exposure to the enemy's fire, he moved around among the wounded men and administered first aid to them. After he had done so, he carried each of them to a position of relative safety. Once, when the situation was very critical, he grabbed an automatic rifle, jumped up on the parapet, and delivered such a withering volume of fire that the enemy stopped the attack at that point.

As usual, our I and R Platoon was very active during this period. And just as usual, the platoon found a large enemy force near the village of

Kowan. Finding an enemy force larger than their own had become almost routine with these men, but they always gave a good account of themselves.

Mounted in jeeps, which gave the platoon leader more mobility and flexibility, he had his scouts well out to the front, flanks and rear. This diamond-type formation provided the platoon with a built-in warning system whenever it encountered the enemy. It also provided some protection from the fire of a machine gun or the burst of a mortar or artillery round.

It indeed was fortunate that they were in such an open formation on this occasion, for as they moved toward the village, the lead scouts received a burst of machine gun fire forcing them to scramble for cover in a nearby ditch. Seeing his men hit the dirt, the platoon leader yelled for the other men to do the same. He then tried to make his way forward cautiously to get a better view of the situation, but before he could move an inch, the entire platoon began to receive a heavy barrage of machine-gun and artillery fire.

Knowing that that was no place to be, the platoon leader tried to work his men around the flank of the enemy, all creeping and crawling on hands and knees or bellies. But every time a head or a rump came into view, the enemy would let fly with an even heavier volume of fire. For the time being at any rate, it seemed as though the platoon was in for a bad time of it. At this point, Pfc. Roberto Carreras got into the act.

Seeing that the platoon and the platoon leader were almost helpless, he climbed into his jeep and headed straight down the road toward the enemy. When he arrived at a point where he had a good view of their position, he stopped the jeep and opened fire on them with a .50-caliber machine gun. For those who have never seen one of these weapons in action, it can be described as a gun with a lot of punch and power — and it might be added that the NKPA and the CCF both had a very healthy respect for it. To begin with, the steel-jacket bullet is about three inches long, weighing more than five hundred grains and when fired, it travels about 2,750 feet per second. When it hits a man, it can amputate an arm or a leg or sever a man's head quicker than can be done with a surgeon's scalpel. When it hits a man's torso, it leaves a hole big enough for you to put your arm through.

Though Carreras opened up on them with this terrifying weapon, and the Chinese could see the tracer bullets, they continued to fire at him. Completely unconcerned with his own safety, he continued to stand up in his jeep and fire away. And it wasn't long before the Chinese got the message, for they soon called it quits and headed out for the hills behind them.

After several weeks of operations like these, it soon became apparent that there were still a lot of the NKPA in the area. The remnants of the organized NKPA units and some guerrilla types had not been the targets of our offensive operations for some time. They had been content to lie low, regroup, and prepare for the winter by stealing and battering the natives around until they gave them food. But when the X Corps units began pushing in and cleaning them out, it became a different story. The Reds reacted sharply and with increasing strength.

This increasing enemy build-up and the action resulting from it not only began to have an impact on us but on our high command as well. This became distinctly evident when in one twenty-four hour period we received four separate and entirely different movement orders, each one of them requiring us to move in a different direction and, consequently, on a different mission.

The first of these directed that we launch an attack to secure the high ground in the vicinity of Songha-dong, a small village about thirty miles to the west of Yonghung. These orders were received on the afternoon of 30 November, and we spent the rest of the day and night laying our plans and positioning our troops, as the attack was scheduled for the following morning. We exercised particular care in planning that operation, because we knew that a very large enemy force was in the area. We also wanted to be quick on our feet, prepared to beat what is called "a hasty withdrawal," or in layman's language, to run like hell if the situation so dictated. But just several hours before the kickoff, we received a second order that canceled the first and directed that we move north to Hamhung.

Since orders for the attack had already been issued and the troops had started to move toward Songha-dong, it took some doing to get them turned around and headed for Yonghung, where they arrived late in the evening of 1 December. After a few hours of rest, the advance guard of the 1st Battalion headed out to the north and Hamhung, to be followed by the remainder of the battalion and finally the entire RCT. But the head of the column had no more than cleared Yonghung when we received the third set of orders. These orders directed that we reverse our direction of march and proceed south to Wonsan.

At this point we began to wonder what the problem was: had the situation changed so fast that we were all about to be scooped up in a big enemy drive or was this just indecision at the higher levels? At any rate, the columns were turned around once more and headed toward the south.

That move was not completed either. The lead battalion had no more than reached the new destination when we received the fourth, and final, set of orders from corps — to again reverse our direction of march and proceed north, back to Hamhung. Since no explanation was given for these changes, I must admit that I was a mite confused; the troops must have thought that we were all out of our minds, for they had been marching and countermarching like yo-yos.

But turn around we did and headed for what was to be our final campaign in North Korea and a place where history was to be made. This occurred at Hamhung on Christmas Eve 1950, where, to the best of my knowledge, we staged the only amphibious operation in reverse — a withdrawal across a beachhead — ever made by the United States Army.

Before describing our combat activities in and around the Hamhung-Hungnam complex, however, I would like to mention one other operation which we started at Yonghung and continued wherever the 65th was located thereafter. This was our own civilian aid program, which we called "civil affairs." In Vietnam they called it the "pacification program." Our main purpose was to prevent disease and unrest among the civilians in our area from interfering with our military operations. We could really have cared less about pacifying anyone, for our motives were purely selfish.

Our civil affairs program really got started shortly after I had sent the note to the mayor of Yonghung warning him about his people harboring or aiding the NKPA or the Chinese. We worried about the dirt and filth prevalent throughout the city causing an epidemic of some contagious disease. The job of cleaning up the place was assigned to a major on my staff who was given a small detachment of men from the regiment and the authority to call upon our supply agencies and others for assistance.

Working through the local government, he organized civilian work parties to clean up the debris, restore some of the public buildings, and repair the utilities. More important, he arranged for several of our doctors to conduct health clinics for the examination and treatment of the sick and disabled, particularly the children. We did not have many medical supplies, but we had picked up some extras with the airdrop, and some of these were used in this program.

One other major effort was the rehabilitation of an old steam engine and several rail cars that we later used to haul surplus coal from the Yonghung area to several other villages to the south where we traded it for rice and other commodities. We also discovered that the people of Yonghung had hidden a large quantity of rice in the mountains to the south, to keep the NKPA and the CCF from stealing it, and periodically we used the train to haul some of it back to the village.

"Operation Turnabout" 4 December 1950

A constabulary form of police force was also organized and local law and order restored to the hands of the civilian authorities. These police were also used by the local government to enforce the rules of sanitation and cleanliness which we posted throughout the city. Anyone caught throwing paper or other refuse in the public areas, or otherwise causing a nuisance, like defecating in the streets, was sure to receive a sound whack on his backside, or even a clout on the head from a long nightstick. I have often reflected since that time that some of this same type of law and order might improve the living conditions in a few of our own metropolitan areas.

It is interesting to note the following letter which I received from the mayor of Yonghung shortly before we departed from there.

Letter of Thanks

You came thousands of miles and you are fighting bravely for the eternal peace and freedom of mankind and the final extermination of the Kim Ill Song Communist thieves.

I express our sincere sense of gratitude for your trouble in the name of Yonghung citizens. I am sure that your distinguished service will shine on the history of mankind forever and will be remembered by all the Korean hearts.

We 10,000 citizens of Yonghung worship and respect you. Though we have hardly made any reward for you.

You gave us plenty of relief commodities. It is difficult to express our gratitude for you by any words. I will distribute your affectionate commodities to my citizens. I swear that we shall make our best for the unity and peace of Korea and for the relief services in honor of your sincere affection.

25 November 1950

CHIEF, YONGHUNG DISTRICT OFFICE
[Signed] CHU YOO CHIN

Almost simultaneously with the receipt of this letter, I had a feeling that we were allowing ourselves to become a bit lax in our awareness of the fact that we were still in enemy country. Men in all of our units had learned the gruesome lesson of ambush, the sudden attack of burp-gun fire from darkness or other concealment. They had learned that they were never completely safe from sneak attack, that there was never a time when danger could not appear from any point of the compass. The baggy trousers and long outer garments of Korean civilians, once considered only with curiosity, must be observed with suspicion. To insure that we did not have a recurrence of the reception we had received that first night, I issued a word of warning.

24 November 1950

Subject: Surprise
To: All Commanders 65th RCT and attached units

I know that you are all in a mood to yawn at the many times each day, and the three times before breakfast, that I have cautioned everyone concerning the inexcusable blunder of being surprised. At the calculated risk of more jaw relaxation, I wish to repeat again, if for no other reason than emphasis, the necessity for all commanders to be constantly on the alert; to make anticipatory plans; to watch every move made by his own men as well as those of the enemy; to avoid being surprised.

It is believed that a military commander can make any mistake in the book (except being surprised) and yet he *may* have a plausible and acceptable explanation. But *never* to my knowledge, has history ever excused, or justified, the inexcusable, and unjustifiable, blunder of a commander being surprised.

We know from our short experience in Korea that it is this very element of military tactics which is most effectively employed by the raggedy-pants guerrilla forces which we have encountered in this country.

Since our mission is primarily an offensive one, it is desired that you intensify your activities to include out-guerrillaing the guerrillas. Such tactics will not only produce the enemy information which we need, but they will also materially assist us in preventing our own troops from being surprised.

[Signed[W. W. HARRIS
COLONEL, COMMANDING

Now back to the combat area. The move to the Hamhung-Hungnam area itself was relatively easy compared to the job of getting the troop columns turned around and headed toward our new objective. Operation Turnabout took time, however, for it was 4 December before we reached Hamhung.

Initially, our missions there were to:

A. Prepare defensive positions on the Charlie Line (See sketch page 121) from the boundary with the 7th U.S. Infantry Division on the right to the George Line on the left;

B. Oppose a large enemy force coming from the North;

C. Defend the village of Majon-dong to the north of Oro-ri;

D. Clear the main supply route (MSR) from Majon-dong to Sudong (just north of Koto-ri) of enemy forces;

E. Protect the withdrawal of the 1st Marine Division from Hagaru-ri where it had been surrounded by an enemy force estimated to be four Chinese armies (instead of the two that had been originally estimated) — Smitty's predictions to me at Wonsan were now coming to light.

Prior to this time I had not known that the 1st Marine Division had preceded us into the area, but it had. Now it was in trouble in the vicinity of the Chosin (Changjin) Reservoir. It had run headlong into the main Chinese force; had it not been for the quick footwork of Gen. O. P. Smith, the division commander, the entire division would have been overrun. It should be remembered, of course, that a division of sixteen thousand to eighteen thousand men is mighty hard to push around. But the Chinese with their four armies could have gobbled them up in time if they could have managed to cut them off from their escape route back to the Hamhung-Hungnam area.

To assist us in accomplishing our missions, the 3rd Division commander assigned the 3rd Battalion of the 15th RCT and the 3rd Battalion of the 7th RCT to the 65th RCT. With the attachment of these units, we started an organization of the ground in much the same way as we had done for Operation Portrex, and we planned much the same type of an operation, a mobile defense, i.e. fire and fall back, when forced to do so.

As the regiment arrived in the area, our 2nd Battalion was positioned at Oro-ri, the 3rd at Majon-dong, while the 1st of the 65th, the 3rd of the 15th, and the 3rd of the 7th RCTs were disposed along Charlie Line from left to right in that order. With these dispositions we started immediate preparations for what we anticipated would be a fight for our lives.

Eventually a special task force was formed to move north to Koto-ri. This consisted of the 2nd and 3rd Battalions of the 65th RCT, Batteries A and B of the 58th Field Artillery, the 999th Field Artillery Battalion (the reconstructed Corps Artillery that had been with me that first night at Yonghung), and the 4th Chemical Company. Under the command of the 3rd Division assistant division commander, this task force was given the job of establishing the forward covering force through which the 1st Marine Division withdrew initially.

The plan was for the marines to come barreling down the pike, followed by the forward covering force. The troops on the Charlie Line would hold the Chinese, who would be in hot pursuit, while the marines loaded on the ships in the Hungnam Harbor for evacuation to Pusan. The troops on the perimeter defensive line around the Hamhung-Hungnam complex would then be withdrawn from Charlie through Tare-King,

Mike-King, Peter-Queen, Able, and finally Fox, in successive delaying actions until it was manned by only the 3rd Division, at which time the 7th U.S. Infantry Division would out-load. The 3rd Division would then be the last unit to leave the area.

But that again is getting ahead of the story, and we should return to about 6 December when we initially occupied our assigned blocking positions to assist in the withdrawal of the 1st Marine Division. In accordance with our plans, Allen's battalion had taken up a position just to the south of Majon-dong and on a ridge that paralleled the road leading south from there to Hamhung. From that position, he could control several miles of the road as well as the areas adjacent to it. Since the Chinese were trying to get in behind the marines and cut them off from this escape route, they had to drive Allen off that ridge and occupy it themselves.

But Allen knew this as well as the Chinese did, and he had planned his defenses well. He had organized three company strong points on the most prominent features along the ridge and had interspersed his machine guns and other automatic weapons to cover the best avenues of approach to it. One of these machine-gun and recoilless-rifle sections was commanded by 1st Lt. José Vega, Jr.

He knew what to expect and took great pains in personally selecting the positions for his guns and supervising their emplacement. He sighted the guns to cover the expected enemy approaches, assigned the crews interlocking sectors of fire, and then assured himself that his men were well dug-in. Having completed these fortifications, he then turned his attention to ammunition and food and water supply, posted his sentinels, and sat down to wait for the Chinese to make their move. This was not long in coming.

About three-thirty in the morning they hit — blowing whistles and bugles and yelling their fool heads off with their usual bloodcurdling screams. But the men of the 65th had heard these before and they didn't scare easily. They just cut loose with their machine guns and their recoilless rifles (intended for use against tanks) and mowed 'em down — but on they came, wave after wave of screaming Chinese. Then, near disaster struck right in the heat of the battle: two of Vega's machine guns stopped firing.

This was not a particularly unusual occurrence, even for the Browning water-cooled machine gun, for there are many things that can cause it. Knowing that their very lives, as well as the safety of the marines, depended upon getting those two guns back in action, Vega scrambled across that bare, open, bullet-swept twenty yards or so and got the one gun back in operation without being hit himself. But when he reached the other, he found that none of the usual reasons had caused the stoppage — his gunners had been killed. Vega then took over the firing of the gun in addition to directing the fire of his other guns. As a result he saved his section from encirclement and ultimate annihilation.

Concurrently with that attack, the Chinese also hit another unit of the 3rd Battalion. This time it was K Company. Literally hundreds of Chinese soldiers came charging up the hill, penetrating one of the platoon positions and almost completely cutting off one of the squads. Had it not been for the quick thinking and positive action by the platoon leader, 1st Lt. Charles H. Fleming, the entire platoon would have been wiped out.

I mention these two actions because as a result of these two units holding their positions, the 3rd Battalion held; and the marines were able to pass through the entire battalion holding position. And as they passed through their area the 3rd Battalion hooked onto the tail of the column and followed them on into Hamhung. Then for some unknown reason the Chinese did not try to attack the column again until after it had passed through Dammer's 2nd Battalion at Oro-ri, and he had in turn joined it with his unit.

This action occurred early on the morning of 9 December, several hours before daybreak, when Dammer moved his battalion down off the high ground to join the rear of the 3rd Battalion. When he did so, he designated G Company to be the rear guard for the battalion and also directed the company commander to leave one platoon on the hill as the rear party. This latter mission was assigned to the 1st Platoon by the company commander who also directed that the platoon follow the company at an interval of about three hundred yards.

Now as we all know, the mission of the rear guard is to stop any enemy attack from that direction by slowing him up, making him deploy his forces so that he cannot attack the main body from the rear. The first unit to become engaged in such action is obviously the rear party. Should that unit not be strong enough to halt them, the remainder of the rear guard may have to be employed. And, in turn, other elements of the main body may be required to stop the enemy attacks. This is a successive build-up type of an operation in which the minimum number of troops are employed to do the job.

So it was in this case, a minimum number of troops employed to do the job — one man. And that man was Pfc. Felix G. Nieves. Nieves was in command of one of the squads of the 1st Platoon. As the platoon leader ordered his men to start moving down the hill at the directed in-

Captured enemy equipment, October 1950; 120 mm mortar, Russian make, captured by L Company.

Russian-made guns and equipment being stored at headquarters, Kumchon, Korea. U.S. ARMY PHOTO

Enemy ammunition removed from dump at Yonghung, November 1950.

Rations being attached to L-5 plane wing to be dropped to the men of Company B trapped by communist forces near Majon-dong. U.S. ARMY PHOTO

Company G positions at Hamhung, 18 December 1950.

Chinese communist soldiers captured by 1st Platoon of Company C, 1st Battalion; Humhung, December 1950.

Marine helicopter evacuating wounded of 1st Battalion, Hungnam; 21 December 1950.

Time out for a baseball game: GI's of the 3rd Signal Company of the 3rd Infantry Division and men of the 65th.

Landing craft pulls up to the U.S.S. *Freeman* as the last troops of the 65th are evacuated from Hungnam area. 24 December 1950. U.S. ARMY PHOTO

Members of the 65th Infantry enjoy Christmas dinner aboard the U.S.S. *Freeman*.

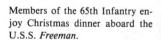

terval behind the remainder of the company, the enemy attacked the position. It was not a massive attack, but there were enough of them that they could have held up the entire rear party and possibly even caused the entire rear guard to deploy to stop them.

At any rate, when the enemy hit, Sergeant Nieves ordered his men to continue on behind the platoon. Then he took up a position on the top of the hill and opened up with such a terrific volume of fire from his automatic rifle that he stopped the enemy in their tracks. That was the end of that attack. When the dust finally settled, Nieves had killed eighteen of the enemy and caused the rest to flee for their lives.

By the thirteenth of the month, the marine division and the entire covering force had withdrawn within the protective lines of our defense, and once more we dug our heels in for the next attack. Our 1st and 3rd Battalions started organization of the ground along the Charlie Line while the 2nd Battalion moved through them to positions on the Mike Line, with the enemy hard on its heels. We had just about completed digging positions for the crew-served weapons on Charlie Line when the enemy hit, and it was B Company which took the brunt of it.

The battle raged all day the thirteenth and throughout the night and on the morning of the fourteenth. St. Clair was able to mount a heavy counterattack with parts of B Company, all of C, and a platoon of tanks, and finally drove the enemy back. We lost four men KIA and fourteen others wounded, but the enemy suffered twice that number in killed alone, and we took some twenty or more prisoners.

During this action, on the night of December 13-14, Sgt. Julio Martinez was in charge of a listening post approximately one-half mile in front of B Company's position. With two other men, he had located the post in a small draw or ditch where they could observe anyone silhouetted against the skyline who tried to move over the crest of the hill in front of them. Because it was a cold, crisp winter night, with little breeze, the sounds of anyone moving around could be heard for hundreds of yards.

About two o'clock in the morning, Martinez and his men heard a slight shuffling crunchy noise to their front, and they knew that it had to be the enemy. But instead of firing on them, Martinez let them go past him and then quietly notified his company commander what was going on and what he planned to do.

When the enemy had moved about halfway up the hill, Sergeant Martinez led his men in a yelling, screaming attack up the hill after them. This bold and fearless action not only alerted the men on our side, but it also so unnerved the enemy that they started to run in all directions. It was a simple matter for the men of B Company to round them up. It was also fortunate that Martinez and his men were not killed or wounded by our own men during the daring maneuver or during the confusion that followed.

It soon became evident, however, that this group of enemy was only the forward element of a larger force which attacked the company a few hours later. This time they tried something new: something like a power play in football, where the offense masses several guards and halfbacks ahead of the ball carrier and then hits one small segment of the defensive line. When they hit, one area of our position was penetrated and about fifty of the enemy charged into the company CP, seriously wounding the company commander, Capt. George E. Armstrong.

He refused to be evacuated, however. Gathering elements of his headquarters group, he moved them to a new location on higher ground. There he reorganized his CP, helped to evacuate the wounded, and then continued to direct the firefight even though he was bleeding profusely. Nothing but an outstanding sense of duty, extreme courage, and a firm determination could have permitted a man to carry on as Captain Armstrong did that day. His troops held their positions until help arrived. At daybreak on the morning of the fourteenth, St. Clair personally led a counterattack, and the enemy broke off contact and withdrew.

In the succeeding days enemy pressure continued to build up, and on the fifteenth one of I Company's platoons came very near to being mousetrapped. Had it not been for the quick thinking and courage of the company commander, Capt. Alfonso Palmer, that unit would have been scooped up by the Chinese, and we would never have heard from them again.

Palmer's unit, along with the remainder of the 3rd Battalion and the 1st Battalion, were on the Charlie Line when they received orders to make a daylight withdrawal to the Tare Line. Because they were still in close contact with the enemy, this became quite a sticky operation. During the withdrawal, one of Palmer's platoons came near to being cut off from the rest of the company. When he saw what was happening, he reversed the movement of the remainder of his company and personally led the charge back up the hill and rescued the surrounded platoon. This was not the first time, nor was it to be the last, that Palmer displayed that almost indefinable trait *courage,* or bravery.

There was no question that the enemy build-up was progressing at a rapid rate, for the intelligence maps were literally covered with Red symbols designating their units, and they were not too far away from our positions at the time. As a result of this increasing build-up of enemy forces, the original concept of a deliberate withdrawal to successive lines at the rear had to be changed. Originally it had been planned that the 1st and 3rd Battalions of the regiment would move back from the Charlie Line to the Tare Line and were to hold there while the 2nd passed through them and took up a position on the Mike Line. The 2nd would then hold that position to protect the 1st and 3rd Battalions, if and when they were forced to move back to the Peter Line. Then they would, in turn, hold there while the 2nd Battalion leapfrogged to the Able Line, and so on. But the enemy pressure was too strong, and a new plan was devised — one that speeded up the entire operation.

Under this concept, the 1st and 3rd Battalions (along with the other elements of the 3rd Division) were to hold on the Tare Line while the 2nd passed through the Mike Line all the way back to the Peter Line. The 1st and 3rd Battlions would then move to the Able Line. And finally, we (the 3rd Division) would all then move to the Fox Line, the Main Line of Resistance (MLR), where we would make our final stand. Presumably the following events would have occurred by this time:

A. The 1st Marine Division would have out-loaded on the troop ships which were waiting in the Hungnam Harbor to transport all of us back to Pusan;

B. The same for the several hundred thousand tons of supplies, ammunition and equipment and,

C. The 9,000 North Korean refugees;

D. The 7th U.S. Infantry Division would have been completely withdrawn from the line and in the process of out-loading.

Then, as I saw it, this would leave only us chickens of the 3rd Division to man the Fox Line perimeter. When we got to that point, anything could happen — and I didn't care to speculate on what it might be.

Later when we implemented these moves, the enemy continued to keep the pressure on us with one attack after another. No large-scale operations, just small harassing probes looking for a weak spot in our defenses. These small-unit attacks were repulsed, and some new heroes in the 65th were born: Pfc. Candido Colon-Fonesca, 1st Lt. Elmo L. Bundren, M. Sgt. Domingo Ortiz-Perez, Cpl. Domingo Miranda-Rosando.

The 2nd Battalion moved on without further mishap to the Mike Line and through it to the Peter Line, where they arrived late in the afternoon of 17 December. The 1st and 3rd Battalions likewise were able to complete the planned moves without too much difficulty. The entire 3rd Division now sat on the MLR with all regiments tied in together.

What we all wondered at the time was why the Chinese hadn't really hit us. We certainly were vulnerable to a degree, and in the face of their hordes, we could have been almost completely destroyed. I do not know even to this day why they didn't hit us with their full force. Possibly the answer lay in the fact that we completely controlled the air and the sea. Nor do I think that our command had any really good explanation for the enemy's delay either. Nevertheless, they were not taking any chances, which is why we were hauled back from the Able Line to the MLR with unhurried dispatch and calm, dignified haste. This is the don't-run-but-walk routine, called a "hasty" withdrawal.

But now we sat on the MLR while the 7th U.S. Infantry Division, the Korean units, the refugees, the supplies, ammunition, transport and the like were out-loaded. The 3rd Division was to hold until it became our turn to be ferried out to the ships anchored about five hundred yards offshore. With the Chinese pushing from our front and the Sea of Japan to our rear, we had no other option.

My records show that the 7th Division completed its out-loading on the evening of December 23, and orders were issued for the 3rd Division to commence loading. As this move was taking place, the 65th was drawn into a tighter perimeter defense around the harbor itself. By late afternoon on the twenty-fourth, when most of the division had completed loading, we were ordered to start embarking on the Liberty Ship *Freeman*. My diary shows that my small command group loaded on the last LCT with elements of the 2nd Battalion at 1430 hours on 24 December 1950. So far as I know, we were the last to leave the area.

In the afternoon of one of these last days, however, when we were on the beach waiting our turn to load and I was giving our navy liaison officer some targets for the big guns to shoot at, I was called to the telephone. St. Clair wanted to talk to me.

"Hi, Saint," I said. We had by now abandoned any talk in code; the Chinese knew where we were, our strengths, our location, and our intentions, so there was little necessity for secrecy.

"Good afternoon, Colonel. I just wanted to report that our men have taken two U.S. Merchant Marines prisoner. They're from one of our Liberty Ships in the harbor — I've forgotten the name of it. I have sent them on to your headquarters."

"What's that? Will you please play that back?"

"I said that we just captured a couple of prisoners, and they turned out to be merchant marines; and I am sending them back to your headquarters."

"That's what I thought you said. What in blazes were they doing?"

"Well, sir, as nearly as I can piece the story together, we found them wandering around up in the front lines. At first our men paid no attention to them, thinking that they were probably on some kind of a mission.

Maybe they thought that they were 007 agents or something. At any rate, they reported it to the company commander, and he sent some men out after them.

"When I questioned them, they said, so help me, Colonel, they said that they were United States citizens and taxpayers and that they wanted to see how their money was being spent. And, Colonel, they are drunker than skunks."

"I hope that you bent them over and gave them a good kick."

"I sure felt like it — but they probably would have written to their congressman and complained that we had mistreated them."

"You're probably right. Where are they now?"

"On their way to your headquarters, sir."

I later sent them on to division headquarters and never heard what ultimate disposition was made of them.

Saint then gave me the details of the action I had heard about from the previous night.

In the early morning hours of 22 December, a force of approximately two thousand Chinese attacked his battalion. About two hundred of the enemy concentrated their rifle and mortar fire on the machine gun which Corporal Santos and his assistant gunner, Corporal Calderon, were manning. There was no question that they had to neutralize it before they could ever close in on St. Clair's position.

At one time during the fight, a mortar fragment knocked their gun out of action, but miraculously neither Santos nor Calderon was injured. Then, instead of abandoning the gun, the two of them calmly repaired it and got it back into action, while the enemy frantically tried to kill both of them.

When the mortar and automatic-rifle fire became so heavy that they knew it was only a matter of time until they received a direct hit, the two men picked up their weapon and carried it to an open field where they had an even better view of the enemy, although they themselves were considerably more exposed than before. Disregarding their own safety, the two men calmly set up their weapon and again opened fire until the enemy was forced to withdraw, leaving about half their number either seriously wounded or dead.

Several weeks later, I had the privilege and pleasure of pinning the Silver Star on those two brave men. They were joined in that ceremony by another gallant soldier, Lt. Col. George W. Childs, my executive officer. Childs had commanded the two battalions of the 65th when they became a part of the task force sent to the north to assist in extricating the 1st Marine Division, and he had done a magnificent job. This was the second Silver Star that "Chick" had received, for he had been decorated as a battalion commander during World War II.

On the morning of the twenty-fourth, our last day in Hungnam, another incident occurred that came very near to being disastrous. At the time practically the entire regiment was in position, circling the dock, and the 2nd Battalion, my reserve, was actually bivouacked on the dock itself. For some unknown and inexplicable reason, I had a sudden urge to leave my CP and walk along the dock area where the troops were loading on the LCTs. At one point I noticed a long string of boxcars sitting on the dockside railroad spur. For no other reason than curiosity, I looked into them and found that they were loaded with thousands of rounds of artillery shells. I had seen the navy Seabees preparing the dock for destruction, but I had given this little thought until I made the next discovery. On closer examination of the cars, I discovered several wires protruding from them. When I followed these, they all led to a hand-generated detonator sitting in the middle of the dock, unguarded. Anyone could have walked up to that box, pushed down on the handle, and the entire 65th would have disappeared.

To say that I was angry with this discovery would be putting it mildly; I was furious. As soon as the chief of the navy's beach party could be located, I had him disconnect the detonator and then made him personally responsible for placing a guard over it until the time it was to be used by the Seabees. Later, as the last of us climbed aboard the *Freeman,* the Seabees detonated the charges, and the entire dock area went up in flames and smoke with a blast resembling that at Yonghung when an enemy mortar hit the 999th Field Artillery's ammunition dump.

With all of the excitement and all of the worried anticipation over the Chinese hordes who never came, the 65th completed loading on the *Freeman* just about dusk on Christmas Eve, the most unforgettable one I have ever had, a logistic and strategic miracle.

But we soon forgot all about the Chinese, the cold weather, and the other hardships of combat, for the navy went out of its way to make all of the creature comforts available to us during the five days we were aboard ship. We really luxuriated in the hot showers, in the clean sheets and bunks, and at the mess tables.

For my part, the hot showers did the most to boost my morale. Getting a bath or shower anytime in combat is a real problem, but it was particularly so during those early days in Korea. Except for the time when we were fighting along the Naktong River, we seldom saw a freshwater stream. Any that might have been in the Yonghung-Hungnam-Hamhung area were completely frozen and therefore of little use for that purpose. Ramos had helped me solve the problem, however, by bringing me a large galvanized container about four feet deep and three feet in diameter which we would place in a warm tent or adobe building and then fill with scalding water. Faced with the choice of either freezing to death or being stewed alive like some unfortunate missionary in the hands of a tribe of cannibals, I chose the latter. But even then, I was able to use that pot only about every ten days or two weeks, for it was also used by the cooks for boiling our potatoes or rice.

The time aboard ship also gave me an opportunity to reflect upon what had happened in the slightly over three months since our first arrival in Pusan. Reflecting on the problem of getting a bath brought to mind the fact that the Puerto Ricans had fought in some of the most severe weather that any American troops had been subjected to. Born in a semitropical climate — most of them had never seen snow — they had lived and fought through it all without complaint. As a matter of fact, we had no more nonbattle casualties than any other American unit and in the case of some units, not as many.

In addition to the human factor, the extreme cold weather in the North affected our combat capability as well. The malfunctioning of weapons was a constant hazard, particularly the automatic weapons. We quickly learned, for example, that if an excess amount of grease or oil were allowed to remain on them after they were cleaned, they would jam and fail to fire. If this should happen when the Chinese were launching one of their mass attacks, it would be disastrous.

Sleeping or even just trying to exist in that climate was a problem, too, because of the constant threat of frostbite. Though we had received our winter clothing and arctic sleeping bags by this time, everyone had to be alert for that telltale patch of yellow-white on the cheeks and nose and, more particularly, the hands and feet, which are more susceptible to this painful affliction than any other part of the body. We learned, too, that there is an art in preventing frostbite. If rubbed too vigorously, the skin tissue is injured; a gentle, delicate pressure or working of the flesh is the answer. This must be done with the hands. Unless it is done with care, they can become frostbitten too. Great care had to be exercised, too, to insure that the men washed their feet and changed their socks daily. We charged each commander with that responsibility; foot inspection each day, even during combat, became routine.

The problem of trying to march and fight with the multiple layers of thick woolen clothing we wore was sometimes frustrating and even dangerous. Between the long-sleeved woolen underwear, the successive layers of woolen shirts and trousers, tightly woven cotton jackets and trousers used as wind breakers, a sweater or two, and finally a pile-lined, fur-collared overcoat, muffler, pile cap with built-in earmuffs, and air-insulated snowpack overshoes, the most we could do was waddle like Christmas-fed ducks.

Though I had no way of verifying it, I was told at the time that the temperature got as low as minus forty degrees Fahrenheit during some of our cold nights. If it did not reach that low, the cold winds blowing down from the steppes of China and Manchuria certainly felt like it. Sometimes they were so strong that the driving snow looked like a horizontal waterfall. Our clothes and sleeping bags would become heavy with frozen condensation and would creak and crack like an old-fashioned, fringed-top surrey out on a country road on a winter's night. Sometimes when the wind stopped blowing, there would be a deathly, eerie silence; and if there was a sound, it could be heard for miles.

Most of the time, the potatoes or rice that we received were as hard as rocks or pebbles and would take hours to cook; eating was done at a jog around whatever fire was available. Such an existence became almost a way of life, and yet the Puerto Ricans did not complain. Absolutely stoic in their emotions and indifferent to any pain, they went about the business of being combat infantrymen just as though they had lived and worked in such a climate all of their lives.

Those of us more fortunate than others had a potbelly stove that we carefully transported from CP to CP and installed in some adobe building, preferably a large schoolhouse, which we would use as my headquarters. Most of these buildings would have no windows and sometimes only a partial roof or one wall would have been blown in as a result of a direct hit from an artillery shell. Our headquarters personnel would make the necessary repairs and then poke the stovepipe through a ready-made opening.

From the stoves we learned another lesson about living in such cold temperature. As a matter of fact, we almost learned the hard way by having several people very nearly overcome from carbon monoxide. The stoves were equipped with a small carburetor which regulated the amount of diesel oil fed into it. On most nights this was kept wide open, which made the whole contraption sound more like a blowtorch than a stove. Then suddenly, sometime during the night, a reverse flow of the air would occur, and the room would be filled with a heavy black smoke that nearly became fatal on several occasions. We finally determined the cause: we found that the column of cold air that formed in the upper part of the chimney would gradually build up, overcome the upward draft, and suddenly rush down and blow the smoke into the room instead of out the pipes. To remedy this, we found that if we covered the top of the smokestack with a piece of burlap and heated the top of the stove-pipe with a blowtorch until it was red-hot, by jerking the burlap away, the stove would function properly until another down draft occurred several hours later; we would repeat the process several times during the night.

With all of the hardships and all of the battles that we had fought with the thousands of Chinese, I noted from the casualty reports that we had lost thirty-six men KIA, seventy-five wounded, and twelve MIA (missing in action) during the month of December compared to almost eight times that many lost by the enemy in their engagements with the regiment. There was no question that the Puerto Ricans had by now established an enviable record for themselves as fighters, and this was recognized by not only the military authorities but the press as well. One reporter from the *Charleston* (S.C.) *Gazette,* who had been an eyewitness to a lot of combat, wrote:

> One of the most cheering reports coming from the recent evacuation of our troops from the Hungnam Beachhead is that which has to do with the actions of the 65th Infantry Regiment. From all reports this regiment distinguished itself above and beyond the call of duty in the bitter fighting which preserved the beachhead and made possible the redeployment of the X Corps which had been isolated in Northwestern Korea. The men of the 65th Infantry Regiment are United States Infantrymen who have lived up to the fine traditions of that fine service. So, a salute to American fighting men — especially the 65th Infantry Regiment.

In another accolade from the 3rd Infantry Division commander, which was published within the division at about the same time, was the following:

Headquarters 3rd Infantry Division

Subject: Combat Infantrymen
To: All Divisional Units

A good infantryman uses the weapons available to him.

A report which just crossed my desk today contains the following facts:

For two days G Company, 65th Infantry, was engaged in close combat with a numerically superior force on Hill 698. On the 11th of December 1950, the 2nd Platoon was ordered to withdraw and Sergeant Nieves and his squad undertook the mission of covering the platoon's withdrawal. An enemy column of twenty or more tried to assault the squad's position, and Sergeant Nieves gallantly faced the attackers, and with his rifle and several grenades, killed eighteen of the enemy, and drove the others away. The courageous act of Sergeant Nieves enabled the platoon and his squad to withdraw without a casualty.

[Signed] ROBERT H. SOULE
MAJOR GENERAL, U.S.A. COMMANDING

Still another article which was handed me after we boarded ship was the following, written by S. Sgt. William Colton of the *Pacific Stars and Stripes.* It is quoted in part:

Puerto Ricans Are Rough and Tough

Last September the American Puerto Rican 65th Infantry Regiment steamed into Pusan Harbor via troopship. The men along the rails observed the hut-lined hills. As the ship neared the dock, they noticed red-striped boxes and many people waiting for them. They decided they were in for a Royal Welcome. Instead, when they landed, they were handed M-1 rifles from those boxes and sent straight to the front.

On the front lines, the Puerto Ricans earned the reputation of being some of the wildest and toughest troops in Korea. Oddly enough, these same infantrymen are also known for their courtesy, reserve, and well-mannered behavior.

In talking to Corporal Ruiz of Rincon, Puerto Rico, he said, "We are proud to be part of the United Nations Forces, and we are proud of our country. We feel that too many people do not know anything about Puerto Rico; they think that we are all natives who climb trees. We are glad for the chance to fight the Communists and also for the chance to put Puerto Rico on the map. It will be a great accomplishment if we can raise the prestige of our country in the eyes of the world."

In my view, Corporal Ruiz expressed the feelings of every man in the 65th, and he expressed it very well. For my part, I thought that the men of the 65th had performed superbly, just as I had expected that they would. As an expression of that feeling, I issued the following memorandum aboard ship on Christmas Eve:

Headquarters 65th RCT
Office of the Commanding Officer
APO 468 c/o PM San Francisco, California

Subject: Greetings
To: All Personnel 65th RCT

I find it very difficult to adequately express my feeling of pride in having served with the 65th Infantry and the high esteem that I hold for each of you. During the past seventeen months that I have commanded this regiment, I have frequently reiterated my complete and unbending confidence in the fighting ability of the men of the 65th. On the date of our departure from Puerto Rico, I stated this conviction publicly and today that opinion remains unchanged.

That record speaks for itself. But that record stems from the specific part which each officer and man of this regiment has played in these military campaigns; and without those loyal and tireless efforts this regiment could not have carried on.

With humble sincerity, I congratulate and thank all of you. To each of you, I extend my very best wishes for a Merry Christmas and a Happy New Year.

[Signed] W. W. HARRIS
COLONEL, INFANTRY COMMANDING

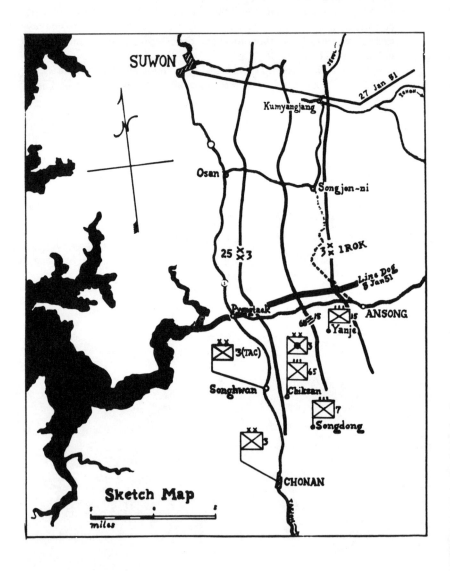

Main Line of Resistance, 8 January 1951

7

WE REJOIN EIGHTH ARMY

Because of the backlog of personnel ships in the Pusan Harbor await-ing orders to unload, it was New Year's Day before we docked. Not that we were in any hurry, for the navy was taking pretty good care of us, but I heard that Eighth Army had ordered a twenty-four-hour dock operation in order to get X Corps up and into the line. We also heard that the Chinese had been staging a build-up in front of Eighth Army, forcing General Walker to give ground. The first situation report that I received after we landed was that the enemy had launched a pretty heavy attack that very day, driving General Walker's units still farther south.

This news sounded much the same as it had the first time we landed in Pusan in September, but this time the 65th was not being rushed in to chase guerrillas. We were to be given a rest period, or so I thought when I received a radio message from division that we were all being detached from X Corps and assigned to I Corps commanded by Lieutenant Gen-eral F. W. Milburn. We were to proceed to a place called Ulsan, about forty miles north of Pusan, and remain there for a period of from a week to ten days in the status of what is called "rest and refit." Then we were to move north.

However, on 5 January, we received hurry-up orders to prepare to move north at once. It had taken two days to assemble the trucks and move us to Ulsan, so we actually had a total of three days there; I do not recall ever having our shortages replaced before we went back into battle.

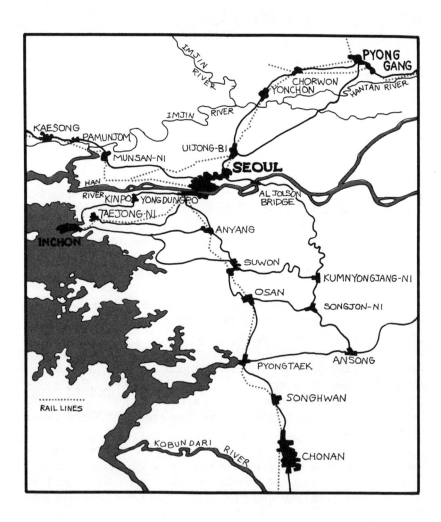

Area of Exploitation

Initially, we were to move to a village named Pyongtaek, about forty miles to the south of Seoul. But these orders were changed while we were en route, and we were directed to proceed to a place called Chicksan, just a few miles to the east of Pyongtaek.

My records indicate that the regimental headquarters opened in Chicksan on 8 January, and our orders were to:

A. Take position within zone on Line Dog (See sketch page 138);

B. Seize a village named Song-golchon, about ten miles north of Chicksan;

C. Destroy all enemy in our zone of action; and,

D. Protect the right, or east, flank of the 25th U.S. Infantry Division (part of I Corps).

Now, for one of the few times since our arrival in Korea, we were part of a homogeneous line of troops stretching across most of the Korean Peninsula. Most of the time we had fought as a separate RCT, with no friendly troops close by. But now Line Dog was the main line of resistance (MLR). To the north about ten miles was Osan and twenty miles to the north was Suwon and forty miles north was Seoul. Somewhere between Osan and Pyongtaek were the forward elements of the so-called Chinese Volunteer Forces.

Once in place, which took about two days, we seized the village of Song-golchon with very little trouble, established our contact with the 25th Division, and proceeded to sweep our assigned sector for the enemy. We had just started on the latter mission when we received word that General Walker, the Eighth Army Commander, had been killed in a jeep accident. It was simultaneously announced that Lt. Gen. Matthew B. Ridgway was being flown in from Washington, D.C., to take command of the army.

Shortly after the arrival of General Ridgway, the differences between these two senior officers became evident. General Walker had ordered a general withdrawal (a walk-don't-run procedure) because of Chinese pressure; when General Ridgway took command a few days after Walker's death, he immediately reversed that concept and ordered an attack.

Now in fairness to General Walker, some officers felt that the Chinese were about at the end of their string when he was killed. They felt that the Chinese had just about reached their maximum capability to supply that many men over such a long distance and would sooner or later have stopped their offensive tactics and taken up a defenseive posture. Then, so the theory went, General Walker would have started his attack.

But whether the Chinese were having difficulty in supplying their troops, whether they would have halted their attack, or whether Walker would then have reversed his strategy are all academic questions. As it was, our withdrawal was abruptly halted, and we were told that henceforth we would attack and keep on attacking until we drove the Chinese back across the Yalu.

The first order we received to implement this new philosophy was named Operation Wolfhound — aggressive patrolling to the north. Though we all assumed this new aggressive posture physically, I am afraid that many of us were still in a mental posture of walk-don't-run to the rear. Several months before his death, General Walker had detailed certain troops to prepare successive defensive positions to the rear, just in case we did not have the time to construct them as we withdrew.

Even though we, the troops, may have felt uncertain, I am quite sure that General Ridgway did not. In less time than it takes to say, "The quick brown fox jumped over the lazy dog," we had orders to launch a coordinated attack. Called Operation Exploitation, our mission was to secure the south bank of the Han River. In less than forty-eight hours we had gone from a general withdrawal all along the line to a general attack.

Along with the orders for Operation Exploitation was an overlay sketch (See page 138 and page 140) which showed that directly to the north in the 3rd Division zone, on the far bank of the Han River, was the city of Seoul. But more important to the 65th was our location within those boundaries. If we stayed in that zone astride the main road — Pyongtaek, Osan, Suwon, Seoul — it was a lead-pipe cinch that we would be given the job as the lead element of the division in the hostile river crossing.

Since this is a dangerous and tricky operation at best, we decided that as soon as the daily tasks permitted, we would make some definite plans for it, even have several dry-run rehearsals to practice and improve our techniques. There was little doubt in our minds as to the kind of reception we would receive from the enemy on the far shore. For the moment, however, we kept all river-crossing plans in the back of our minds.

Now the general offensive was about to get under way. The new directive made provision for a bit of a tiptoe advance should the Communists again become obstreperous. Well-identified phase lines to which we could advance were established. Should any unit reach one of them before the units on his right or left, the first unit was to hold at that position until the others arrived. The objective, of course, was to enable General Ridgway to exercise control over all units of the Eighth Army and permit him the option of assuming a defensive posture, or even withdrawing, if it came to that.

The attack jumped off early on the morning of 15 January. By the afternoon of the sixteenth we were on the Queen Line, about ten miles north of the Dog Line (See page 140). We had started out from the Dog Line with the 2nd Battalion on the right starting from a village named Youngjang-ni and the 3rd Battalion on the left from its position near Sungdung-ni. The 1st Battalion was in reserve near Joagan-ni, ready to be employed in either of the forward sectors should the assault battalions run into trouble. Additionally, we were ordered to put out a screening force in advance of our assault battalions.

This force had the following missions:

A. Secure the village of Song-golchon;

B. Destroy the enemy in zone;

C. Disrupt the enemy lines of communications; and,

D. Protect the right, east flank of corps.

Within hours after we had formed that task force, we were ordered to organize another one which was to be attached to the 25th U.S. Infantry Division on our left. This was a most unusual order, and I never did fully understand why we had to provide a screening force for another division. But we did. When it did not encounter any enemy after several days of probing, it was returned to my control.

Since other units of the corps were apparently having the same negative results, the corps commander must have concluded that the enemy was not bracing himself to make a firm stand on that terrain, for he ordered a coordinated attack by both the 3rd and 25th U.S. Divisions. Corps order also provided that the 65th RCT be the screening force for the entire corps. In order to accomplish this dual mission, we split the responsibility between the regimental I and R Platoon and a task force composed of A and B Companies — the former to work the area in front of the 25th Division and the latter in our area ahead of the 3rd Division.

But even this general offensive met no resistance until the morning of the eighteenth when the 2nd Battalion uncovered a strong, well-dug-in group of about fifty Chinese on the high ground near a village called Songchon. We concluded that they were the rear guard of a larger force not too far ahead of us, because shortly after Dammer deployed two of his companies to attack them, they hightailed it out. The following morning our estimate that this group was only a part of a larger force was fully confirmed when, about two hours before daybreak, both the 1st and 2nd Battalions were hit by at least two Chinese regiments, an estimated two thousand men.

The enemy attack started with the usual whistles, bugles, and Commanche yells. St. Clair's position was the first to be hit, or at least his men were the first to discover the enemy coming up the north slope of the

WE REJOIN EIGHTH ARMY

hill, and were the first to open fire on them. Then like a string of fire-crackers, the rifle shots rippled around his position until they had made a complete circle. Within minutes after we discovered them, the enemy opened up on St. Clair's position with a very heavy mortar and artillery barrage.

My own CP was located not more than five hundred yards away on another piece of high ground, and the rattle of the rifle fire brought all of us to our feet in a hurry. Though there were not too many men in our perimeter defense, we had most of the tank company surrounding our position. With their fifty caliber machine guns and the riflemen of the headquarters company interspersed between the tanks, we had a pretty good wall of defense. The tanks also gave me a good, fast mobile reserve. While Childs was alerting the commander of that unit and I was trying to contact the 1st and 2nd Battalions by phone, heavy fire broke out in Dammer's direction.

"Chick, guess you had better tell him to be ready to go to Dammer's position too."

"Right, sir. Will do."

"What's going on over there, Saint?"

"I'm going to call both of them and see how they are making out. If you will, get the tanks saddled up and ready to make a sweep of either one or both of those hills. Tell them we will give them specific instructions after we've found out what the situation is in both places."

I then placed my first call to St. Clair.

"Well sir, they hit us pretty hard at first, but the action has slackened off a little now. From a couple of prisoners we learned that the Chinese attacking us are from the 149th and 150th CCF Divisions. They are from two different regiments, so we estimate that there must be at least a couple thousand men attacking our two positions."

"OK, let me know if you need any help."

I then called Dammer and asked how he was making out.

"We're OK, sir. Little trouble at first, but I think we can handle it."

As it turned out, neither battalion needed any help, although both of them took a pretty good drubbing before the enemy broke off contact about daybreak. It was also about midmorning before either battalion was ready to resume the attack, so there was no question that they had been shaken up a bit. But they had held their positions and had not given up an inch of ground to the enemy.

After Pagani and his men of the I and R Platoon returned to my control from the 25th Division, they were assigned their normal missions of reconnaissance in front of the RCT. I was always less apprehensive when they screened our movements, because if there were any enemy in our zone, Pagani and his men would find them. Only this time, in addition to locating the enemy, they came up with the biggest prize of the war — as far as the 65th was concerned, that is.

About noon on 29 January, I was observing our advance from a small hill when I received a call on my radio that Master Sergeant Pagani had brought in a bag of prisoners, one of whom was believed to be the regimental commander of the 447th Infantry Regiment, 149th CCF Division. Since I was only a few minutes drive by jeep away from our POW cage, I headed out in that direction at once. When I arrived, I found Pagani and one of our interpreters questioning the man they thought was the regimental commander.

As I walked up to the group, Pagani handed me a map with supporting documents, which he said was the complete layout of the CCF 149th Division's defenses; they were located directly to our front. It was of course all in Chinese, and I was unable to make much out of it, but with the interpreter's help I became convinced that they were correct in their analysis; it actually was a schematic drawing, to scale, of that Chinese division's defenses. It showed not only their entrenchments and the areas covered by their automatic weapons but also the locations of their mortars and their artillery pieces, their CPs, and even where their reserves were located — the entire plan.

The staff and I made plans to exploit this booty to the fullest. We decided to use the information in a piecemeal fashion, just as though our units were discovering these enemy positions in the natural course of events. When one of our battalions hit some resistance, and the commander determined that it was from one of the positions on the map, he would call for mortar and artillery fire and attack in accordance with the plans already worked out. The artillery commander was to work out the fire plans now for both our mortar company and his artillery.

The same system would apply to enemy mortar and artillery positions. The whole idea was to use the information which we had just as though we had come by it through observation, deduction, or the use of our enemy artillery detection devices. We hoped that it would take some time for the information to filter up to the division headquarters that one of their regimental commanders had been captured and even then not be aware we also had a map of their defensive plans.

I thought that we might start our real drive on the 149th the following day to give Dammer and St. Clair a little breather. Besides, we were well ahead of the units on our right and left and could afford the delay without slowing up the whole works.

Certainly all military people know there is no shortcut to the capture of a piece of enemy dominated terrain, especially when it is high ground and defended by a determined and well-fortified enemy. Nor are there any movie-like tactics acceptable to the military tactician that can be used to take that high ground. In the final analysis it comes down to who has the more firepower and which of the two antagonists is the more determined to win. Just plain sweat, tears and, hopefully, as little bloodshed as possible is what it takes.

As we fully expected, when the attack got under way the following morning, our units had advanced only five or six hundred yards when the enemy opened up on us. The heaviest firing seemed to be coming from the two hills in the vicinity of Suwon, directly in front of us: Hill 449 in the 1st Battalion zone and Hill 262 in the 2nd Battalion zone. Both of these enemy strong points were shown on the captured map as being right in the center of their main defensive position, and we really went to work on them with everything we had.

In addition to our normal attachment of one battalion of artillery, we had been assigned the direct support of three battalions of 155 mm (heavy artillery), and all of them were prepared to lay down what is called a TOT (time on target). In layman's language this means that the fires of all of the battalions were concentrated to hit in a specified area at the same time and for a specified period. Each battery would fire as fast as the men could load. And that is a lot of artillery fire.

Even so, it took us the better part of three days and nights before we captured those two hills. As Saint and Dammer began their approach to the enemy positions, Childs started his concentration of mortar and artillery fires, searching out the targets ahead of the attacking troops with the help of our artillery spotter plane. Usually Charlie Boyle was the spotter.

As the battle for the two hills continued and our battalions progressed up the slopes, Childs shifted his fire partly on instinct and partly from information relayed to him from Saint and Dammer. When they received mortar or artillery fire, Childs just called for counterbattery on the known enemy artillery locations. On several occasions, Childs called in our supporting air strikes for both machine-gun fire on well-defined targets and napalm bombs where the targets could not be defined as well. In that connection, it should be mentioned that the piston-engine aircraft were the most suitable for our support, more so than the jet type. We soon learned that the jets were so fast that the pilot could not pick up a target unless it were defined as, "the west side of the hill at coordinates 423-631, — half way up the hill." On the other hand, the piston-type aircraft were slow enough for the pilot to locate more specific targets.

Knowing beforehand where each strong point was located, where the automatic weapons, the mortars and the artillery pieces were located gave us a greater advantage and, more important, saved many lives.

During the hours of darkness the fighting slackened off somewhat, though we used flares to light up the battlefield for short periods of time. During those bright periods we were able to preselect certain spots where our squads or platoons could move to better their positions and at the same time move closer to the top of the hill. It was tough going, but we took our time for we knew that we had them boxed in and sooner or later we would take the two hills. And of course, Childs kept up his hammering of the Red positions throughout the night.

Finally, on the morning of the third day both Saint and Dammer led their troops on an assault for the top of the hill. In closing with the enemy, the men of our two battalions fixed bayonets and charged straight at the enemy positions. Apparently the sight of that cold steel in the hands of the Puerto Ricans so unnerved some of the Chinese that they made the fatal mistake of starting to run down the far side of the hill. When they did, our men just picked them off like cottontails in a corn field.

When our forward elements got beyond what had been the 149th CCF Division's area, several of us made a tour of it. There was no doubt that we had captured their defensive plans. Our mortars and artillery had literally lifted the ground from a depth of about three or four feet and turned it over like a cook would flip pancakes on a griddle. And what the mortars and artillery did not accomplish, the foot troops completed. The whole area was a shambles of tangled barbed wire, broken logs, busted equipment, and dead bodies. With the number of prisoners we captured, our total "bag" since we had arrived in Korea was increased to 1,543. Our "body count" of dead enemy for the month showed an official count of 307.

One other result of our textbook attack was the hurried withdrawal of the enemy in front of us. There was nothing deliberate about it either, for it turned out to be a race between them and a task force which we sent to cut them off before they reached the Han River. They won the main race, but we did manage to capture another 150 prisoners.

The entire operation had gone like clockwork, just as we had planned it. Like most operations, several interesting stories emerged later which bear repeating: one of them amusing and the other nearly tragic. The first had to do with the capture of the CCF regimental commander and repeated here in the words of the I and R Platoon leader, Master Sergeant Pagani in his after action report to me.

I was ordered to patrol the area north of our headquarters at Chicksan to a point near Osan (about ten miles to the north) to determine how far south the enemy had located his troops. The terrain was very open, with almost no cover to conceal our movements.

We moved out, thirty-three men, and for the first seven miles there was no enemy activity. I stopped the patrol and called Staff Sergeant Gartegena to inform him that I considered the terrain too open for us to continue moving as a group and that I would continue forward with only one squad, while he was to establish a base of fire with the other two squads and the platoon headquarters. This would give us protection in case we had to withdraw hurriedly; it would also provide a getaway unit in case we were cut off.

I sent Sergeant Borrero and Pfc. Delgado Ismael to go forward in one jeep as scouts. Pfc. Paul Torres, the radio operator, and I followed in the second jeep. Sfc. Eric Cestero, the second in command, brought up the rear in the third jeep with Pfc. Heriberto Rodriguez.

We moved toward Osan until we came to a point about a mile and a half from that village when I noted a small hill about two hundred yards from our position. We had been expecting to find the enemy ever since we had left our headquarters, so we were particularly apprehensive about the hills to our left front; if we were lucky, we would find only a few Chinese soldiers, but we could also find a very large group of them.

We dismounted from our jeeps and spread out to reconnoiter the high ground. It appeared that there were no enemy in those hills, and I was about to radio back to headquarters that the area up to this point was clear when suddenly a burst of enemy fire from a small Korean hut hit Private First Class Delgado, and from the way that he fell, I thought that he was dead; his parka was on fire, and as he rolled over into a ditch out of sight, a heavy burst of automatic-weapons fire swept the entire area.

When the sudden burst of machine-gun fire hit us, the main body of the patrol in jeeps was able to withdraw without being hit. However, six of us were caught in the crossfire and pinned down. I knew that we couldn't stay there very long, so I made my way to better cover. Here I bumped into Sergeant First Class Cestero who said, "Sergeant, I think that we are the only ones alive."

He had hardly finished making that statement when we noticed someone approaching from the direction of the small hut. The man looked like a Chinese, so Cestero opened fire on him, and then this Chinese started to yell in Spanish not to fire on him that he was "Chicken," the nickname of Pfc. Delgado. Cestero ceased firing immediately, and Chicken came running to where we were.

He said that when he was hit, he fell into a crater that was filled with water and that he was able to extinguish the fire from his parka and his hair. He then removed all of his clothing except his underwear, and that was why we had mistaken him for a Chinese soldier.

Soon we came under mortar fire, and again we had to scramble for cover. We made our way from small hill to small hill, with the Chinese firing at us all the way. Finally we saw two of our jeeps come racing up the road, firing their machine guns at the Chinese. When our men spotted us, they whirled their jeeps around while we jumped into them. After picking us up, the drivers, Corporal Valazquez and Private First Class Carreras, found Sergeant Borrero and Pfc. Rodriguez, and we were able to escape.

During the fight, however, we captured several prisoners and one of them turned out to be a Chinese officer who had a map on him that showed the defensive positions of the 149th CCF Division.

We returned to the headquarters and reported the results of our reconnaissance; our mission was accomplished, but Chicken was still in his underwear.

The other story that came to light, several months later, was the capture of Sfc. Alfonso Garcia and Corporal Centero by the Chinese and their subsequent escape. The following are excerpts from Sergeant Garcia's report of that experience:

During the month of January I was a squad leader of G Company, and we were ordered to attack several hills south of Suwon. The attack was successful, and we received orders to stay in that position for the night and hold the line until the following day.

About two o'clock in the morning, the Chinese counterattacked. We were holding pretty good except that there were too many of them, and suddenly we saw that they were where our 1st Squad was supposed to be. Then they infiltrated into our position and Lieutenant Vasaldua was killed by a grenade. One of the fragments hit me above the right eyebrow, and I killed the Chinese who threw it. Meanwhile the Reds overran our position and Corporal Centeno and I were captured.

They took our weapons away from us and marched us to their CP; en route, they captured another man from my company, Pvt. Ramon Rodriguez. When we arrived at their headquarters, we were questioned by many Chinese officers. One of them, who spoke English very well, pointed his pistol at me and said that he was not satisfied with the answers we had given to their questions. He then said something in Chinese and one of the soldiers hit me in the head with his rifle; I do not remember how long I was unconscious. The same thing happened to Corporal Centeno.

Later they marched us every night from 1800 hours to 0600 hours, and at one of the daytime stops to rest they started to talk about some Communist books. They said that anyone wishing to read the books could ride in the trucks, otherwise we would walk. None of us took the books, so we all walked. There were sixteen of us in all — eight British and eight GIs. One night one of our men was too weak to walk so they ordered one Chinese soldier to take him out of the line and stay behind with him. Later we heard a shot and the guard showed up alone.

Corporal Centeno and I had planned to escape from the first day, but there was a platoon of guards around us during the march, and at night the place was full of Chinese. One night during an air raid we had our chance, and so kicked in the door of the hut where we were being held and started to run to the top of a nearby hill. When the Chinese saw us they started to fire at us but we managed to get away.

We then started to follow the Southern Cross because we had been traveling north all the time we were prisoners, and we knew that sooner or later we would get back to our own lines. One night when we were following a trail through the woods, I suddenly bumped into a Chinese soldier. It was very dark and when he said something to me I hit him with all my might, and then I strangled him. We took his rifle and some food, mostly rice, and continued along the trail. By morning we came close to a village which was full of Chinese and were almost recaptured but again we managed to escape.

Several days later it began to snow so hard that we could hardly see and decided it would be better to walk during the day and rest at night. Finally we came to a river but I had to carry Centeno across the deep parts because Centeno could not swim. After that we were so cold that we couldn't walk and had to go into a cave to get out of the wind. We stayed there for several days until the Chinese got too close, and then we moved out. One day we found an old Korean who told us that troops were coming up from the south. They turned out to be an ROK patrol, and they took us to the 65th.

During the time we traveled south we had many encounters with the enemy, but we were always able to escape. We were then sent back to a hospital in Japan where we were treated for frostbite, but there was nothing else wrong with us though it had been two months since we were captured. One month was spent marching north from one POW cage to another in freezing weather without either enough clothes to stay warm because the Chinese had taken most of them away from us or enough food to really stay alive. The other month was spent in trying to get back to the regiment, and although we came close to both freezing and starving to death, we managed to survive.

This account is an important part of the overall history of the 65th that first year of the Korean War for several reasons. First, there were few prisoners who ever escaped from the Chinese. Secondly, there were even fewer men who could have managed to make their way across those frozen wastelands, with as little food, clothing, and shelter as they had and still survive to tell about it. Lastly, their self-reliance, stamina, courage, and bravery were characteristic of all of the Puerto Ricans of the 65th.

After our capture of Hills 449 and 262, we encountered little resistance until about 29 January. But from that date until about February 5 or 6, we fought many vicious battles with the enemy as we drove him back across the Han. Turung, Sanuisil, Yongin, Kalgok, Nubong-dong-ni, Suwon, Chongson-gok, Tongchon-ni, Songhongdong, and Chomchon — the names of the villages where most of these engagements took place will long be remembered by the men of the 65th. For the record, from the time that we had arrived in Korea until we reached the river, we were officially credited with killing 1,125 of the enemy and taking 1,543 prisoners — a record which I doubt was equaled by any other regiment in Korea.

During this period of little enemy activity we worked on our plans for the river crossing. As a matter of fact, it seemed more urgent now than before because we were getting nearer to the river each day, and we were still in the zone of action which was on a collision course with the city of Seoul.

In our initial preparations for this operation, we had made a detailed study of the map, and from selected points of observation we compared this with the actual terrain to select the best avenues of approach to the river. Wooded areas or ravines that would permit us to reach the river without being seen or fired upon were noted. These were essential because we knew that the crossing would have to be made during daylight hours — the hazards of a nighttime operation were completely unacceptable.

We then studied the area for the best landing sites on the far side of the river, sites which would afford us the maximum protection from hostile fire while we disembarked from our rubber assault boats and scaled the bluffs where the enemy was entrenched. Included in this survey was all of the data we could gather concerning the river itself — the width, the rate of flow, sandbars that might obstruct our crossing, the nature of the soil on both sides, and other essential items that might help us. Later, when we reached the south bank, we were able to refine these data.

While all of this planning was being done, we requisitioned a sufficient number of rubber boats, both six- and eight-man types, to lift two battalions across at the same time. Fortunately, Eighth Army had brought those rafts far enough forward so that we could obtain them quickly. When they arrived, we had our battalions organize their crossing parties and rehearse their procedures and techniques for this hazardous venture. It was somewhat amusing, though not too much, that even though our request for these craft had to go through the 3rd Division headquarters before it was acted upon by army, no comment was made about it, nor did they question why we wanted them. No orders had been issued for us to start training for this hostile river crossing. We just figured that we would be selected to do the job and so initiated the training program on our own.

Finally we coordinated all of these plans with the support elements to insure their maximum effectiveness: the mortars and artillery, the engineers, the signal people, and our own supply of ammunition and other essentials, and lastly, the TACP which would provide us with the air coverage during the crossing. As for the latter, this eventually would be included in the overall corps plan for the operation, but we wanted to make sure that the air force personnel already assigned to us knew the details of our plan.

But early on the morning of the twenty-ninth all thoughts of a river crossing came to an abrupt halt. As indicated earlier, it was on this date that the Chinese slammed into both the 1st and 2nd Battalions, and we lost five men KIA, twenty-four wounded, and three missing in action.

The first unit hit was A Company located near Turung. In accordance with our usual custom, we had halted the attack shortly before dusk the night before, and each battalion had gone into its normal perimeter defensive position. The 1st Battalion had taken up position on the high ground near the small village of Turung, and St. Clair had designated three areas along the ridge as company strong points: two of them on the forward slope and the third in a supporting position behind them. A Company was on the right, B Company on the left, and C Company located in the third strong point. Each position was mutually supporting with the other, and A and B Companies were tied in with the units on their right and left — the 15th Infantry (3rd Division) on their right and our 2nd Battalion on the left.

Shortly after midnight about two hundred Chinese managed to slip through somewhere between the right flank of A Company and the left flank of the 15th Infantry and attacked A Company from the rear. Normally we were particularly alert to establish good contact with adjacent units at the boundary lines because they are usually the most vulnerable points in any defensive position. But somehow the Chinese managed to find a soft spot and take advantage of it. Almost with the first shot that was fired, the enemy was in on top of A Company's CP, completely surrounding the company commander and the four or five men with him.

Had it not been for the quick thinking and heroic action of 1st Lt. Paul Lavergne, the company executive officer, the small group might have perished. He was the first to discover the enemy, and when he did he jumped out of his foxhole and in full view of the charging enemy, opened up on them with an automatic rifle. This sudden and unexpected action so startled the enemy that the company commander was able to deploy his men and hold the Chinese until St. Clair could order C Company to counterattack and restore the position.

But even with the help of the support company, the situation was touch and go in the hand-to-hand fighting that followed. The C Company commander had ordered his men to fix bayonets, and when they landed in the middle of those two hundred Chinese, the fur began to fly. In short order it became a rifle-butt swinging, bayonet jabbing, close-range shootout, where it was difficult to distinguish friend from foe. When the fight was finally over, however, there were more than a hundred dead Chinese on the ground, and the rest were taken prisoner.

However, we did not escape completely unscathed in that melee, for A and C Companies lost three men KIA, fifteen wounded, and two MIA, and one of those KIA was Lieutenant Lavergne. He had been in the thick of it from the beginning and was the rallying point around which our men made their stand. Had it not been for his heroic leadership, the enemy might have overrun the entire A Company position.

In addition to this attack, another enemy force hit Sanuisil, where the Headquarters Company of the 1st Battalion was located. Apparently it was a part of the same group that had been able to get through our lines at the boundary between A Company and the 15th Infantry. However, other than temporarily driving one platoon back a short distance, this attack did not get very far, primarily because of the prompt and effective action taken by the company commander, 1st Lt. Julian F. Lockerman. He had his jeep with a fifty caliber machine gun mounted on it sitting alongside his foxhole, and when the enemy struck, he jumped up on the vehicle and opened fire on them. He delivered such a heavy and devastating volume of fire on the attackers that he quickly drove them out of the company position. The company had only one casualty.

In the action on our left flank, the 2nd Battalion was able to stop the enemy attack almost before it got started. Its position was really an extension of the 1st Battalion along the ridge, and here the enemy tried a frontal attack, which turned out to be poor judgment. The outpost Dammer had posted discovered the enemy well before they reached the bottom of the hill and immediately called for mortar and artillery fire to be placed on them. When that barrage hit, the enemy broke and ran.

This sequence of events for the twenty-four hour period of 28-29 January became almost a daily routine until 9 February when we finally reached the Han River. Each day we would continue the attack to the north against only minor, if any, resistance. About sundown we would halt for the night and take up our normal wagon-wheel defensive positions on the nearest high ground. Promptly, several hours before daybreak, the enemy would launch an attack on us. As a matter of fact, with the exception of short periods of time, this became SOP for the remainder of time that I was in Korea and accounted for our having so little opportunity to sleep.

During the early hours of each night the enemy would pull back some ten or twelve miles so that we were unable to locate them in any strength. Then several hours before daybreak, down the ridges they would come, hundreds of them running at top speed, and hit us during the early hours before dawn.

The secret to this technique, we finally realized, was their superb physical condition and their logistical system. As for the former, we had witnessed their almost unbelievable strength since the day of our arrival in Korea. As for their logistical system, it was very simple and uncomplicated. No ration trucks, no chuck wagons, no long string of trucks behind them carrying supplies of rations and ammunition. They did not require what we call a "division slice." Before they started out on a mission, they were given a small sack of rice, a canteen of water, and a bandoleer of ammunition for their weapon, and that was it.

However, the Puerto Rican soldiers were quick to learn all the tricks, and they continued their search for the enemy. When they located them, they charged their positions with courage and daring. If the enemy wanted a fight, that is what he got, to the death. If they surrendered, our men would calmly round them up and send them to the rear under guard of maybe only one man. It was a ludicrous sight, and I witnessed it many times, to see a long line of maybe fifty or seventy prisoners coming down the road toward our POW Cage, and way in the back — at the tail of the column — one lone Puerto Rican rifleman.

But where the resistance during the daylight hours had been fairly

Men of Company G, 2nd Battalion, digging fox holes at the front; January 1951.

South Korean refugees fleeing south from the Kum River.

Rice being distributed to civilians at Kaesong-dong, February 1951.

Lieutenant General Matthew B. Ridgway, Commanding General Eighth Army, and the author, ready to observe the crossing of the Han River by the 2nd Battalion of the 65th Infantry; 16 March 1951. U.S. ARMY SIGNAL CORPS PHOTO

General MacArthur and the author. 24 March 1951.

The author (left) with Lieutenant Colonel Ojeda, Commanding Officer 10th Battalion; the Philippine unit commander.

light over the past few days, it now began to increase as we neared Suwon and the approaches to the Han River. Again our 1st and 2nd Battalions took the brunt of it; the last day of the month was the worst. At the time we were in the same formations that we had been earlier in the month, with those two battalions leading the assault. The 25th U.S. Infantry Division was on our left, and the 15th Infantry Regiment (3rd Division) was on our right.

Not too far ahead of the 1st Battalion, almost on the boundary between our right flank and the 15th Infantry and near a village named Kalgok, about ten miles or so southeast of Suwon, there was a large, ominous-looking hill mass which we were quite sure would be defended. Since there was no way that we could go around it, St. Clair had to take it if we were to continue our advance.

In preparation for this attack, he deployed A and B Companies abreast. With C Company in reserve, he commenced his approach march on a broad front, giving the men plenty of interval. When the lead elements reached a point about two hundred yards from their objective, the enemy opened up — mortars, artillery, rifle and machine-gun fire. Every man of the two assault companies immediately hit the ground and began to engage the enemy with his own fire. But each time the company commanders tried to advance their men, the enemy poured such a heavy volume of fire down on them that they were forced to halt and seek cover. For several hours it appeared as though the fight was a stand-off, with each side holding its ground.

It was at this point in time, however, that one of the scouts of A Company, Pfc. William Hernandez, suddenly jumped to his feet and started to charge the hill in a one-man attack. Running at full speed and in a zigzag fashion, he made his way toward the enemy, firing as he went. About every ten yards or so he would drop down in the knee-high grass, roll over several times to conceal his exact location, and then leap up and continue.

To the men of the company who were watching him, it appeared only a matter of time before he would be hit. But on he went, drawing the fire of almost every enemy rifleman above him. In the meantime, his distraction of the enemy permitted both A and B Companies to continue their advance. By the time they reached the forward slopes of the hill, Hernandez was almost at the top, alternately firing his rifle and heaving hand grenades at every enemy soldier he encountered. When the two companies finally reached the top of the hill they could see Hernandez still chasing the enemy down the reverse slope — still blazing away at them as they ran for cover.

A little later that same day, 31 January, several other men of the regiment distinguished themselves above and beyond the call of duty. Among these men were Cpl. Pedro Pagan of B Company headquarters and M. Sgt. Federico Martinez of G Company. Each of these men was responsible for leading the attack of his unit to restore the company position after a fierce enemy attack.

Some part of these actions, possibly all of it, was witnessed by the new army commander, Lt. Gen. Matthew B. Ridgway, for he spent the thirtieth and thirty-first observing the entire regiment — quite an unusual amount of time for an army commander to spend with one regimental combat team.

When I heard that he was coming to visit us, I selected the two tallest Puerto Rican soldiers I could find over six feet, tied several dummy hand grenades to their field jackets, and then gave each of them a long knife (this in addition to their M-1 rifles). I then smeared some black soot on their faces and posted them as guards to the entrance of my CP. It will be remembered, of course, that General Ridgway was the commander of the 82nd Airborne Division during World War II, and every picture that I had ever seen of him showed him with several live grenades suspended from his web shoulder harness. It was something of a trademark as far as he was concerned. I must admit that I do not know what he ever expected to do with them, but like other high-ranking officers, he had his own battle image. Georgie Patton had his: the twin, Hirsch bone-handled pistols. General MacArthur had his: the braided, sloppy cap.

So we presented an image: two of the biggest, toughest-looking characters I could find, actually tough fighters but also two of the most pleasant and kindhearted men I knew. They were our image — impressive, even if I do say so myself.

The day after Ridgway returned to his own headquarters, he sent me a radio message which is exactly the same as the one incorporated in the following letter which he wrote some days later to Colonel Colberg of the Puerto Rican National Guard.

Headquarters Eighth Army
Office of the Commanding General

5 March 1951

Dear Colonel Colberg:

Thank you for your letter of 1 March 1951, inquiring about the 65th Infantry Regiment.

I think my respect and admiration for their soldierly qualities is best summarized in a message which I sent to Colonel W. W. Harris, the Commanding Officer of the 65th Regimental Combat Team on 31 January 1951. In that message I said,

> "What I saw and heard of your regiment reflects great credit on you, the regiment, and the people of Puerto Rico, who can be proud of their valiant sons. I am confident that their battle records and training levels will win them high honors."

Since that time, their conduct in battle has served only to increase the high regard in which I hold these fine troops. I am confident that the 295th and 296th Infantry Regiments will measure up to the high standards set by their brothers in arms here in Korea.

Sincerely,

[Signed] M. B. RIDGWAY
LIEUTENANT GENERAL, U.S. ARMY COMMANDING

At the same time an article written by one of the war correspondents quoted General Ridgway as making the following statement during an interview:

> These boys [referring to the men of the 65th] are fine soldiers. I am highly impressed with their ability. We are damn lucky to have them here at this time. They have put the fear of God into these Commies.

And then the reporter continued with some observations of his own about the 65th. He said:

> They climb the hills with the tenacity of a goat, and they force the Communists to surrender at the point of a bayonet. They ask no quarter and give none. Whatever assignment the Eighth Army delegates to them, the Puerto Ricans accept without complaint and discharge with skill.

It was about this time, too, that we received a copy of the Puerto Rican newspaper, *El Mundo*, which contained an open letter to the 65th written by Maj. Gen. Luis Esteves, a highly respected regular army officer who later became chief of the Puerto Rican National Guard. The letter follows:

Hail the 65th
by
Major General Luis Raul Esteves

While back in 1918, while I was serving with the Regular Army and was assigned to Camp Las Casas during World War I, my first impression of the Puerto Rican soldier was very poor. When I saw our weak country boys of that time compared with the Continental, Regular Army soldiers which I had been commanding, I could not but prefer my 23rd Infantry Battalion I had commanded, than the Puerto Rican soldiers to fight with. But after a few months, I admired the physical change that was taking place in our boys. I could appreciate the spirit, discipline and military pride inherited from our ancestors. I changed my opinion, and I felt proud in serving with the Puerto Ricans. Because of this, at the end of World War I, I insited upon the organization of our National Guard, since from that time on, I was convinced that the Puerto Ricans could be as good soldiers as the best from any other country in the world.

During the years between the first and second wars, I had the opportunity of making a detailed study of our military history and a close study of the Puerto Rican soldier. The glorious military achievements of our ancestors made me enthusiastic about our soldiers, and the conduct of the 65th Infantry and our National Guard made me feel proud as a Puerto Rican. I was, therefore, expecting that at the outbreak of the Second World War, the Puerto Rican troops would have the opportunity to show that they were worthy descendents of Andino, Vizcarrondo, Amezquita, Sosa, Diaz, and many other Puerto Rican military heroes, partially forgotten by our people.

I was greatly discouraged when the blindness of the Federal Military Authorities in Puerto Rico denied us that opportunity. It was the opinion of some of these officers that the Puerto Rican, although they were valiant individuals, could not be trusted in his collective abilities and valor. Others argued that the language problem, the Puerto Rican replacements, and even the special rations, made difficult the use of our troops on the fronts. I objected energetically to these opinions, asking for an opportunity for our boys. When my arguments and efforts with the department failed, I went to see Governor Tugwell, who understood my reasoning and promised to see President Roosevelt about the matter on his next trip to Washington. Upon his return from the Federal Capital, he announced to me proudly that not only one, but two Puerto Rican Divisions were to be organized and that they would have the opportunity to show in combat my contention that our troops were as good as the best in the world.

I was again greatly disappointed when President Roosevelt's promises were not fulfilled, probably due to the objection of the War Department, wrongly informed by the Military Department of Puerto Rico, and although our troops honorably accomplished their missions in World War II, they never had the opportunity to participate in active combat as a unit.

With the change in policies of the Military Department in Puerto Rico initiated by Generals Bissel and Porter, and followed firmly by the good friend of Puerto Rico, General Sibert, the 65th Infantry has the glory of demonstrating the valor and military ability of the Puerto Rican soldiers . . . Borinqueneers of the 65th . . . with your conduct in Korea, you are breaking the strings that, due to lack of vision and unskilledness of some commanders, our troops were tied with. You are destroying the discrimination which hurt us so much during the war; you are writing a glorious page in our history . . . Puerto Rico is proud of you . . . We, your comrades in the National Guard, wish you good luck and success in the New Year.

There was no question that General Esteves had correctly expressed the sentiments of the War Department with regard to the Puerto Ricans as combat soldiers, but he was in error about who was responsible for sending the 65th to Korea. Although I am sure that both Generals Sibert and Porter would have recommended it had they been asked, the officer actually responsible for it was my old friend — and former commander when I was chief of staff of the 17th Airborne Division — Maj. Gen. Wayne C. Zimmerman. At the time, he was chief of the Plans Division, Headquarters Army Ground Forces, Fort Monroe, Virginia, and was responsible for compiling the troop lists for Korea. Several years after the war he told me that he had personally selected the 65th for inclusion on that list.

But just who selected the regiment for combat duty, or why they had not been selected sooner, was of little consequence to the men of the regiment in 1951. The important fact was that they had by this time more than proved their capability. They had established a reputation for themselves as combat soldiers that was second to none. And, in their inimitable fashion, all of these accolades showered upon them had little or no effect on their demeanor, for they went about their daily tasks with the same quiet, reserved determination and firmness of purpose as they had from the day that I joined the regiment.

The battle toward the south bank of the river went on, with the enemy resistance increasing day by day as they fought for every inch of real estate that they gave up. Once we captured the high ground south of the river, the city of Seoul itself was in jeopardy, and its loss by the Communists would have had political (loss of face) as well as military implications.

Enemy resistance was general all along the entire division front, but in our zone of action it was particularly heavy in and around Suwon and the villages north of there to the river. But we finally drove them back and reached the heights overlooking the river on the afternoon of 9 February.

Some of the bitterest fighting prior to the ninth took place near the small village of Songhongdong, where the enemy had dug in like moles along a small ridge that we called Hill 582. Company K had the respon-

160   WE REJOIN EIGHTH ARMY

sibility of seizing it, and 1st Lt. Charles H. Fleming was in command
of the lead platoon.

As he and his men reached the base of the hill, they were suddenly
fired on from the front and both flanks. Again it was a question of staying
at the bottom of the hill and being subjected to such withering fire that
he stood a chance of losing his entire platoon, or charging the heights
in an all-out assault. Fleming chose to do the latter. Calmly moving out
in front of his men, he ordered them to fix bayonets and follow him.
As he led the charge up the hill, he of course immediately became the
main target for the enemy's rifle and automatic-weapons fire and was
mortally wounded. Despite his wounds, he continued to lead the assault
and finally captured the objective.

Still another action, which involved Lt. Col. E. G. Allen's 3rd Battalion, occurred near Nubongdong-ni as he attempted withdrawal to
more favorable terrain to establish a defensive position for the night.
His unit had been deployed on our left flank to plug a gap that had suddenly appeared between us and the 25th Infantry Division. Having successfully accomplished that mission, he was attempting to consolidate his
position and secure himself for the night when the enemy struck.

The attack came in such a direction and manner that the battalion
supporting weapons (mortars and artillery) were the first ones hit. This
was really a fluke and normally wouldn't happen. Realizing the gravity
of the situation, Colonel Allen personally led a counterattack against
the enemy, and though he was subjected to continuous heavy rifle and
automatic-rifle fire himself, he succeeded in driving them out of the besieged positions.

At Tongchon-ni, a village just to the northeast of Suwon, Colonel
Dammer had ordered an attack to drive the enemy off the high ground
to his front, and the 2nd Platoon of F Company had the mission of capturing Hill 297. As the platoon advanced up the steep slopes, firing on
the well-dug-in enemy, Sfc. Felix Jimenez, of his own accord and with
complete disregard for his own safety, ran forward of his own platoon
and started to throw hand grenades at the enemy. He repeated this action
five times, and each time he destroyed a portion of the enemy's defenses
and killed several of them. Though they continued to fire at him each
time he ran forward, the suddenness of each of his one-man assaults
and the effectiveness of his grenades so demoralized the enemy and so
inspired his comrades that they charged the hill and occupied it without
a single casualty.

On 1, 2 and 4 February, the Chinese made their final stand just before
they crossed to the north bank of the Han. The action on those three

days involved several different companies of all three battalions. On the first, we encountered heavy resistance from Hill 299 in front of A Company and at Hill 298 in front of E Company; but because of the heroic actions of two men, both companies were able to take their objectives with a minimum of casualties.

Those hills were the last two really dominant pieces of terrain in our sector, and it was essential that we occupy them if we were to control the south bank of the river. Since they were in the zones of the 1st and 2nd Battalions, St. Clair and Dammer were given the mission of taking them.

St. Clair's plan of attack was to move forward in a column of companies in order to allow himself the maximum flexibility in the employment of his reserves. A Company led the assault in somewhat the same formation but with the platoons echeloned to the right rear. The 1st Platoon, commanded by 2nd Lt. Pablo Ramirez, was in the lead.

As the company began its approach, the lead platoon started to receive a very heavy volume of mortar and artillery fire. The shelling continued at a moderate rate until the platoon reached the bottom of the hill and prepared to assault the crest. At this point, the fire increased in volume considerably; one man was killed and several more were seriously wounded. This created some confusion among the men of the 1st Platoon, A Company, and for one decisive moment they faltered, not knowing where to go or what to do.

Quickly realizing the seriousness of the situation and knowing that he had to take immediate action to rally his troops, Lieutenant Ramirez yelled for his men to follow him and charged up the hill alone. Seeing this, his men regained their confidence, jumped to their feet yelling words of encouragement to Ramirez, and then stormed the hill after him. In the vicious fighting that followed, the 1st Platoon either captured or killed every enemy soldier on that position. But sometime during the final minutes of the battle, Lieutenant Ramirez was mortally wounded. There was no question that his inspirational leadership, initiative, outstanding courage and bravery had been the basic reasons for the platoon's taking its objective with a minimum of casualties.

In the other zone of the regimental sector, a similar amazing feat of daring and bravery by one man brought about the capture of Hill 298. In this case, the 1st Platoon of E Company commanded by M. Sgt. Manuel Acevedo, Jr., was held up by very heavy fire from one well-placed machine gun which had stopped the attack in its tracks and threatened to wipe out the entire platoon.

Seeing that every man of his platoon was helplessly pinned to the ground, Sergeant Acevedo realized that he had to take some action, and fast, to knock the gun out before they were all killed. He thought his best chance was to make his way to a small ditch some fifty feet or so off to his right flank that appeared to lead directly to the gun position.

Jumping to his feet, he raced toward the ditch, and within a fraction of a second the enemy gunners picked him up in their sights and followed him with a stream of bullets until he finally reached cover. Then they continued to rake the area, hoping to hit him as he made his way in their direction. While the enemy was firing at Acevedo, however, his men were able to get to their feet and rush to the bottom slope of the hill.

Arriving within about twenty yards of the gun, Sergeant Acevedo started to lob hand grenades into the position, and this further distracted the crew, allowing his men to make a rush to the summit. Charging in, they engaged the enemy with bayonets and pointblank rifle fire, killing all of them and silencing the weapon.

Thus ended the major effort by the enemy to keep control of the south bank of the river. They did not give up completely, however, for on the two following nights they launched an attack against our positions on Hills 298 and 299. One of these hit G Company on Hill 298, and the other was met by I Company of the 3rd Battalion, which we had moved forward into position on Hill 299 along with the 1st Battalion.

In the fight on Hill 298, we had another one of those one-man army stands. One of the squad leaders was mortally wounded, the squad became disorganized and was driven back several hundred yards to the rear of its original position. The platoon leader, Sfc. Felix G. Nieves, rushed to the breach in the defensive position and, completely exposing himself to enemy fire, allowed his body to be employed as an aiming stake so that friendly machine-gun and mortar fire could be directed at the advancing enemy. Defiantly shouting at the enemy, throwing grenades, firing his rifle, blowing a whistle, and brandishing his bayonet, Sergeant Nieves singlehandedly held an area normally assigned to an entire rifle squad. Because of this one-man action, the enemy was thrown into a complete state of confusion, and the squad position was retaken.

The last little skirmish that we had on Hill 299 occurred on the night of the fourth when Colonel Allen attempted to move his men to a more dominant position and encountered about a platoon of enemy that had managed to work its way back to the top of the hill. When one of I Company's platoons was suddenly hit by a large volume of small-arms and automatic-weapon fire, several of the men were reluctant to move forward.

Seeing this hesitancy, Private Cirino-Rivera, the radio operator attached to the platoon, rushed forward, shouting for the others to follow him; he charged straight into the enemy ranks. This display of courage, determination, and complete disregard for his own safety so inspired the other members of the platoon that they immediately charged after him and drove the enemy off the position. During the melee, Private Cirino-Rivera was mortally wounded.

With these actions completed, we now sat firmly on the Boston Line, which ran along the high ground on the south bank of the river. The 65th was the first I Corps unit to reach this army objective, and on the following day, 10 February, we were ordered into division reserve in the rear area. This was to be the second time since our arrival in Korea, five months before, that we were to be given some rest. But something quite unexpected came up, and our rest period lasted exactly four hours.

8

PRELUDE
TO THE BIG BATTLE

As the 15th RCT relieved the 65th Boston Line, we were ordered to move into reserve. We were given no specific area to move to, just to pick our spot and notify division headquarters of our location after arrival.

Since this was only the second time we had been out of contact with the enemy, this move soon took on a rather festive air.

The move to the rear was by both truck and on foot, in other words a shuttle. This added to the gaiety of it all, for it was seldom that we had the good fortune to ride anywhere. Chick, Allen, Dammer, St. Clair, and I led the procession in somewhat of a picnic fashion. Occasionally we would halt the entire column and take a C-ration break — lousy coffee, and even worse, some hard biscuits. But it was fun, and as we headed on down the road I began to look for a place where we could go into that reserve status with nothing really to do except eat and sleep.

The most promising looking spot that I could see from a distance was just about where we knew the 3rd Division CP to be located. Off in the distance we could see three hills about five or six hundred feet high, located so that they nearly surrounded the command post. And since it was just SOP for us to look for high ground, that's where we decided to go. Three hills, three battalions, one for each of them. No formal orders were necessary to get the battalion commanders headed in the right direction. I just pointed at each of them, indicated which hill each was to take, and that was it. No fuss, no feathers, no further to-do about it — just move on up there and enjoy yourselves while you can — which turned out to be a very short time.

As the battalions moved out, I drove by the division CP and reported our location to the staff. Since I had already decided to stay there close to the division commander, I arranged for both radio and telephone communication with my battalion commanders. Our Regimental Headquarters Company, the Engineer Company, the Tank Company, and other ancillary units just paired off with whatever battalion combat team they wished to spend the holidays.

As for my little "command group" of Charlie Boyle, Ramos, Vargas, my radio operator and myself, we just pulled our jeeps and my paneled trailer under a small group of trees in the CP area and acted just like any other group of tourists. I forgot to mention that this paneled job had arrived back in my supply dump about the time we reached the Boston Line. It was a gift from the army commander, and I suppose that each RCT commander received one.

The first thing we did after finding our spot was to take a sponge bath. That means a helmet full of water, some soap, and a towel, and — oh yes — a toothbrush. And you performed all of these niceties with one helmet full of water.

"Showered down" so to speak, we all gathered near my trailer and started supper. Beans, hash, hard biscuits, jam, and coffee were on the menu. Then into our down-filled sleeping bags.

We had only recently acquired these new bags. The first ones we had received were the open-at-one-end type. Once in them you sometimes had trouble getting out of them. This was particularly true when you were in a hurry — like when you were being attacked by the enemy with fixed bayonets or carrying those deadly machetes which most of them did and they got in close before you discovered them. We did actually lose some men in the early days who were stabbed to death before they could get out of those damn bags. The new ones had a ripcord which you could pull from the inside and pop out like a jack-in-the-box.

The last thing I remember before falling asleep was how nice it was to be in the rear area where we didn't have to worry about the damn Chinese. The very next thing I knew I was standing barefoot on the floor of my trailer screaming at the top of my voice, "Forgodssake whatenhell was that?"

In absolute disbelief at what was happening it took me a few minutes to recover my wits — but there was no mistaking that now very familiar sound: whompf — whompf — whompf — zing — zing —zing.

The entire division command post was under attack; and the way it sounded it wouldn't take long before the entire staff, division commander, and, even more important, us — Charlie, Ramos, Vargas, the radio operator and I — would all be dead or captured. I immediately grabbed my telephone and got all of the battalion commanders on the line at the same time.

"Saint, are you there?"

"Here, sir, what's going on?"

"Hang on a minute and I'll tell you."

"Herm, are you on?"

"I'm on, sir."

"Jerry, how about you?"

"I'm on, sir."

"Good, guess you can tell by the shooting that we're under attack down here."

"That's what it sounded like to me," Dammer replied.

"Well, that's exactly what's happening, but don't ask me how they got here. Now here's what I'd like for you to do — I want all three of you to join hands and come in on these bastards in a circle formation."

"Herm."

"Yes, sir."

"Suppose you come straight west since you are almost due east of us."

"Right, sir."

"Jerry."

"Here, sir."

"Suppose you swing around slightly and hit us from the south."

"Right, sir."

"Saint."

"Here."

"Suppose you come in from the north — then, when you get close enough to do so, all of you close the circle. Any questions?" When I received a negative reply from all of them I said,

"Go get'm."

And man, did those Puerto Ricans have a ball. They moved down out of the hills and swarmed over those North Koreans so fast they didn't know what had hit 'em. When the smoke and noise had cleared away several days later, the 65th was officially credited with the following: counted NKPA dead bodies — 560, NKPA prisoners — 276 for a total of 836.

When we finished processing the prisoners and burying the dead NKPAs, we found that they were from the First North Korean Regiment of the 8th NKPA Division. But with all of that good luck, we also suffered some casualties ourselves. We lost one man KIA and six wounded.

A few days later we received the following communication.

Office of the Commanding General
APO 358, United States Army

Subject: Commendation
To:　　Major General Robert H. Soule
　　　　Commanding General
　　　　Third United States Infantry Division
　　　　APO 468, United States Army

1. I wish to commend you and your officers and men for the action just completed by the Third United States Infantry Division, one more in a lengthy history of such exploits.

2. On the night of 13-14 February 1951 the First North Korean Infantry Regiment of the Eighth North Korean Division launched an attack against the center of your Division, with the mission of penetrating the Division sector and continuing South towards Kumyangjang-ni, to cut and disrupt lines of communication in that area.

3. By morning of 14 February, through the alertness and steadfast courage and determination of combat, service and headquarters elements of your division in the threatened area, the enemy had been stopped far short of his objectives and rendered incapable of further cohesive action. Throughout the remainder of the day and night units of the Division fiercely engaged the trapped enemy, hunting him down and relentlessly driving him before them into the weapons of other waiting forces. Broken remnants of the enemy force attempting to escape north of the Han River were brought under withering fire by your artillery.

4. Today, with your zone cleared, the results of this magnificent action have been assessed: 671 counted enemy dead; 338 shaken enemy prisoners of war; the 1st NKPA Regiment destroyed and a demonstration given to the forces opposing this Corps of the tactical skill and fighting caliber of the American Army.

[Signed] F. W. MILBURN
LIEUTENANT GENERAL, U.S. ARMY COMMANDING

1st Indorsement

3DCG
(15 Feb 51)
Subject: Commendation

Headquarters Third Infantry Division, APO 468, 17 Feb. 1951

To:　　The Officers and Men of the Third U.S. Infantry Division

1. I desire to add my commendations to those of the Corps Commander.

2. Each and every one of you participated in this action and fully per-

formed your duty as a member of the Division fighting team. I am proud of you and the division's record on this occasion.

3. The cooperation and fighting spirit shown will assure us of victory over our enemies.

[Signed] ROBERT H. SOULE
MAJOR GENERAL, USA COMMANDING

2nd Indorsement

Headquarters 65th Inf., APO 468 c/o PM San Francisco, Calif. 24 Feb. 51
To: All Personnel, 65th Inf. Regt. APO 468

1. It is with just pride that I pass on to you of the 65th Infantry this commendation from the Corps Commander, Lt. Gen. F. W. Milburn, and the additional commendation of the Division Commander, Maj. Gen. Robert H. Soule.

2. The part played by this regiment in achieving the successful action cited by Lieutenant General Milburn was as a principal and was a part well attested by the 268 POWs taken by the regiment and the 537 enemy dead credited to the regiment.

[Signed] W. W. HARRIS
COLONEL, INFANTRY COMMANDING

I was slightly amazed to receive such a general commendation because the 65th was just about the only unit of the division which had participated in the fight. Some rear-area units of the division had participated — like the cooks and bakers of the Division Headquarters Company. Likewise a part of the Division Reconnaissance Squadron, but that was about all. The rest of the division, the 7th Infantry RCT and the 15th, for example, weren't within ten miles of the action. Yet the division commander had commended the entire division for its good work. Somebody forgot to tell somebody what had happened. Instead of being commended, someone should have been chewed out for letting an entire NKPA regiment of over one thousand men get through the front lines. I was a bit irritated, but the men of the regiment just laughed it off as another slight for what they had done almost singlehandedly. Then, a few days later we forgot all about the "Shootout at the 3rd Division CP" when we received a copy of a letter written to Mr. Eugene Wright of the *Puerto Rico News* by General Douglas MacArthur.

General Headquarters
Supreme Commander for the Allied Powers
Office of the Supreme Commander

Tokyo, Japan
12 February 1951

Dear Mr. Wright:

Reference is made to your letter of January 19th.

The Puerto Ricans forming the ranks of the gallant 65th Infantry on the battlefields of Korea by valor, determination and a resolute will to victory give daily testament to their invincible loyalty to the United States and the fervor of their devotion to those immutable standards of human relations to which the Americans and Puerto Ricans are in common dedicated. They are writing a brilliant record of achievement in battle and I am proud indeed to have them in this command. I wish that we might have many more like them.

Faithfully yours,
[Signed] DOUGLAS MACARTHUR

This was indeed a fine tribute to the men of the 65th, and they greatly appreciated it. As had the Filipinos, the Puerto Ricans had established an empathy with General MacArthur. Following that now-famous letter from General MacArthur, I received another testimonial to the men of the regiment in the form of a concurrent resolution of the Senate and The House of Representatives of Puerto Rico. The Resolution was sent to me by the secretary of the Senate, Mr. Jose Cestero Guardiola (see Appendix).

We reproduced the resolution for the information of all the men of the regiment, as we had done with the copy of the letter from General MacArthur. And I also responded to the Eleventh Special Session of the Seventeenth Legislature of Puerto Rico and to the people of Puerto Rico with a letter to the secretary of the Senate, Mr. Jose Cestero Guardiola (see Appendix).

There were many stories told after the action was over, and two that I recall were about what happened to Cpl. Victor Cintron and Lt. Jamie Colozo. Cintron said that he caught a large number of NKPAs trying to sneak up a draw where they could again attack our troops. He described them as looking like a small forest of trees. Standing there at the top of the draw he calmly pulled the pins on several hand grenades and just lobbed them down into the crowd as you would a soft ball. Killing four of them in this fashion he then knocked off three more with his rifle. As for Colozo, he led his platoon on three separate charges down into the valley and captured forty-four of the enemy.

Following that "rest" in the reserve location we again moved up onto the Boston Line (see page 174) and relieved the 7th Infantry RCT.

It was now 15 February. We were located directly across the river from the city of Seoul, a position that made it quite clear that we would be required to make the initial hostile river crossing.

Occupying the area just south of the river gave us our first opportunity to probe the enemy positions on the far bank. The 2nd and 3rd Battalions were given the positions in the forward area while the 1st was placed in reserve. One effective ploy we used to good advantage was to send quite a strong patrol across to the far shore fully expecting it to be driven back. But, as the patrol fell back to our side, the patrol leader would leave one or two men in place as a listening post. Two days later a similar patrol action would cross and pick up the two men. Credit should be given to L Company for thinking that one up; it worked to perfection.

From the observation reports we received, we learned that the enemy was well dug in along the banks of the far side. What was equally disturbing were the reports of the steep slopes we would be required to scale after crossing the river. In the midst of our preparations, division and corps artillery started a twenty-four-hour barrage throughout a division depth of their defensive position. As we found out later this had done terrific damage.

And mentioning Corps, it was about this time that we received the following Order of the Day:

Headquarters I Corps
Office of the Commanding General
APO 358, United States Army

Order of the Day

I Corps stands firmly on the south bank of the Han River.

A simple statement of an accomplished fact, made possible through an equally simple truth: the power of confident, fighting men and their commanders when given the opportunity to come to grips with a tangible enemy.

A month ago today this Corps seized the initiative from the forces of the Communist Chinese with a series of quick armor-infantry thrusts. Caught off balance by the rapidity of these moves the enemy could only fall back to successive defensive lines.

We pressed him relentlessly, fighting him yard for yard and hand to hand in treacherous terrain, throwing off his nightly counterattacks. In the open valleys the superiority of our troops, training and firepower over-

whelmed him. As the full fury of our offensive mounted, he threw in everything he had, and it was not enough to stop us. We drove on through to
the final objective.

Once he attempted to recross the Han River but found us ready and
waiting. The regiment that made this attack against us no longer exists as
a military force.

*This sweeping tactical success will rank high in the recording of military
achievements.* All forces of this Corps have done their part and done it well.

[Signed] F. W. MILBURN
LIEUTENANT GENERAL, U.S. ARMY COMMANDING

Note: Italics are author's.

On the morning of 17 February, I received word that General Mac-
Arthur was going to visit us. The time was not specified, but it was estimated that he would arrive somewhere around midday. No specific
instructions were given regarding his visit except that I was to meet him
at my headquarters. Even so I knew that he would want to hear about
our plans for the river crossing and I prepared for that.

I also felt quite sure that he would want to speak to Ojeda, the CO
of the 10th Philippine Battalion which was attached to us. The empathy
between General MacArthur and the Filipinos was well known. The
Puerto Ricans also held the supreme commander in high regard and I
only hoped the troops wouldn't pull out of front line position to visit
MacArthur at my headquarters. I asked for, and received the assurances
of all my commanders that it couldn't happen.

About noon in came the caravan with General MacArthur in the lead
jeep. Following along behind, like a string of elephants with each holding the tail of the one in front, came a column of twenty or thirty other
jeeps. Each was loaded to capacity with assorted air force and army generals, admirals and other ranks. It was quite a show just to see the procession wheel into my headquarters.

After the salutations, General MacArthur asked me if my troops were
still doing their same fine job, and when I replied in the affirmative, asked
what my plans were for the crossing. While I was going through what
had now become a routine briefing, I happened to look up beyond the
column of jeeps. Incredible as it may seem, we were almost completely
surrounded by at the very least five thousand of our soldiers. I almost
swallowed my tongue. I gasped for breath and I came very close to passing out like a plebe at parade. Imagine the situation! When I finally recovered sufficiently, I continued my briefing knowing that at any moment
the axe would fall.

Would you believe it — General MacArthur didn't bat an eye. He just sat there silently until I finished my spiel and then thanked me. After a few more pleasantries he drove off and, just as he did, he said to me, "Felicitations upon you."

I saluted and did a double take — "Felicitations upon you." Now what did he mean by that? I had to go in and look it up in the dictionary. And when you think about it, only General MacArthur could have thought of such an expression, to say nothing of saying it.

After he was out of sight I just looked around with a sickly smile and went into my headquarters. There was no sense in making a fuss about the damn thing. It hadn't bothered him, apparently, so why let it bother me.

Another event of import to me and to those who participated, was a small front-line ceremony when I pinned the gold bars of a second lieutenant on the shoulders of six men whom I had recommended be given a battle field promotion. They were: M. Sgt. Victor M. Navas, M. Sgt. Eladio Lopez Ayala, M. Sgt. Federico Pagani, Jr., M. Sgt. William Dominquez, M. Sgt. Ignacio Garcia, M. Sgt. David Stover.

Now once again we turned our thoughts to what General Milburn had said, reminding us that we now stood on the south bank of the river. The only remaining thing to do, of course, was wait for orders to cross it. So we continued our training.

I began to notice an increase in the number of refugees, particularly in our rear area. I had previously noted this same phenomenon elsewhere in Korea. When the war seesawed back and forth, the refugees just flowed with the tide. When we withdrew, the refugees streamed back with us. When we moved forward, they just followed along behind. What I feared most was that the enemy would use these columns of people to infiltrate into our positions, and we did indeed discover some enemy pockets of resistance isolated in our rear areas.

To clean out these nests I directed the 1st Battalion (reserve) to work forward toward the front lines and mop up; the front-line units were to work the area back to the regimental headquarters. Because the effectiveness of battalions and larger units is judged by what the small units, like the squads, sections, and platoons can do, I would like to relate several incidents that occurred at that time.

On 14 February, Company C was trying to clean out one of these pockets near the village of Hoha-dong. As the 1st Platoon moved up the hill where the enemy was known to be, it came under intense rifle and machine-gun fire. After thirty or forty minutes it became quite obvious that the platoon was in trouble. As hairy as it was, it could have become worse had it not been for the quick thinking and positive action taken by Cpl. Eduardo Maisonet-Zeno. Entirely on his own initiative he jumped to his feet and ran zigzag fashion nearly seventy yards toward the enemy. Since he was on open ground, with no cover or concealment, he immediately became the center target of the enemy's fire. When Maisonet-Zeno reached a point within throwing distance of the enemy's position, he calmly raised his hand and signaled for his platoon to hit the ground and cease firing. Then, in the same cool and collected manner, he started to heave grenades into the enemy's position. About three of those did it, for in short order the heavy firing ceased and the platoon was able to advance. Once on the position, the other men of his outfit were able to polish off the rest of the enemy in the pocket.

In another attack on one of these isolated spots, one of our companies tried to take a knoll we called Hill 88. As usual, the company again came under heavy machine-gun fire. The company called for mortar and artillery fire, but even that did not neutralize it. It was then that one individual stood up to be counted. Though it was not his responsibility to do so, 1st Lt. Harry J. Sternberg asked permission to attack it with hand grenades. Sternberg was the forward observer for our mortar company, and had he been just another individual, he might have just sat it out until help arrived. But being a man of action he proceeded to crawl forward until he reached a point about thirty yards from the enemy and then started to lob grenades at them. After several attempts to knock them out he realized that he would have to try from a different direction. Creeping and crawling around about the pillbox until he was on the opposite side, he again started to pitch his grenades. This time it worked, for the chatter of the gun stopped. The remainder of the company then cleaned up the hill, and that was the end of that story.

We moved into the month of March, which was fairly quiet, at least in the first half. This gave us more time to prepare for that crossing, and for this I was thankful. From a probable time schedule it now looked as though that operation would come off about the sixteenth. We increased our patrolling of the area and called for all the artillery fire that division and corps could give us to plaster the enemy positions along the riverbank and beyond.

One other effective means we found to reconnoiter the enemy positions was discovered by Charlie Boyle. He had found out from questioning the prisoners that the Chinese commanders had ordered their troops not to fire on low-flying aircraft. The idea was that doing this would only bring the heavy artillery and air bombing down harder. So, Charlie would fly as an observer in one of our light aircraft and have the pilot skim the tree tops, and he could get a really good look.

During one of these low flights Charlie saw two of our men struggling

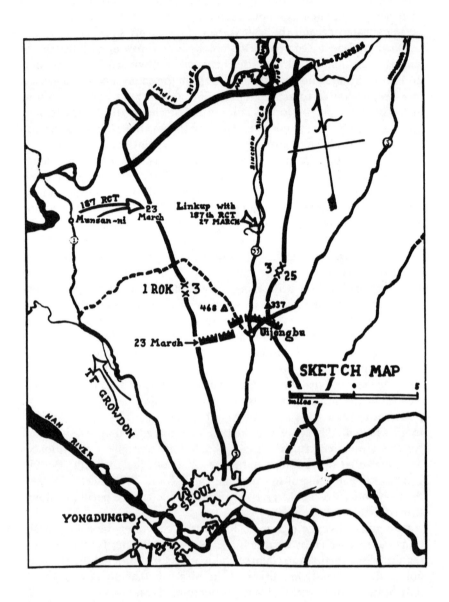

"Operation Tomahawk"

to cross a sandbar in the middle of the river, one was trying to drag and carry the other. Signaling to the pilot to land, Charlie loaded the two men in the aircraft and told the pilot to take off. He did this knowing full well that it would be well over an hour before the pilot could return to pick him up. Fortunately, the pilot did get back and pick up Boyle before dark.

It was also during this slack period that the 65th was to be given another honor, a combat infantry streamer for our flag. In a fine little ceremony not far from the front lines, the division commander made the presentation.

During this period we did learn some interesting things about the enemy. Fully nine out of every ten prisoners we captured were willing to surrender unconditionally and voluntarily because they were getting fed up with the Communist propaganda. Unquestionably, something was amiss across the river, because this was the first time we had had any indication that the Chinese weren't just as gung ho as ever. This could have been one of the reasons for what happened a short time later — this and the artillery and air bombing that we had been laying on them.

When the fateful day for the crossing finally arrived, we commenced our advance which would carry us to the water's edge. I shuddered every time I thought about it. Our patrols moved out; our boat crews prepared to launch; and our follow-up troops swung their light packs and rifles into place when we received our first air reconnaissance report. I couldn't believe it — the Chinese were pulling back in a general withdrawal. The Good Lord must have had his hand on our shoulders, for that crossing could have been murder.

The Chinese must have known that they could have cut us to ribbons — they couldn't help but know — yet here they were pulling back. It was almost unbelievable. Why they did what they did, we will probably never know. But with this good news we quickly halted our advance and made other plans.

These other plans consisted of sliding to the east and making our crossing on what was left of the Al Jolson Bridge — I don't know where this name came from. Opposition was so light that the entire operation became more of a Sunday stroll than a firefight.

As we continued down the road west to Seoul we became a bit more cautious. We noted some hastily placed land mines and other booby traps, which indicated that the Chinese were high tailing out and trying to gain time while they did so. It looked like they, too, were making one of those don't-run-walk withdrawals.

We were concerned, too, about the city itself. If the Chinese decided to stop there and make a stand, it could become pretty tough. But as we entered the outskirts, it became apparent that they had kept right on going — probably to the village of Ujonbu about thirty miles or so to the north. There is high ground there, and it does make an ideal place to defend.

We soon found that our estimate was correct, for the enemy did offer some resistance — about that of a rear guard action, for we pushed them back quite easily. Then the race was on. The Chinese literally took off in hurried flight, and we followed in hot pursuit. And I mean *hot*, for at times we actually had to run to keep up with them.

It was then that the high command decided to stage Operation Tomahawk. Eighth Army decided to drop the 187th Airborne RCT, Westmoreland commanding. The object was for "Westy's" outfit to cut off the retreat of the main elements of the Chinese force. The hooker as far as we were concerned was that the 65th was to hurry forward as fast as possible to give aid and assistance should the 187th run into trouble. (See sketch page 174.)

The drop zone was some fifteen miles or so north of our position, and I didn't really know how we could go any faster than we were going at the time. I mentioned this to the corps commander in a mild complaint. His reply was to the effect that the 187th had been in the theater for several months and had not seen any action and that the army commander thought that they should be "exercised."

If that's what they needed, they might relieve the 65th, and they would get all the exercising they wanted. I personally thought that it was an exercise in futility. But we just plugged along without saying any more and soon caught up with them. As it turned out, the Chinese had already cleared the drop zone and when last seen were still moving rapidly to the north. They didn't actually stop to make a determined stand until they reached the Imjin-Nantan River, but this turned out to be a real nasty one.

Draining the higher elevations around Ujonbu, this branch of the Imjin flows southwest, finally emptying into the Yellow Sea. Narrow and swift, with high banks on each side, it made an ideal defensive position. But even though the Chinese put up a stiff fight here, it really turned out to be only another holding action while they prepared for a counteroffensive.

This time, however, it was the British Brigade that was given the mission of making the initial crossing. They tried desperately two or three times to cross, but the strong, well-organized defensive position was too much for them. After some very serious losses to the brigade, the corps commander ordered them withdrawn, and the 65th was given the assignment.

I think that it should be pointed out that their failure to cross the Imjin should not in any way reflect upon the bravery, courage, and determination of the British. Our solution was no different from what the British had employed. They had assembled in a wooded area with short approaches to the riverbank, and we did too. They had started their assault at daybreak, and we did too. They had built rafts out of the trees from the wooded area in which they made their assembly. And so did we. They had plenty of mortar and artillery-support fire. They had their automatic weapons well placed to cover their movement across. Their boat crews seemed well disciplined. And I can go right on down the list and just say, "We did too."

To do this miserable job I selected the 2nd Battalion. We had an unwritten policy that we rotated the battalions on the "toughies," and it was the 2nd Battalion's turn. I was indeed glad that we had spent so much time preparing for the Han crossing, even though we had had it easy on that one. The training would certainly come in handy here. However, I missed Herb Dammer. He had been with me for the entire two years that I had commanded the 65th, but it was time for him to go on to something else.

Dammer's replacement was Lt. Col. L. A. Johnson — a fine officer, but I knew nothing about him. Dammer and the other battalion commanders I knew well. I knew what they would do under any kind of conditions, but I didn't have that knowledge about Johnson. I'll admit that his was the first shoulder I felt obliged to look over. I went over his plan of operation with him, and it seemed all right to me. I had nothing to add, so I told him to have at it. But I watched every move that he and the battalion made.

I did arrange for artillery fires to support him and gave him an air liaison officer to operate directly between him and our air coverage. And then, I just watched and prayed, for it was going to be tough.

Promptly at daybreak, Johnson launched his attack. The mortars and artillery opened with a terrific barrage while his automatic weapons concentrated on the enemy positions along the river bank. All was well so far, but then there was a considerable lapse in time before I saw any rafts hit the water. When they did, the two- and three-man boats launched first, followed by the six- and seven-man ones. There were even men hanging onto the sides of these rafts — and what was even more startling, I actually saw men swimming across. Not content to wait for the rafts to deliver their cargo and return, those men struck out on their own. This proved to be costly, for the enemy could and did pick them off like ducks in the pond. Those on the rafts had a bit more protection, for they could get down behind the logs on the top of the raft, but those swimming were just bobbing targets. And the drift of the rafts worried me, too, for they seemed to be going more downstream than across. This gave the enemy longer to fire at them. The quicker they got across the better.

As morning turned into afternoon, and the shadows began to appear, I thought that if we got caught with darkness and still not across we would sure be in trouble. Then the picture began to change, for I saw some of our men on the far shore engaged in hand-to-hand combat. At least we had gained a foothold, and with some luck maybe we could get the follow-up troops over in time to secure it. And this Johnson did. The entire operation proved successful for no other reason than that the Puerto Ricans were determined that they would not let the Chinese stop them. They had accomplished their mission against terrific odds.

As we were to see later, this delaying action at the Imjin was only intended to hold us up while they prepared for an even more stubborn defense farther down the road. This did not come immediately, for we were able to continue our advance for several more weeks. Thus, the month of March passed into history. The following month was a different story.

9

THE CHINESE
SPRING OFFENSIVE

April started off with little offensive action by the Chinese, and we spent a goodly portion of our time in aggressive patrolling in order to maintain contact. Toward the middle of the month, enemy activity began to increase. By the end of the month the situation burst wide open, and once more we found ourselves in that now familiar routine of walk-don't-run-to-the-rear called an "orderly withdrawal."

I guess that you could characterize that time as one of those seesaw operations. It included such events as: our further move to the north; our occupation of Line Kansas just south of the 38th parallel; attacking missions into North Korean territory; our occupation of the Utah Line still farther to the north; our breaking up of an enemy all-out attack on us while we occupied the Utah Line (See sketch page 180); and then our withdrawal to prearranged defensive positions which included the 65th's designation again as division reserve located in the city of Seoul.

Operations such as these always produce a large number of casualties and ours were no exception. By the end of April our official records showed our battle casualties to be: KIA — 133, WIA — 577, MIA — 33 for a total of 743 since our arrival in Korea.

As a footnote to these casualty figures it should be mentioned that most of our nonbattle casualties were returned to us, and the total loss was therefore minimal. As an example, for the month of April we had 186 nonbattle casualties. During the same period, we had 164 of the same category and 6 battle casualties returned to us. Most of our nonbattle losses were due to eye, ear, and throat problems caused by the dusty roads. Other causes were listed as fractures, joint ailments, dental con-

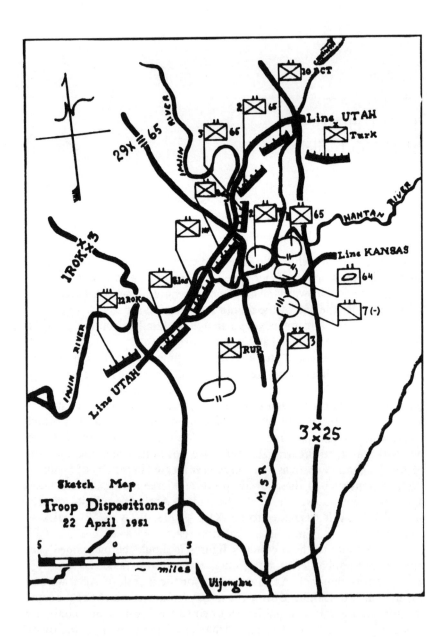

sultations, and chicken pox. We had few foot problems because of our continued daily inspection by all commanders, even during combat. And our self-inflicted wounds were almost nonexistent.

As for the latter category, we had jumped onto that one very early in the game after our arrival in Korea — about the time of the Hamhung-Hungnam affair — when for the first time we were confronted with the hordes of Chinese. It was then that we noticed a sudden rash of fingers and toes being shot off as a result of enemy action. All of these men were recruits inducted into the service as fillers. They had not yet learned all the traditions of the proud 65th. I wasn't too concerned at the moment, but should the trend continue, it could get out of hand.

Our solution turned out to be a fortunate one — a lucky guess I suppose you could call it. First, we appointed a summary court officer for each battalion aid station. When a suspected case of this nature came in, the summary court officer would try the case with all witnesses present. In most cases the man was found guilty of "inflicting a wound upon himself in order to avoid hazardous duty" and given a minor sentence like, "to walk back to his front line unit." In some cases this was a pretty good punishment, but the real punishment came when the man later applied for his veterans benefits and found out there were none. His conviction of a self-inflicted wound negated any benefits, and it didn't take long for everyone to realize that it wasn't worth it.

Comparing our losses, all of them, to the number of enemy we were officially credited with either capturing or killing it was quite obvious that the 65th was inflicting a far worse punishment on the enemy than he was on us. The official records by the end of April showed that we were credited with: POWs captured as of 31 March — 1906; total captured as of 30 April — 2,005; total enemy killed as of 31 March — 3,261; total enemy killed as of 30 April — 3,261; total KIA for the month of April — 2,188. Comparing our losses with those we inflicted on the enemy, we had a ratio of 10 to 1 in our favor.

Now, back to the operation and our position on the Utah Line: We had crossed the Imjin and had advanced north of the 38th parallel when suddenly the Chinese started to play their high cards. As I recollect, it all started on 23 April, when we encountered very heavy resistance.

Up to that time they had been steadily withdrawing, and we had only maintained contact by aggressive patrolling, but this time they held fast. Suspecting the worst, we prepared for a counterattack; it was fortunate that we did, for they really hit us. E and F Companies were the first to get it when shortly after midnight of the twenty-fourth about one thousand Chinese smashed into the 2nd Battalion. The attack was so fierce that Johnson had to pull back several hundred yards and consolidate his positions.

In the meantime, our 3rd Battalion was able to hold in place, but the Philippine Battalion, which was attached to us during this period, was forced to withdraw to more favorable ground.

As for the 1st Battalion, it was able to hold until about three in the morning when it, too, was forced to move back. In the dark such a move becomes extremely difficult. In fact, about four that morning my CP came under terrific artillery fire, and we were forced to move in the dark too. It was as though the enemy had laid hands on our defensive plans just as we had theirs at an earlier date.

The Chinese were putting heavy pressure on our entire line, for I heard shortly after we moved my headquarters that the Turkish Brigade had fallen back some ten or twelve miles. They were on our right and with that much gap on my flank, we could have been in deep trouble. It was my observation that as long as the Turks were on the offensive and the Chinese were running, the Turks were pretty good. But when the going was tough, they were hard to find. As a matter of fact, it took me a day or so before I could convince the corps and army staffs that the Turks were not where they said they were.

On our left flank we had that reliable, unflappable British Brigade, and they really caught hell. They were on the army left flank, and one of their battalions was overextended to the front. As I reconstructed the Chinese attack later, it seemed to me that the main thrust had been at the 65th and our boundary with the British. I believe that the enemy attack bounced off us, spilled over on both sides of us and then concentrated on the British and the Turks. I didn't realize how critical the situation was in the British sector until about 2 or 3 A.M., the morning of the attack, when Shorty Soule called me on the phone and ordered me to go over to the brigade position and see if I could give the brigadier some help in extracting his Gloucester Battalion.

I reminded Soule that everything I had was already engaged, and that we were fighting for our lives. Our condition didn't seem to concern him at the time, for he repeated that he wanted me to go over there and see what I could do. So off I went. It was only a few miles, no more than a forty-minute drive, and I arrived there just about daybreak. What I saw and heard scared hell out of me.

Their CP tent was actually being hit by rifle bullets, and the entire area was being bombarded with heavy mortars. I didn't really know whether I should stay or take off. What in hell I could do to help them I didn't really know. Soule had said something about helping them extract the Gloucesters, but it seemed to me that the brigadier himself was going to need some help.

When I walked into the tent they were having a staff meeting. I had seen a lot of the British during World War II, so I was not at all surprised to see them doing what they were doing. Seeing me enter, the Brigadier came over to welcome me and then offered me tea.

With that, the four of us made ourselves as comfortable as possible under the circumstances. I had brought along my artillery and air liaison officers and my tank company commander. Believe me, it was worth the price of admission to see the look on each of their faces. This was the first time any of them had seen such a display of complete indifference to what was going on around them. All the time we were sitting there the bullets were whizzing through the top of the tent and the mortars were exploding around the outside — if one of them had registered on the tent it would have been just too bad for all of us.

When the brigadier finally finished his staff meeting, he walked over to where we were and said something to the effect that he really didn't know what good I could do, for the Gloucesters had been cut off for over twenty-four hours. He also said that he had been warning Shorty Soule for the previous thirty-six hours or so that if they didn't authorize him to draw them back they were going to be cut off. It seems as though Soule had said that he would keep a good watch on the situation and would authorize the withdrawal if and when it became serious. The brigadier was furious, and I didn't blame him.

After a short discussion, I believe it was the consensus that there was little we could do to help under the circumstances. I did agree, however, to send the one tank platoon that I had available, but we all knew that that was sending too little too late. This ultimately proved to be the case. The Gloucester Battalion of over eight hundred men was lost. Perhaps two or three were able to escape, but that was all.

In fact, I was sure that the entire incident would be considered a major catastrophe by the British government and that a formal investigation would be made. Very frankly, I would have done just that had I been in their position. Feeling so strongly about it, I had Chick make an investigation of our own. He took testimony from all the witnesses available. When he completed it, we were found to be not at fault in any way. I did not intend to be the fall guy, if it came down to that. So far as I know, no investigation was ever made.

By now the Chinese pressure was beginning to build up stronger than ever. And we continued to give ground, slowly at first and then later at a dead heat. Finally on the twenty-seventh the entire 3rd Division was

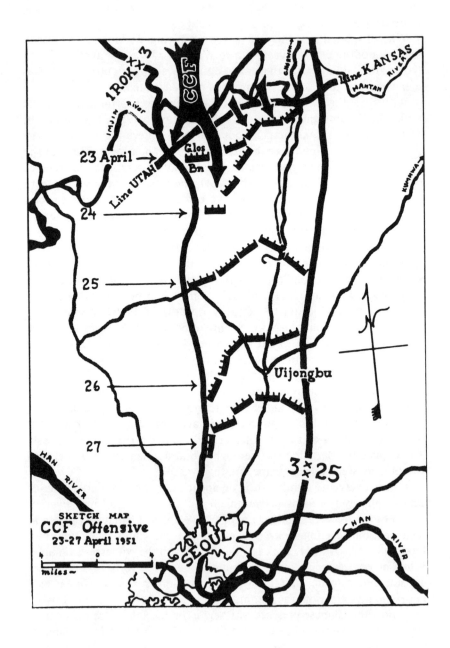

SKETCH MAP
CCF Offensive
23-27 April 1951

miles~

ordered back to Seoul in corps reserve. There we were to start the forti-fication of the city while the other troops of the corps moved back. It had been decided that we would not let them push us back across the Han; we would make our stand in the city.

However, between 24 and 27 April, the regiment was engaged in some pretty heavy action. (See sketch page 184.) I became particularly con-cerned that we not have a battalion or a company cut off as had hap-pened to the Gloucesters. The timing of our battalion withdrawals became highly important to insure that we didn't leave one of them hanging out in the breeze. In fact, at one point it took an actual bayonet charge by the combined forces of B and K Companies before the 1st and 3rd Battalions could continue their moves to the rear. In that fracas those two companies killed an estimated 150 Chinese.

Initially I guess that the 1st and 3rd Battalions were the hardest hit, but then the 2nd didn't fare much better. As an example, in one engage-ment one company and the battalion headquarters were completely sur-rounded by the Chinese. Caught up in this melee was the regimental Mortar Company, which had to abandon all of its mortars. We quickly executed a strong counterattack and recovered all but one of the mortars.

As we pulled back and beat off the constant enemy pressure, we were finally able to reorganize our ground positions and hold in one position long enough to organize the next spot to the rear. These holding posi-tions were given us in not only the 3rd Division sector but in the others as well. For example, we were directed to provide two battalions to help the 25th U.S. Infantry Division extract themselves from the hordes of Chinese. At another time we were ordered into a blocking position behind the British Brigade, and so it went, on back toward the city of Seoul. All of this was of course labeled an orderly withdrawal, but at times it became pretty hairy.

When we finally arrived at the outskirts of the city, we did breathe more easily because some rather extensive defensive emplacements had been set up there. We had sent a few troops back there even before we arrived, and they had already started on these fortifications. Individual foxholes, connecting trenches, positions for the crew-served weapons, command posts, and much, much barbed wire. I believe that those em-placements were worthy of any ever built during World War II. In fact, they greatly resembled those that we had built for the Vieques maneuvers.

We set to immediately finish the job of digging in. While the troops were doing this, the staff was busy making plans to counterattack.

The United Nations Forces had been hard hit, but our withdrawal had been orderly even though I may have joked about it from time to time. What's more, the Chinese had paid dearly for their recklessness.

The number of the enemy both killed and captured by the 65th has already been shown, and its record of achievements had become common knowledge. Known not only on the battlefield and in Puerto Rico but in the United States as well, the Borinqueneers of the 65th had by now established themselves as fierce combat soldiers. The *Far East Command Stars and Stripes* carried an article about how the "hot news" of the 65th took precedence over any other news and that letters and pictures got almost unlimited space in the papers.

A truly fine tribute to those extraordinary Puerto Rican soldiers. But, I guess the most tangible accolade which the men of the 65th received was this:

Carlos E. Seijo
P.O. Box 3364, San Juan, PR

Colonel William W. Harris
Commanding Officer
65th Inf. Regiment, Third Inf. Division
APO 468, San Francisco, California

Dear Colonel Harris:

Today I am shipping one hundred cases of Don Q rum as a compliment of Destileria Serralles, Inc. to you and your brave Regiment that have put the name of Puerto Rico so dear to our hearts.

For months we have been trying to ship this, but today we have authorization from the Commander-in-Chief of the Far East Command, so, you have to pardon the delay on the arrival of this present.

Everybody in Ponce — Fao, Tito, Geno, Armando, Adrian, and Poppy — are sending their best wishes and regards and we all expect the finishing of the war and see you back once more in Ponce.

With my sincere wishes and the best of luck, I remain,

Sincerely yours,
[Signed] CARLOS E. SEIJO

I had met all those whom Don Carlos had mentioned and had found all of them friendly and warm toward the Continentals in the 65th. And so I responded immediately to his letter, thanked him and the Destileria Serralles Corporation for their kindness, and asked to be remembered to all my friends both in Ponce (the location of the destileria) and elsewhere on the island.

The prospect of getting one hundred cases of Don Q rum was almost as good a feeling as the evacuation from the Hamhung-Hungnam perimeter. I had received this letter just before we were ordered back to Seoul, so I hoped that the rum would arrive while we were there. What joy to be in reserve and with one hundred cases of rum.

But the more I thought about it, the more convinced I was that the shipment would probably be sent to Pusan, and that was several hundred miles away. Anything could happen to it en route. One hundred cases of rum would be a temptation to both Korean and American personnel at the base section. They would also be the target of what might whimsically be called the train crew, like the "engineer" who tooted and whistled down the track until he had attracted the attention of the guerrillas who attacked us when we arrived in Korea. Then I remembered that Brig. Gen. Paul F. Yount, a West Point classmate of mine was in command of the base section at Pusan, and I decided to call him from the field telephone in my headquarters.

It took about twenty-four hours before we could make a decent hookup, but I finally got him. I told Paul about the shipment and then asked him if he would place a guard around it until I could get a detail down there to pick it up. Paul promised that he would, and then I told him to keep one case for his trouble.

Our convoy and guard detail made the trip down and back without incident and arrived at our headquarters just the day before we pulled into our reserve location in Seoul. Much planning had gone into this operation — as much as any of our plans for the withdrawal. We decided, for example, to split the cache, issue one half to the top three graders and then save the other half for a later date. When the issue was made, we suggested to the noncoms that they share with all ranks.

The issue was made and I would hazard a guess that the fifty cases lasted all of fifty minutes. With over five thousand troops, the mathematics of the number of swigs it took to consume the lot are apparent. The other half was placed under guard as we had planned, and as we moved into our reserve position in Seoul we hauled it with us. Now for the last half.

But that moment didn't come, at least not when we had planned it. I no more than drove into our new CP when I was told that we had been ordered to hit the trail again. It seemed as though the Chinese had been able to penetrate our eastern flank, and the 7th ROK and the 2nd U.S. Division were in trouble. The 3rd had been ordered to move as rapidly as possible clear across the width of the Korean Peninsula, some one hundred miles or more to the east, and plug the gap — and there went another of those rest periods in reserve.

We didn't even stop the columns moving into our new location, just wheeled into the CP area and kept right on going — north and east. Other information regarding the situation was relayed to me by radio as we traveled. Apparently the Chinese had hit at the boundary between the 7th ROK Division and the U.S. 2nd near a village named Changpyong-ni. It was reported, too, that the Chinese force consisted of both the 12th and 27th CCF Armies — quite a sizable attack. It resulted in the 7th ROK Division exploding and going in all directions. This left the American 2nd Division with its right flank completely exposed, and it was being mauled a bit too.

Our move of over one hundred miles to the east was made more difficult because we were cutting directly across our own north-south supply lines, and the flow of refugess streaming back and forth. By traveling day and night we were able to reach the area in about thirty-six hours. We had also kept abreast of the situation by radio and were, therefore, fairly well informed when we arrived there.

To say that the situation was confused is an understatement, for North Korean, South Korean, and Chinese troops were intermingled in one great big scrap. And I am afraid that none of us could tell the difference between any of them. As a result, the usual orders, which were now SOP, prevailed. They were if you don't know or cannot recognize the soldiers confronting you, take them prisoner — or kill them if they resist. Simple and direct orders.

We had seen the danger of assuming that because soldiers were dressed in ROK uniforms they were automatically South Korean troops. For instance, not long after our arrival in Korea we heard the story of some supposedly South Korean soldiers who drove into the CP of the Dutch Brigade. They said they were out of food, ammunition, and medical supplies and would the Dutch help them. The brigadier summoned his staff, ordered each of them to give what assistance was required and then stood and talked with the "South Korean commander" of the detachment. The "ROKs" helped themselves to all of the goodies, formed in two ranks, saluted the generous brigadier, marched off fifty paces, wheeled about, and killed the entire Dutch staff, including the brigadier. I had decided then and there that we didn't want any of that. We trusted no one, and we didn't get into that kind of trouble the entire time we were in Korea.

For several days we tried to restore order out of the confusion. Then I received word that the ROK Commander of the 7th Division was "upset" because the 65th had disarmed and placed under guard at least three-fourths of his division. I immediately sent him my apologies and informed him that if he could identify to me which were his troops, I would have them released at once. This took some doing because I was not about to release anyone just because he happened to be wearing an ROK uniform. But it all worked out. After several days he had his troops back under control and no serious diplomatic error had been committed. We were now ordered back to our original assignment with the I Corps and positioned near the village of Samsan-ni. From our location to Samsan-ni was about one hundred and fifty miles, and we arrived back there on 31 May.

Great credit I think is due our regimental supply section under the able command of my supply officer, Maj. Augustin Ramirez. We had traveled across and back the entire width of the Korean Peninsula, a total of over three hundred miles, without a major incident or a breakdown of our vehicles — a major accomplishment in itself. The really remarkable part of that story is that most of our vehicles were the same ones that had gone through the Vieques maneuvers and the war up to this point. It should be remembered that just prior to that maneuver Ramirez had told me that our vehicles were in bad shape. What's more, with very few minor exceptions, we never had a serious breakdown in our supply position. Ramirez was truly a great supply officer and a fine gentleman.

With the close of the month of May the official records showed that the 65th had been credited with the following: POWs captured — 2,086; Enemy killed — 5,905. As I recollect, these totals would just about add up to the equivalent of one NKPA or CCF Infantry Division. Now back to the Western front.

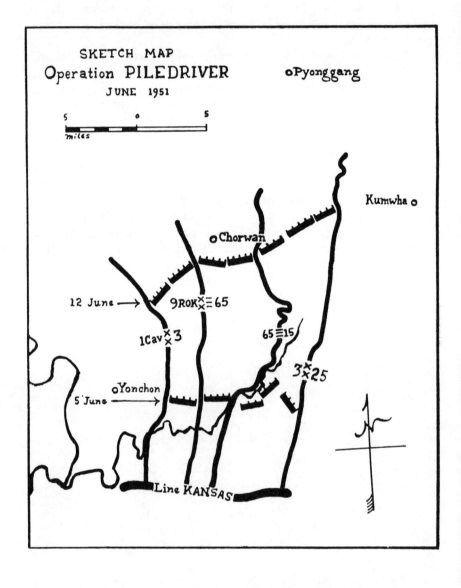

10

CHORWAN
AND THE IRON TRIANGLE

Back with I Corps, enemy action was light. We took the opportunity to celebrate our fifty-second anniversary. A one-battalion parade, a holiday, some special food, and the last of our Don Q rum were the principal items on the program. We also received some congratulatory messages which are reproduced in the Appendix.

On the first of June, orders were issued for the I Corps to again take the offensive. The Corps plan was part of the general offensive of Eighth Army with the principal objective being to "secure the village of Chorwan and control the Iron Triangle."

Our intelligence agencies had determined early in 1951 that the main Chinese depot for both personnel and supplies was located north of one branch of the Imjin River in the small village of Chorwan. It was the center of a north-south, east-west road and rail net that reached across the peninsula; we called it "The Iron Triangle."

Eighth Army believed that if we could seize that valley and control Chorwan and the Iron Triangle, we would break the backbone of the Chinese defenses in Korea. And as usual, when the 65th took its place back on the line in I Corps, we found ourselves pointed due north at the principal objective, Chorwan. (See sketch page 190.)

Named "Operation Piledriver," the new offensive jumped off by our relieving the Canadian Brigade on Line Sword. This was on the south bank of the Imjin River, that old familiar stream where we had met up with the British Brigade. This time, however, the Canadian Brigade had already pushed the Chinese across to the north side, and at least we didn't have that problem staring us in the face.

With the 1st Battalion on the right, the 2nd on the left, and the 3rd in reserve, we pushed off on schedule with the other troops of the I Corps. We hadn't moved more than a mile or so before we encountered heavy resistance and then one counterattack after another. The 1st and 2nd Battalion got the worst of it, and I believe that those encounters were from June 1 to 4. By the seventh, however, we were securely positioned north of the river starting our preparations for the final drive toward Chorwan.

Operation Piledriver was soon in full swing. I don't believe the fighting was nearly as heavy, though, as some of our other skirmishes had been — the Spring Offensive of the Chinese, for example. I could be wrong, but it seemed to me at the time that the high command in Peking had decided "to hell with it — it wasn't worth it." Chinese losses had been terrific.

Most of the action we participated in consisted of company or smaller-unit fighting. There was no need for the employment of battalions or larger units. No question about it, the Chinese were falling back. However, some of the small-unit action was pretty bloody. A few that I remember though were decisive, because winning the little ones enabled us to continue our advance without serious interruption.

One of these small-unit actions consisted of one man. Here is how the 3rd Division newspaper, *The Front Line,* reported it:

Borinqueneer Manhandles MG
to Keep Reds Lying Low

The Hollywood style of shooting a thirty-caliber machine gun from the hip may not always be practical, but Cpl. Armando Rosa of D Company, 65th Infantry has found it quite effective.

The corporal, attached to elements of B and C Company during a recent Chinese attack, used this method of keeping the enemy from breathing down the necks of the Puerto Ricans as they effected an orderly withdrawal.

On a foggy morning the enemy attacked near Rosa's position at the forward point of the defensive line. Rosa leaped up from his hole, firing from the hip, and backed from the enemy with the gun blazing. He crossed two ridges in this manner, keeping the Chinese forward movement at a slow crawl. He enabled the rest of his company to take up defensive positions by his action. No accurate account of the enemy killed by Rosa is available, but he fired a total of 3,500 rounds by himself, and all from the hip.

Another of those little ones occurred near the village of Sunbong-ni. Here the Chinese had selected a piece of high ground to make a stand where it absolutely dominated our route of advance. We called it Hill

466, and when we got within sight there was no doubt in our minds that we would have to control it if we were to continue on our present route. It rose from the middle of the valley floor, and I estimated that while it was only about seven or eight hundred feet in height, any enemy sitting on top would definitely be in a commanding position.

From where I stood several miles to the south viewing it through my field glasses, there didn't seem to be any reason why we shouldn't be able to take it. It didn't really look much different from all of the other hills we had encountered. However, the sun was still low in the sky and the entire area was obscured by a thick haze, and I couldn't make out too many of the details.

By the next afternoon when we were a little closer to it and I had a clearer view, the whole picture had changed dramatically. Instead of the usual thirty- or forty-degree slope, this one was scraggy and precipitous for the most part. The cliffs seemed to jut out from the side of the hill and then drop straight down fifty feet or more. They were not quite like the Cliffs of Dover, but that's the general idea.

However, cliffs or no cliffs, the capture of Hill 466 was essential; it was the key to our advance up the valley toward Chorwan. After some discussion with my staff, we decided that with our disposition of the 1st Battalion on the right and the 2nd on the left, we would let St. Clair have the first go at it. Our 2nd Battalion would then be prepared to attack from the west, if that became necessary, and the 3rd would be prepared to follow up wherever.

We prepared mortar and artillery fires and air support missions, initially in support of the 1st Battalion, with secondary targets on the west slopes, and finally with TOTs on the top of the hill. Since this could turn out to be a pretty good fight, we gave the Tank Company some direct fire missions on the west slopes. Not wishing to leave anything to chance, we also notified the 15th Infantry on our right and the 9th ROK Division on our left of our plans.

Particular attention was given to the 9th ROK because I still didn't trust our Korean Allies. And just to make sure that they didn't pull some uncoordinated move while we were attacking Hill 466, I sent a liaison officer to their headquarters. He spoke fluent Korean, and he had a radio tuned into my command net. I wanted to know every move they made — before they made it.

As planned, the attack jumped off at first light the morning of 3 June, but it didn't go very far. Both assault companies came under heavy fire immediately — rifle, automatic rifle, mortars and artillery — and were pinned to the ground. Movement from there on was slow and dangerous because of a lack of communications. When the troops deployed, they had about fifty or one hundred feet between riflemen in an irregular pattern, and each man was more concerned with finding maximum cover and concealment than with staying in communication with his squad or platoon leader.

But to be effective, squad, platoon, and company commanders, especially, must be in close contact with their units. New targets, targets of opportunity, shifting of fires, concentration of fires, changing direction of movement, and other actions are necessary to meet changes in the situation. And only with well-trained and disciplined troops can this be accomplished. We had fortunately spent many training hours on such techniques, and our leaders were able to maintain that very necessary communication.

And a good thing, too, for Saint realized that if his men stalled in their present positions, they would soon be wiped out, and he ordered his company commanders to move forward by squad rushes. Within two hours or less we were at the base of Hill 466. The question now was how to get to the top and close with the enemy. A Company faced an immediate climb up the cliffs, while B would have a more gradual slope of several hundred yards before reaching the steep part of the hill. In either case, however, the cliffs were there to be scaled.

After we had discussed it, Saint decided to employ both companies at the same time. He figured that he would have several advantages by doing it this way. First, it would save time by not having to wait to find out whether one or the other of his companies could make it. Secondly, by having the two companies attack at the same time, the enemy would not be able to concentrate his fires on any one area. The overriding consideration was time — Saint just did not want his men to be fighting on those cliffs after dark.

Our biggest problem in making this ascent was the lack of mountain-climbing equipment. We didn't even have materials that could be used as substitutes for pitons, grappling hooks, or spiked shoes. We did have some picks, but they were of the construction type; too heavy for climbing mountains. But this lack of professional equipment did not stop the men of A and B Companies. As stated, "They climbed the hills with the tenacity of a goat." However, from what I saw and heard later, I doubt whether even a goat could have gone where some of those men climbed.

The case of Pfc. Monserrate Vega-Vega and some others are typical examples. Stripped of all of his equipment except his canteen and medical kit, with his rifle slung across his back, Vega began his climb. Slowly, inch by inch, he made his way up those scraggly cliffs by pure brute

Rifle crew of M Company, 3rd Battalion, with a 75mm recoilless rifle, guarding a valley north of Chorwan. 15 June 1951. U.S. ARMY PHOTO

Battle weary soldiers return to safety behind the lines after two days of being trapped north of the Han River, June 1951. U.S. ARMY PHOTO

Guarding the Chorwan Reservoir; 19 June 1951. U.S. ARMY PHOTO

Men of the 65th kneel in prayer at a memorial mass honoring their fallen comrades.

strength and determination. Stopping to rest from time to time, with his life hanging in the balance every minute of the way, he finally reached a small ledge not more than ten feet or so from the top of the hill. So far so good, for he had been climbing for about three hours, and the enemy had still not discovered him.

In the meantime, other men of the two companies had started their climb up the cliffs. Some of those others whom I know made the climb and blazed the trail were: Pfc. Julio C. Torres, Sgt. Carlos Bonet Morales, Pfc. Juan F. Rodriguez Forty, Lt. Sherman K. Burke, Lt. Armando Medina Olivera. I only regret that I am unable to list the names of every one in A and B Companies who followed along behind that initial group without giving it a second thought.

Watching his men as they neared the top without being discovered, Saint figured that the enemy must have decided that those cliffs were too difficult to climb and had concentrated its attention on the western slopes. Hoping to take advantage of this mistake, he called me on the radio and informed me that he was going to commit C Company to the west side of the hill. I agreed with his decision and assured him that the other battalions would be alerted to come to his rescue in case he got into trouble. If he could only keep the enemy's attention fixed on the west slope, it would improve the chances of Vega and the others of reaching the top before dark.

Then, to give a further assist to Saint, we ordered our mortars and artillery to lay down a concentration of fire on the top of the hill ahead of C Company. Air strikes in the same area were called in. With all of this firepower, the company was able to make good progress.

The climbers fared well, too, and a large number of them were able to reach the top before they were discovered. It was then that the real scramble got under way. Neither side was able to get a good shot at the other because of the irregular features of the terrain, the rocks and boulders, so the fight started out as a grenade-throwing contest. But as the build-up of our troops continued and our numbers increased, our men started a bayonet charge across the top of the hill and literally herded those Chinese into the arms of the men of C Company. Caught between these two forces, it was only a matter of minutes before all organized resistance was eliminated.

By this time it was dark and our men spent the rest of the night organizing their positions and trying to eliminate individual snipers. When morning arrived it was all over, for it became a simple process to either capture or kill the rest of the Chinese and take control of Hill 466.

From here on in the road to Chorwan was comparatively easy. We did encounter some small resistance, but by and large it appeared that the Chinese had decided to withdraw back to the North, possibly even back across the Yalu. We came to this hopeful conclusion, for it was just about this time that we heard the first rumors of a peace conference. These were carried in several articles in the *Stars and Stripes* and apparently had originated in Peking. It appeared that the Chinese were ready to talk peace, and if my memory serves me correctly it was 18 June 1951. On that day we were sitting on the high ground overlooking Chorwan and the roads to Pyonggang and Kumwha — the Iron Triangle.

Sitting peacefully with nothing to do was never a part of my life with the 65th, and this was no exception. Within four days after our arrival at Chorwan, I received a call from Col. Edgar T. Conley, G-1 of Eighth Army. Conley informed me that since I had had command of the 65th for over two years, it was now time for my reassignment. He further stated that Brigadier General Milburn, the G-1 of General MacArthur's headquarters, wanted me assigned to his office in Tokyo. I did not know *this* Milburn, but I understood that he was either a cousin or some other relative of my present corps commander, Lt. Gen. F. W. Milburn. I told Conley that I would give the idea some thought and call him back later.

My corps commander had also asked me what I would like to do when time came for my reassignment. I replied that I had hoped to be assigned as a student at the National War College, and that was still my preference. A short time later I was advised that both Maj. Gen. Robert H. Soule, the 3rd Division commander, and the corps commander, Lt. Gen. F. W. Milburn, had recommended to the Department of Army that I be selected to go there. Shortly thereafter I received a copy of General Milburn's recommendation to the Department of Army. A copy of this recommendation follows:

CICCG 230.2   11 May 1951

Subject: Recommendation for attendance at the National War College
Thru: Commanding General
         Eighth Army
         APO 301, U.S. Army
To: The Adjutant General
         Department of Army
         The Pentagon
         Washington, D.C.

1. I strongly urge the consideration of Colonel William W. Harris for attendance at the National War College. Colonel Harris has commanded the 65th Infantry Regiment since July of 1949, bringing it into Korea and

combat in the fall of 1950. In that capacity he has been under my direct observation and I am personally familiar with his work and qualifications.

2. His service during that period has been outstanding in every way, earning him universal respect. Through his superior leadership the 65th has developed into a fine fighting unit, and his direction of that unit in combat has clearly demonstrated his even greater potential for the future.

3. He possesses the requisite attributes for such schooling to a marked degree and is a most promising officer.

[Signed] F. W. MILBURN
LIEUTENANT GENERAL, U.S. ARMY COMMANDING

As it turned out I did not attend the National War College that year but was assigned as a student for the class of 1952-53. As for Conley's call to me, it appeared from where we sat that the war was over. We had orders to sit tight — no more advances, no more artillery bombardment. Peace talks were in the offing, and no one wanted to rock the boat. And so the more I thought about it, the more the idea appealed to me. I was tired, and the thought of some physical rest in a staff job was too good to turn down. I told Conley I would accept.

The 65th, of course, remained in Korea for another year or so and was then returned to Puerto Rico. Shortly thereafter the regiment was inactivated in accordance with the Pentagon's reduction in force policy.

Telling Conley that I would take the job was the easy part, however, for leaving the 65th was a bit emotional. We had a small parade as a departing ceremony. We hoisted a few drams of rum in a gathering of all the officers after the parade, then I said a few words to the assembled noncoms and quickly jumped into my jeep and departed for Seoul — I wanted no prolonged and agonizing departure, and that is what it could have been had I delayed any longer.

But while at the time I thought that my departure was a bit on the emotional side, it was minor compared to my feelings upon receiving the following two letters after my arrival in Tokyo.

Headquarters 65th Infantry

22 June 1951

Colonel W. W. Harris
Commanding Officer
65th Infantry Regiment
APO 468, U.S. Army

Dear Sir:

As senior Insular Officer present in your command I take this opportunity to express to you and to some extent the deeply rooted gratitude and appreciation of myself, and my fellow Puerto Ricans, both military and civilians, for the great and unselfish services which you have rendered above and beyond the normal offices of your position as commanding officer of the regiment.

Our mutual sentiments are that through your tireless efforts, not only has the 65th Infantry become one of the most outstanding regiments of the U.S. Army, but the respect and acceptance of the Island of Puerto Rico and its people have been indelibly impressed upon the minds of our fellow Americans, and other United Nations people; to say nothing of the lasting impression which must be in the minds of our present and potential enemies.

It has been a pleasure and a privilege to serve as a member of your command, and I feel sure that I express the wholehearted opinion of every insular member of this organization when I say that we shall look forward to a time in the near future when we may again have the pleasure of your presence and family in our beloved Puerto Rico, and the privilege of serving under your command.

Sincerely yours,
[Signed] AUGUSTIN A. RAMIREZ

Headquarters 65th Infantry

22 June 1951

Colonel W. W. Harris
Headquarters 65th Infantry
APO 468, U.S. Army

Dear Colonel Harris:

Please, for the purpose of this letter, let me go back to the status I was when the colonel took command of the 65th Infantry Regiment about two years ago.

As your Regimental Sergeant Major and primarily due to your willingness to let your ranks display their initiative I had the privilege and the honor of being one of your closest advisers in the regiment. Colonel, this democratic way of handling the affairs of our regiment permitted me to know personally the big job you had placed on your shoulders, to make out of the 65th Regiment, as it is considered now, one of the best regiments in the United States Army. Not only have you made the 65th one of our best regiments, but in addition you have made the Island of Puerto Rico, and the Puerto Ricans, known to many peoples of many nationalities.

I have the privilege of personally knowing the many times and the many ways you fought and defended our capabilities as soldiers and as citizens. I still remember your words one day, "Somebody has been selling the Puerto Rican soldiers too low." And, "I have never seen a bunch of men more willing to do their jobs even in adverse conditions." Sir, those words were the result of one of your inspections during PORTREX at Vieques Island in 1950 — our first victory under your command. The prelude of the actions of the 65th some months later on the battlefields of Korea.

Sir, a few months after your arrival to take command of this regiment you stated, "I would not hesitate to go into combat with these troops." Those words became a reality and it is my only hope, and I am sure that all members of the regiment feel the same way, that you feel satisfied and as happy as we feel, of the realization of your prediction. Your name, Colonel, will be a part of the history of this regiment; you are deeply in the hearts of all men who followed and will follow you wherever you go. You opened a door, for so many years closed, to the Puerto Rican soldier, a door that I am sure we will keep open in your memory.

Please, Colonel, pardon me for writing so much, but I know so many reasons as to why we are so grateful to you that I am afraid of not being able to express what I feel.

To close, Sir, and on behalf of all Puerto Ricans, please accept our eternal and deepest gratitude for all your kindness and all your valuable efforts made in our behalf.

Please accept my best wishes for health and success in your new assignment and for many years to come.

Sincerely yours,
[Signed] VICTOR M. NAVAS
1ST LT. 65TH INFANTRY

Colorado Command Post
Office of The Former Commander
65th United States Infantry Regiment

16 November 1979

To: Major Augustin A. Ramirez
         1st Lt. Victor M. Navas
         All Former Members 65th Infantry Regiment

Señors,

I regret that it has taken me these twenty-five years to write the glorious history of the 65th United States Infantry Regiment during that first year of combat in Korea. Among other accomplishments, it is my fervent hope that *From San Juan to Chorwan* will express to "Carno" and to Navas, and to all of you, how completely happy and satisfied I am with the performance of the men of the 65th under my command during that first year of the Korean War. You were magnificent.

Not only did you of the 65th fulfill my predictions but by your outstanding performance of duty, your courage, and your bravery, you evoked the praise and admiration of every one there from the rank and file GIs to the most senior of them all, General Douglas MacArthur. They were all proud to be called your comrades-in-arms, and I was the proudest of them all.

I further hope that this history of the Borinqueneers in Korea will convince others what you and I know to be a fact, that the men of the 65th United States Infantry Regiment were the best damn soldiers in that war. Viva 65th.

Vaya con Dios
W. W. HARRIS
BRIG. GEN. U.S. ARMY RET.

AUTHOR'S NOTE —

It had never occurred to me at the start of this narrative how difficult it would be to describe battle. I have participated in many of them, and I just never thought that there would be a problem relating my experiences. Actually there is no real problem describing them; the problem arises in the repetition of the ways to kill a man. You can stab him, shoot him, strangle him, drown him, freeze him, cook him, starve him, beat him, and I suppose there are still other ways that it can be done, but soon you come to an end of the various methods.

So after describing a dozen or more important episodes of hard fighting, I found myself trapped trying to record others equally as important. Soon they all began to sound the same and redundant. To remedy this I employed several methods.

The first was to give the names of the villages where we had experienced some hard fighting and then state that these names would long be remembered by the men of the 65th. Another was to name the general area where some difficult fighting took place and then name the officers and men who had distinguished themselves there. I only hope in doing so I did not overlook some individual or place that should be recorded in history.

APPENDIX 1

Members of the 65th United States Infantry Regiment
who were awarded the Silver Star
and the Distinguished Service Cross
in combat in Korea

Borinqueneers who were awarded the Distinguished Service Cross

Sgt. Modesto Cartagena (also the most
  decorated soldier of the 65th)
1st Lt. Richard W. Durkee

Cpl. Fabian Nieves-Laguer
Pvt. Badel Hernandez-Guzman

Borinqueneer who were awarded the Silver Star

Headquarters and Headquarters
  Company
Pfc. Roberto Carreras
Lt. Col. George W. Childs
  (1st BOLC)
Col. William W. Harris
M. Sgt. Federico Pagani, Jr.

Headquarters 1st Battalion
Capt. Leo Donald Anderson
1st Lt. Julian F. Lockerman
M. Sgt. Ramon P. Martinez
1st Lt. Louis F. Nastri
Lt. Col. Howard B. St. Clair

Company A
Capt. George F. Ammon, Jr.
1st Lt. Armando Amy

Capt. Romeo H. Bucknell, Jr.
  (2d BOLC)
Pfc. William Hernandez
1st Lt. Paul Lavergne
Sfc. Heriberto Medina-Oliver
Cpl. Antonio Pizarro-Mojica
2d Lt. Pablo Ramirez
Sgt. Vidal Reyes

Company B
Capt. George E. Armstrong
1st Lt. Norbert E. Brodowski
Sfc. Jose Ramon Gotay
1st Lt. Walter N. Higgins
Capt. James M. Hill
1st Lt. Robert M. Horan
Sfc. Julio Martinez
Pfc. Francisco McEvedo-Olivio

Cpl. Pedro Pagan
M. Sgt. Isaac Paz-Ayala
1st Lt. Hector E. Pineiro
Capt. Raymond J. Rush, Jr.
1st Lt. Robert Sanders
Cpl. Arturo G. Torres

Company C
Cpl. Catalino Aruz-Perez
1st Lt. Sherman H. Burke (1st BOLC)
Sfc. Donald Joseph LeCouvere (1st BOLC)
Cpl. Eduardo Maisonet-Zeno
Sgt. Albert M. Mendez
Pfc. Joseph L. Mentrie
1st Lt. Benjamin Pagan
Pfc. Juan F. Rodriguez-Forty
Pfc. Monserrate Vega-Vega

Company D
Cpl. Gilberto Calderon
Cpl. Luis E. Maldonado-Matos
Sgt. German Oyola
Cpl. Armando Rosa
Cpl. Antonio Santos

Headquarters 2d Battalion
Capt. Frank Earl Blazey
Lt. Col. Herman W. Dammer (1st BOLC)
Lt. Col. Laurence A. Johnson
1st Lt. Jose R. Martinez
Maj. George A. O'Neal

Company E
M. Sgt. Manuel Acevedo, Jr.
Pvt. Juan Cruz Alicea
M. Sgt. Victor Cartegena
1st Lt. Angel Escribano-Aponte
Pfc. Felix Oerez Figueroa
1st Lt. Melquiades Gavillan
Pfc. Pedro Morales
Cpl. Alfonso Rodriguez-Martinez
Sfc. Angel Luis Ocasio
Pvt. Ramon Alicea Reyes
1st Lt. Luis R. Rodriguez
M. Sgt. Pedro Rodriguez (OLC)
2d Lt. Antonio Rodriguez-Balinas

Sfc. Donato Roman-Reichard
Pfc. Tomas Rosa-Claudio
Pfc. Juan H. Santiago

Company F
Cpl. Hugo Alvarez
1st Lt. Albert E. Carsley
1st Lt. Smith B. Chamberlain (1st OLC)
1st Lt. Pasquale J. Conti
Sgt. David Rivera Diaz
M. Sgt. Victor M. Inglesias
Sgt. Ismael Jiminez-Hernandez
M. Sgt. Pedro J. Zayas

Company G
1st Lt. Cyrus L. Gibbs
M. Sgt. Federico Martinez
Sfc. Felix G. Nieves (1st OLC)
Sgt. Ferdinand Lugo-Ortiz
Pfc. Jose A. Rivera-Carrion
Pfc. Enrique Vega-Lugo

Company H
1st Lt. Albert Martin Garbade, Jr.

Headquarters 3d Battalion
Lt. Col. Edward G. Allen
Lt. Col. John E. Harris

Company I
1st Lt. Elmo L. Bundren
Pfc. Arthur D. Cirino-Ribera
M. Sgt. Heriberto Feliciano
Cpl. Felix Figueroa
Pfc. Joseph L. Gelabert
Pfc. Jose E. Navarro-Rodriguez
Pvt. Santiago Perez-Garcia
Pvt. Filiberto Rivera
Sgt. Julio Rivera
Pfc. Ismael Robles-deJesus
Sgt. Pablo Sierra
1st Lt. Marshall B. Tator

Company K
Pvt. Antonio Berrios-Suarez
1st Lt. Charles H. Fleming

1st Lt. Clarence H. Fuller
1st Lt. Raymond W. King (1st OLC)
Capt. Edward A. Konek (1st OLC)
Capt. Theron H. Perry
Pfc. Arcadio Santiago-Rodriguez
1st Lt. Maynard Weidmann

Company L
Sfc. Candido Colon-Fonseca
Pfc. Victor Lizardy
2d Lt. Jose Rosario-Lorenzana
Sfc. Ramon Santiago-Rogue

Company M
1st Lt. Rudolph F. L. Giglio
1st Lt. Sewall H. E. Johnson
Cpl. Domingo Miranda-Rosado
1st Lt. Jose N. Ortiz

M. Sgt. Domingo Ortiz-Perez
1st Lt. Jose Vera, Jr.

Heavy Tank Company
2d Lt. Dale E. Broughton
1st Lt. Myron Dushkin
1st Lt. James B. Welsh

Heavy Mortar Company
1st Lt. Edmund H. Cave
Capt. Eugene D. Freeman
1st Lt. Harry J. Sternburg

Medical Company
Sgt. Carlos Bonet-Morales
Sgt. Luis M. Marrero
Pfc. Marine Narvarez-Montalvo
Cpl. Guadalupe Ortiz
Cpl. Rafael Rodriguez-Pacheco

APPENDIX 2

Though I know that I have failed to mention the names of many brave men who played decisive roles in the April Chinese offensive, it is only because my records are incomplete or because so much time has passed that my memory fails me. And to those many soldiers and officers of the 65th, my deepest apologies. Some of those whom I do remember and who are mentioned in appropriate correspondence during this period include the following:

Pfc. Felix P. Figueroa, Company E
M. Sgt. Victor Cartagena, Company E
1st Lt. Smith B. Chamberlain, Company E
2d Lt. Antonio Rodriguez-Balinas, Company F
Cpl. Hugo Alvarez, Company F
Sfc. Angel L. Ocasio, Company F
M. Sgt. Victor M. Iglesias, Company F
Lt. Col. Howard B. St. Clair, CO 1st Bn.
1st Lt. Romeo H. Bucknell, Jr., Company A
Capt. Frank E. Blazey, Company E
Maj. George A. O'Neal, Jr., Hq. Co. 2d Bn.
1st Lt. Jose R. Martinez, Hq. Co., 2d Bn.
Sgt. German Oyola, Company D
Cpl. Luis E. Maldonado-Matos, Company D
1st Lt. Albert M. Garbade, Jr., Company H
Lt. Col. L. A. Johnson, CO 2d Bn.
1st Lt. Edmund H. Cave, Mortar Co. 65th Inf.
1st Lt. Hector E. Pineiro, Company H
Sfc. Jose R. Gotay, Company B
M. Sgt. Isaac Paz-Ayala, Company B
1st Lt. James M. Hill, Company B
1st Lt. Robert C. Sanders, Company B
Cpl. Armando Rosa, Company D

Capt. Edward A. Konek, Company K
Pfc. Arcadio Santiago-Rodriguez, Company K
1st Lt. Maynard E. Weidman, Company K
Capt. Leo D. Anderson, Hq. Co., 1st Bn.
M. Sgt. Ramon P. Martinez, 1st Bn. Hq.

Dedicated and brave men all.

APPENDIX 3

Headquarters United States Army Caribbean
Office of the Commanding General
Fort Amador, Canal Zone

AG 201.22 (CG)   10 August 1950

Subject: Letter of Commendation
Thru: Commanding General, United Sates Army Forces
To: Commanding Officer, 65th Infantry Regiment
          Fort Brooke, Puerto Rico

1. Among the graduates of Officers Leadership Course No. 10 conducted at the United States Army Caribbean School, I was pleased to observe that officers from your regiment placed first, third, fourth, and fifth in the numerical standing in the class. This is an outstanding record and one that justifies pride in your organization.

2. The training of junior officers and the development of their leadership qualities is a responsibility of command. Although assistance such as schools, texts, etc., is made available, the commander's responsibility is continuous and the effectiveness of his leadership is reflected in the abilities of his juniors. The splendid performance displayed by your junior officers while attending the Leadership Course is indicative of their excellent training within the regiment.

3. I extend my personal congratulations to you for this enviable record and deeply appreciate the outstanding performance of duty by the officers of your command.

[Signed] RAY E. PORTER
MAJOR GENERAL, USA
COMMANDING

APPENDIX 4

Headquarters USARFANT and Military District of Puerto Rico
Office of the Commanding General

AG 201-Harris, W. W. (O)   New York, N. Y.
                                            25 August 1950

Subject: Commendation
To: Colonel W. W. Harris
          Hq. 65th Infntry Regiment
          Fort Brooke, Puerto Rico

1. Prior to your departure from this command, I do wish to commend you for
your splendid service during the last thirteen months.
2. Since your arrival you have demonstrated every good quality of a leader: enthusiasm, good humor, conscientious concern for your subordinates, imagination, drive and staying power. In the two big operations of the command during
the last year, i.e. PORTREX and 4051, you had a key role. Consequently our successes must in large part be credited to you.
3. You and your regiment take with you the sincere best wishes of myself and
my staff. I have complete confidence that you and the 65th will gain distinction in
the coming campaign.

                    [Signed] EDWIN L. SIBERT
                    BRIGADIER GENERAL, U. S. ARMY
                    COMMANDING

APPENDIX 5

1st Indorsement

AG 201.22

Subject: Letter of Commendation, P. R., 10 August 1950
HG USARFANT & MDPR, Ft. Brooke, P. R., 14 August 1950
To: Col. W. W. Harris
Regimental Commander
65th Infantry Regiment
Fort Brooke, P. R.

It is a pleasure to forward this letter of commendation to you. I join the Army Commander in recognition of the fine record consistently made by the officers of the 65th Infantry Regiment who attended the Leadership Course. That consistent record clearly indicates superior leadership at the regimental level. Please accept my sincere congratulations on the achievement of members of your command in this important training.

[Signed] EDWIN L. SIBERT
BRIGADIER GENERAL, U. S. ARMY
COMMANDING

APPENDIX 6

Senate Concurrent Resolution
of the Seventeenth Legislature of Puerto Rico

To extend and express to the 65th Infantry Regiment, and to our compatriots fighting in Korea, the congratulations and appreciation of the Legislature and the people of Puerto Rico, and for other purposes.

WHEREAS, the 65th Infantry Regiment of the United States Army, which has always been timbre of honor and pride of the Puerto Rican people, has reaffirmed its prestige and consecrated its well-recognized patriotism during the bitter fighting which has been done on the battlefields of Korea;

WHEREAS, the valiant Puerto Rican soldiers of the 65th Infantry Regiment are living evidence of the Puerto Rican people, and represent the thought of the people of Puerto Rico in the face of the problem of universal proportions that the troops of the United Nations are meeting in Korea;

WHEREAS, the valiant Puerto Rican soldiers of the 65th Infantry Regiment have performed such notable exploits of heroic courage, and have discharged the mission which took them to Korea with such fervent determination, that they have earned for themselves honorable mentions and citations for distinguished conduct from their commanders;

WHEREAS, the defense of the democratic principles sustained by the United Nations, and of which the people of the United States are a worldwide exponent, have had in the Puerto Rican soldiers of the 65th Infantry Regiment a firm advocacy and a decided support, and in the service of such democratic principles our compatriots of the 65th Infantry Regiment have exposed their lives, NOW, THEREFORE, BE IT RESOLVED BY THE SENATE OF PUERTO RICO, THE HOUSE OF REPRESENTATIVES OF PUERTO RICO CONCURRING:

FIRST — To express, as it does hereby express, the warm testimony of the gratitude of the Legislature of Puerto Rico and of the Puerto Rican people to the men of the 65th Infantry Regiment for the heroic campaign they have waged on the battlefields of the Korean peninsula;

SECOND — To express, as it does hereby express, the testimony of the appreciation of the Legislature of Puerto Rico and of the Puerto Rican people, for the defense of democratic principles made by our compatriots of the 65th Infantry Regiment, and for the loyalty and courageous patriotism which has informed such defense, which has been made without vacillation of any kind, with a lofty sense of responsibility, and with an unselfish spirit of sacrifice;

THIRD — To express, as it does hereby express, the solidarity of the Legislature of Puerto Rico and the Puerto Rican people with the families of our compatriots of the 65th Infantry Regiment, their satisfaction and pride over the patriotism of our soldiers being likewise the pride and satisfaction of the Legislature of Puerto Rico and of the whole Puerto Rican people;

FOURTH — To declare, as it does hereby declare, that these expressions of congratulations and appreciation of the Legislature to the 65th Infantry Regiment constitute at the same time, because of the sentiments in which these congratulations and appreciation are inspired, a reaffirmation of our faith in democratic principles, our faith in the principles of Universal Christianity, the subversion of which is the purpose of destructive communism;

FIFTH — To express, as it does hereby express, that the Legislature of Puerto Rico and the Puerto Rican people are watching with profound satisfaction and take to themselves as their own, the successes achieved by our compatriots of the 65th Infantry Regiment, and affirm their trust in that those successes will continue to be the pride of Puerto Rico in whose Legislature and whose people the Puerto Rican soldiers fighting in Korea have decided moral support and profoundly sincere solidarity;

SIXTH — That a certified copy of this CONCURRENT RESOLUTION be transmitted to the Secretary of Defense, to General Douglas MacArthur, to the Commander of the 65th Infantry Regiment, and to newspaper and radio press organizations.

President of the Senate
Speaker, House of Representatives
IN WITNESS WHEREOF, I issue,
sign and seal these presents in my
office, this 30th day of January 1951.

[Signed]JOSE CESTERO GUARDIOLA
SECRETARY

Headquarters 65th Infantry
Office of the Commanding Officer
APO 468 c/o PM San Francisco, California

16 February 1951

Mr. Jose Cestero Guardiola
Secretary of the Senate
The Capitol
San Juan, Puerto Rico

Dear Mr. Cestero:

I do not feel that I can adequately express the grateful appreciation of the men of the 65th Infantry for the sincere expression of confidence extended to them by the people of Puerto Rico and the Legislature in its Senate Concurrent Resolution of the Eleventh Special Session of the Seventeenth Legislature of Puerto Rico.

In behalf of those 65th Infantrymen who have made the supreme sacrifice and former and present members of the 65th who have and are continuing to fight willingly and eagerly in defense of our democratic way of life, I wish to humbly acknowledge receipt of the Concurrent Resolution and to reaffirm to the Seventeenth Legislature of Puerto Rico and to the people of Puerto Rico, the firm determination of the men of this regiment to continue to fight to protect those democratic principles.

Sincerely,
[Signed] W. W. HARRIS
COLONEL, INFANTRY
COMMANDING

APPENDIX 7

Headquarters I Corps
Office of the Commanding General

26 April 1951

To: Commanding Officer
65th Infantry Regiment
3d Infantry Division
APO 468, U. S. Army

1. The 20th of May marks the fifty = second anniversary of the date of the organization of the 65th Infantry Regiment. As its anniversary approaches, it is a great pleassure to congratulate your fine Regiment on its splendid record in the past and on the way in which it is adding to that record in the present.

2. The Regiment has been assigned one important role after another since the Third Division joined the Corps and has carried out these assignments in an exemplary manner. It has established a fighting reputation and a standard of combat leadership of which it can be proud.

3. I am confident that the 65th will meet future challenges in battle with resolution and skill and I wish its officers and men continuing success now and in operations still to come.

[Signed] F. W. MILBURN
LIEUTENANT GENERAL, U. S. ARMY
COMMANDING

APPENDIX 8

Headquarters Third Infantry Division
Office of the Commanding General
APO 468, c/o PM San Francisco, California

30 April 1951

The Editor
El Imparcial
San Juan, Puerto Rico

Dear Sir:

I am informed that your edition of 20 May is to be dedicated to the 65th Infantry Regiment, in honor of that distinguished organization's fifty-second anniversary.

The 65th is a very important part of the Third U. S. Infantry Division, which I command. It is a pleasant duty to offer my thanks and congratulations to the Puerto Rican people who offered the valiant soldiers assigned to this splendid regiment.

Your Puerto Rican Regiment is fighting side by side with many fine units of the United Nations Forces and it is recognized as the equal of the very best.

As this is written, the 65th is heavily engaged with the enemy northeast of Seoul. The fact that it is in the line is a great comfort to me as Division Commander. It is also a comforting thought for the units on its right and left, for they know that when the 65th is in defense, *it holds* — when it attacks, *it takes*. In short, its conduct can only be characterized as superb.

Only a fine, liberty-loving people could produce a regiment of the character and ability of the 65th Infantry. Surely victory will soon crown such heroic efforts; then our gallant Puerto Rican soldiers will return to their loved ones in their beautiful island homeland.

In the meantime it is an honor and a privilege to me to have these gallant soldiers as members of my command.

Sincerely,

[Signed] ROBERT H. SOULE
COMMANDING

Communications Center
Third Infantry Division

PRECEDENCE: PRIORITY
From: CO Tenth BCT PEETOK
To: CO 65th Infantry Regiment

Officers and men of the one zero BCT join me in felicitation and congratulating you and members of your command in the recent celebration of five-two anniversary of the six five Inf. Regt. on two zero May 1951. We are looking forward for your success and more power to the six five. Sgd. OJEDA

We also received a message from the Eighth Army Commander:

On behalf of all members of the United Nations Forces in Korea, I offer my sincere congratulations to you and the members of the fighting 65th Infantry Regiment on your 52d Anniversary. The Regiment has a long and glorious record, and its outstanding combat performance in Korea will take its rightful place in our military history and in the history of Puerto Rico. Please convey my best wishes to all members of your command.

[Signed] VAN FLEET

INDEX